V&R

Refo500 Academic Studies

Edited by
Herman J. Selderhuis

In Co-operation with
Christopher B. Brown (Boston), Günter Frank (Bretten),
Bruce Gordon (New Haven), Barbara Mahlmann-Bauer (Bern),
Tarald Rasmussen (Oslo), Violet Soen (Leuven),
Zsombor Tóth (Budapest), Günther Wassilowsky (Linz),
Siegrid Westphal (Osnabrück).

Volume 45

Katalin Péter

Studies on the History of the Reformation in Hungary and Transylvania

edited by Gabriella Erdélyi

Vandenhoeck & Ruprecht

This book was produced under the auspices of the Research Centre for the Humanities of the Hungarian Academy of Sciences and with the support of the National Bank of Hungary.

Bibliographic information published by the Deutsche Nationalbibliothek:
The Deutsche Nationalbibliothek lists this publication in the
Deutsche Nationalbibliografie; detailed bibliographic data available
online: http://dnb.de.

Typesetting: 3w+p, Rimpar
Printed and bound: Hubert & Co. BuchPartner, Göttingen
Printed in the EU

Vandenhoeck & Ruprecht Verlage | www.vandenhoeck-ruprecht-verlage.com

ISSN 2198-3089
ISBN 978-3-525-55271-1

Contents

Part II Confessional Cultures and Beyond

List of Illustrations

List of Abbreviations

EOE - *Erdélyi Országgyűlési Emlékek. Monumenta Comitialia Regni Transylvaniae 1540–1699* [Transylvanian Diet Records], 21 vol. Budapest, 1875–1898.

RMNY 1 - Gedeon Borsa, Ferenc Hervay, Béla Holl, István Käfer and Ákos Kelecsényi, ed. *Régi Magyarországi Nyomtatványok/Res Literaria Hungariae vetus operum impressorum* [Early Hungarian Printings], vol. 1. 1473–1600. Budapest, 1971.

RMNY 2 - Gedeon Borsa, Ferenc Hervay and Béla Holl, ed. *Régi Magyarországi Nyomtatványok/Res Literaria Hungariae vetus operum impressorum* [Early Hungarian Printings], vol. 2. 1601–1635. Budapest, 1983.

WA - Martin Luther, *Werke: Kritische Gesamtausgabe*, vol. 1–73, Weimar, 1883–2009.

Preface

This book contains Katalin Péter's most important works on the Protestant Reformation in Hungary and Transylvania that have previously been available only in Hungarian. Like all selections, this one is also subjective and arbitrary. The editor's role has been very limited but crucial. Even though the author has encouraged many of her students, including me, to publish their major works in English as well as in Hungarian in order to reach an international audience, she has not considered this to be one of her own tasks. Instead of revising and translating her own works, a process that she found boring, Péter has always preferred to venture into new, undiscovered terrains of research. She once wrote in the introduction to a book on early modern marriages:

> After a long period of deliberation I decided to apply the method of everyday cognition in this book. I will walk about in history and I will form an opinion of people who lived in the remote past as I do in everyday life[1]

– a statement which also reflects her concept of history as a livable, knowable, discoverable space. In the present book she follows the same path. Péter starts the story of the Reformation by sharing a personal experience—the museum visit and visual sight of the beautiful and rich Gothic altars, which made her realize that the Church and the faithful had a vivid relationship when the Reformation appeared.

The first part of the book is composed of a work published in Hungarian in 2004 that targets both scholars and the general public. The second part includes five studies published in academic journals that have not previously been published in either German or English. Therefore, we had to omit from this book, among others, an important essay in which Péter issued a pioneering challenge to the influential idea that the new Churches placed the Bible into the hands of the ordinary people.[2]

1 Katalin Péter, *Házasság a régi Magyarországon* [Marriage in Old Hungary] (Budapest, 2008), 9.
2 Katalin Péter, "Bibellesen. Ein Programm für jedenmann in Ungarn des 16. Jahrhunderts," in

In general terms, we aimed to make a selection of works that highlight the Reformation both as a specifically Hungarian and as a generally European phenomenon. The Reformation has traditionally been explained in terms of theology, the corruption of the Church and the roles of princes. Katalin Péter shifts the context of the study of the Reformation to a bottom-up perspective and produces a lively narrative of the experiences and reactions of contemporary actors—including rural town and village communities, local priests and landlords—to evangelical ideas. The evolving historical narrative of the social and cultural dynamic of the Protestant Reformation in all the three parts of divided Hungary, according to the intention of the author, is not only a walk through the past but an intriguing dialogue. The author engages in a dialogue with other historians, which renders her history a part of a discourse rather than a piece of knowledge or the past depicted in detail. And all readers are invited to participate in the process of writing history, during which in certain instances the author refrains from providing a definite answer to the dilemma posed, thus allowing them to come up with their own answers.

The Editor

Iter Germanicum. Deutschland und die Reformierte Kirche in Ungarn im 16.-17. Jahrhundert, ed. András Szabó (Budapest, 1999), 7–38.

Foreword

The recent anniversary of 1517 has brought about a great deal of new results and valuable research on Reformation history, all the more so as the growing activity of historians coincides with substantial changes in the practice of our trade. We no longer believe in a history flying or struggling—the difference depended on the mood of the author—toward a uniform state of affairs all over the world. And we no longer believe in the power of universal laws directing the actions of the agents of the past. With regard to the Reformation, this means that—like all historical phenomena—it became debatable. And the focus of inquiry turned from the great personalities involved in the matter to the people who experienced the Reformation and shaped its impact on history. One may state without too much exaggeration that there are as many Reformations in existence at the moment as there are historians dealing with them.

The studies in this volume treat the Reformation as it happened in Hungary, in my interpretation. I am an old historian who has worked on different subjects, with one of my favorite topics having been the Reformation.

To start the explanation of my opinion with the personal part, I have drawn a somewhat lopsided picture. A colleague who is an excellent expert on the period called my attention to this. He said that he liked my writings on the Reformation but he could not agree with them. "Your conception is as pointed as the other," was his comment. By "the other" he meant the traditional understanding of the Reformation. According to this understanding, the landlords, male and female, were instrumental in the reception of the new tenets. The landowners used, or most often misused, their right to determine the denominational belonging of the church buildings on their estates in establishing the new Church and then the new Churches. The logical explication of this development would be that something similar to the "Princes' Reformation" took place. My reasoning, on the contrary, leaves out the landowners because, on the one hand, my experience is that they did not concern themselves with the spiritual needs of the subjects and, on the other hand, the power and the rights of the lords or ladies over the peasants was unrelated to ecclesiastical matters. The person who had the *ius patronatus* over the churches of a territory was the church patron of the Latin and the Greek Churches as well. That had been the practice in Hungary since the earliest times, and this practice continued during the Reformation. Catholic lords and ladies could be the patrons of Protestant institutions or congregations and Protestants had Catholics under their patronage as well.

The landowners had no interest in changing the faith of the subjects. In addition, there were far fewer people on whom they could count as evangelical ministers than was the need of their immense estates. If, for instance, the three Zrínyi brothers who adopted the evangelical faith in the middle of the sixteenth century had wanted to turn the peasants on their domains Protestant, they would have needed to provide at least a thousand congregations with evangelically minded pastors. This would have obviously been an impossible task.

I put uneducated simple people, called *község* in Hungarian, in the place of the landowners in the Reformation. They were the first to hear of the new tenets and they spread the good news of the omnipotence of faith. As a contemporary theologian wrote in the dedication of a popular book: "you received and heard before others and you glorified and spoke to others the knowledge of God's mercy." That was probably an overstatement at that time and it is likely an overstatement today. To be partial, however, when it comes to writing on peasants, is, so to speak, natural. I have the feeling that history writing on the peasant that involves the historian emotionally, as Theodor Shanin put it in his 1971 *Short Historical Outline*, has not lost its emotive character. And the uneducated people of my studies published in this volume are practically the peasants. I confessed in one of the pieces to my partiality without mentioning Shanin. He came to my mind only after having read the parts together as a book.

In chronological terms, the book covers issues from the middle of the fifteenth century to the middle of the seventeenth century, while geographically it treats events that occurred in the Kingdom of Hungary. Transylvania has been mentioned in the title because it was a fairly separate entity of the Hungarian kingdom in the Middle Ages and became a separate country for a time precisely at the beginning of the Reformation era. The latter development, however, was not connected to changes in religion: it was the result of wars and the Ottoman occupation of a large part of Hungary. I am not sure if one needs to emphasize the separateness of Transylvania, though this is usually done. In the text I use the Hungarian place names of the period, with the names of today and the country in which the localities are located in parentheses. It is impossible to confine the history of the Reformation to the current territory of Hungary because the lives and consciousness of its sixteenth-century inhabitants were based in the domain of shared history that had emerged in the medieval Kingdom of Hungary. It is important to take this fact into consideration, particularly in order to understand that people of various ethnicities and religions inhabited this common space.

The early chronological start of the book is the consequence of the conviction that it is inadvisable to treat intricate occurrences of history in themselves. Through a broad approach it first of all becomes clear that the relationship between the Roman church and its members was harmonious. The main proof of the good connections between the Church and its members was the series of churches with rich and splendid inner decoration, built roughly at the time when the Reformation reached Hungary. Then there was the Dózsa peasant uprising in 1514. According to the interpretation I suggest, the crusade proclaimed by the legate of Pope Leo X, Cardinal Tamás Bakócz, turned into a war against the "infidel" nobility because the simple man and the simple woman—the papal bull on the crusade addressed male and female members of all social standings—were sincerely concerned about their afterlife and were familiar with the language of the church. I would say that the same explanation is valid for the commerce in indulgence slips. It was exactly in 1517 that a local synod in Hungary had to take measures against possible abuses in this regard. A high demand for forgiveness mediated by the church was palpable at the time when evangelical tenets reached Hungary, in the 1520s.

The field was ready for the reception of the message *sola fide.* The new ideas were attributed by both friend and enemy to Martin Luther. We have very few sources on the actual contents of early evangelically minded preaching. Judging by people's deeds, it seems that two tenets were the most alluring for the audiences: the idea of universal priesthood and the serving of the Lord's Supper under two kinds to all members of the congregation. The attraction of the first was reflected in the activity, and long activity at that, of lay people as preachers. And according to denunciations made in the 1520s, these lay preachers were not exclusively of the male gender. The allure of the other feature of the new faith, receiving the Lord's Supper under both kinds, was reflected in the fact that the first indication of turning to evangelical faith was to demand the Eucharist that way. The meaning of the two most popular theological tenets could be summed up as the wish for equality before God.

It would be plausible to conclude that the wish for equality before God has been one of Christianity's main characteristics. That conclusion, however, would be incorrect. The many Catholics we know to have been at the side of the Protestants prove it to be so. I mean not merely the coexistence of different denominations but even more the hard choices. Sources tell repeatedly about some people feeling comfortable in the Roman Catholic Church while others declared themselves ready to die if coerced into its faith. A church visitation record from around 1560 that I used in several studies says that even members of a socially and intellectually homogeneous group living in a village could be of sharply divergent religious inclinations. The Hungarian case warns strongly against regarding the Reformation as the only or imperative solution to social or ecclesiastical problems.

The main benefits of the Reformation in Hungary affected not only the evangelical minded but also people who decided to stay with the old faith. The Reformation presented in this book above all provided members of the community with the possibility to doubt. The new ideas called into question knowledge that had become part of the people's essential being. This applied to everybody—both to those who accepted the new faith and to those who rejected it. During the disputes regarding the new teachings, some people chose to retain the old knowledge, the language they already spoke well, while others chose to accept the new teachings and to learn the new church language. This change was perhaps less traumatic in religiously mixed Hungary than it was in countries where people had previously experienced the ministry of one church only.

We know very little about the shock of changing religion. No direct sources revealing information on this issue have been preserved from the sixteenth century. It was different in the seventeenth century, when from the 1620s on a fairly great return to the Roman Catholic Church took place in Hungary. At the moment of my present considerations, the content of songbooks can be taken as indirect sources. They reveal the fact that the representatives of the churches were not keen on demonstrating theological differences between denominations before the faithful. Their aim was perhaps to soften the blow of conversion. And the same interpretation can be given to the phenomena I treated in the piece *Confessionally Undivided Hungary* in Part II of this volume. The Reformation did not destroy the existing networks of social relationships. To choose the evangelical faith at the time of the Reformation was most probably less staggering than turning from Protestant to Roman Catholic in the age of Catholic Reformation.

The difference between the sixteenth and seventeenth centuries has been treated in several studies. They might seem superfluous in a book on the Reformation, were it not for the fact that the disparity was in substantial measure the result of the actions of Protestant agents. It was the evangelically minded pastors, schoolmasters and typographers who created printed culture in Hungary. Before the sixteenth century we know only of some codices and very few books, whereas beginning in 1528 printed works appeared fairly regularly. The first book in the vernacular we know of for sure was a work in German regarding protective measures against the plague, and the second was the Hungarian translation of the letters of Paul the Apostle. The initiative of the Franciscan Pelbárt Temesvári to publish Latin model sermons for ordinary parish priests—who would then perform them to the laity in the vernacular—had no continuation after his death in 1504. The Catholic clergy and Catholic intellectuals in general were strikingly absent from the period of the profound swing which led from the beginnings of printed culture to the time I call the Golden Age at the end of the sixteenth century.

The Golden Age, in my interpretation, consisted of roughly three decades at the end of the sixteenth century. Its main characteristic was that all vernaculars spoken in the country were put into print. It took 150 years for that to happen again. Besides that, a rich body of material of secular interest appeared in popular form between 1571 and 1600. For the sociological analysis of these phenomena I used the handbook *Régi Magyarországi Nyomtatványok* (Early Hungarian Printings), which gives bibliopolical and thematic descriptions of all printed matter. The obtained figures appear in tables at the end of the *Golden Age and Decay* piece.

Vernacular literature, especially in popular form, was the great gift of the Reformation to the simple people that was devoid of religious considerations. The creators of this literature—Protestant schoolmasters and village ministers—worked with themes that were denominationally unbiased. The community, whether it had chosen the Reformation or remained Catholic, could read it. The importance of this fact is equal to that which we attach to the impact of books and the printed word. The simple folk were offered the opportunity, because there was demand for it, to learn about the world from the printed book without religious partialities. In the next period, after the turn of the seventeenth century, simple men and women were only provided with devotional reading, if anything, in their language. And there was no return of the Golden Age any time later.

Finally, I feel an intriguing concatenation of events in connection with the Reformation would be worth mentioning. It was constructed in Transylvania, where rulers were Roman Catholics for all but a few years during the sixteenth century. These Catholics, one woman and several men, assumed the supreme headship of the Protestant churches. The ecclesiastical and secular representatives of the churches accepted them in that position without the slightest indication of displeasure. The initiator of this curious development was one of the very few leading female political officials in Hungary, Queen Isabella. She sanctioned a law stipulating that "everybody should follow the faith of their choice." As a result, religious tolerance could be used for the political apportion of subjects, which is discussed in more detail in Part II Chapter 4.

There is no space here for the acknowledgements customarily expressed in the introductions of books. I became indebted to very many people during the decades spent doing historical research. Citing their names and saying thank you to all of them would require another entire volume.

Part I
Coercion or Choice?
The Early Reformation in Hungary

An Opening Word

I must first make it clear that although this book concerns matters of religion it does not deal with personal faith.[1] This is a serious shortcoming, since the connection of most people to a religion or a church is based upon faith. Some historians believe that religious themes should be left to theologians, while others decline to deal with issues of faith because they themselves espouse no spiritual creed. I uphold the commonly held conviction that faith manifests itself in deed. Therefore, one cannot stray too far from the mark if one examines the actions of others without dissecting personal faith, though always presuming its influence.

The usage of the term "church" is closely connected to this issue. I use this word in a secular sense in this work to refer to the ecclesiastical organizations of various religious denominations. Although I know that in theological terms there is a single Christian mother church, this tenet can scarcely be applied within the context of a secular historical narrative. The fact that most Christians regard their own denomination as the sole true church and embodiment of original Christianity makes application of this doctrine impossible. Since I strive to emphasize the essential unity within the Christian church in this book, I do not use the distinction between Catholic Christian and Protestant Christian that is expressed so frequently in Hungarian public discourse.

For citations I used *The Bible: New International Version.* International Bible Society, 1973. Many editions.

1 Part I of this volume was first published in Hungarian: *A reformáció: kényszer vagy választás?* (Budapest, 2004).

Fig. 1. Master MS, *The Visitation*

1 Introduction: Art Treasures and Historiography

One of the most surprising experiences of my life took place at the Hungarian National Gallery. After walking through the gallery's permanent exhibition of Late Gothic religious art two or three times, I suddenly realized that the vast majority of beautiful winged altarpieces and church statues on display had originated from the period just prior to the Reformation or during the years around 1520 when evangelical teachings reached Hungary.

Standing right next to the entry of this exhibition of Late Gothic religious art, for example, stands a stunning, larger-than-life-size sixteenth-century carved wooden statue of the crucified Christ bleeding from five wounds from a church in Gyöngyös. It was made sometime in the early sixteenth century. The following room contains Master MS's 1506 painting *The Visitation*, depicting the meeting of the Virgin Mary pregnant with Christ and Saint Elizabeth pregnant with Saint John the Baptist. In my opinion, this is the most beautiful painting ever created in old Hungary. The Visitation is a peerless work, even though from the standpoint of mere dry facts there is nothing exceptional about it. Both the color of the clothing of the two figures shown in the painting as well as the movement with which Elizabeth touches Mary's abdomen are familiar from other depictions of this scene on numerous artefacts. However, no other artist has evinced the harmony of the earthly and transcendent that is embodied in the persons of Mary and Elizabeth as well as Master MS did in *The Visitation*. This painting is rightfully contained in most histories and albums regarding the art of Hungary.

Standing next to *The Visitation* in the Hungarian National Gallery exhibition are elements of altarpieces produced at the beginning of the sixteenth century. To the left of the painting is an ornately carved wooden *Pietà*, a broad-cloaked Madonna with the dead Christ in her lap. This image of a woman whose face is beset with pain, and the male figure showing many marks of suffering, was originally located above the altar of the church in Keszthely. To the right of the *Visitation* painting is an image of John the Evangelist from a church in Okolicsnó (Okoličné, Slovakia). In it, he looks on it like a living person. The *Pietà* and the John the Evangelist works are smaller than life-size. Among the very large winged altarpieces and statues in the next room stands an enormous Saint Nicholas triptych from a church in Nagyszalók (Vel'ký Slavkov, Slovakia). According to the date on the picture, it was made in 1503. The gold statue of Nicholas wearing his bishop's clothing rises up halfway from the opulently gilded background on the central panel of the triptych, while the wings contain panels showing the four episodes of the legend of the saintly bishop. I did not find the half statue and the panel paintings to be particularly captivating.

However, there is a wonderful scene depicted on the predella of the altarpiece. If viewers did not know that the image illustrated figures from the Bible, they might believe that it portrayed an ordinary family idyll: two female figures, a younger one sitting on the left and an older one sitting on the right, with a nude little boy stepping from the former toward the latter. In his hand the child holds a rose branch with bud and open flower. The older woman with covered head extends an apple toward the boy. Because the image is on an altarpiece, it clearly shows the mother Virgin Mary and her mother Saint Anne playing with the child Christ, though any mother or grandmother could imagine themselves in their place.

Certain church paintings and statues, in fact, display the features of genuine people. I consider the most interesting such work in the Hungarian National Gallery to be the votive image of Johan Hütter, citizen of Kassa (Košice, Slovakia). The details on this image are clearly visible due to the fact that it is practically the same size as the 140 cm x 95 cm *The Visitation.* Sitting on the right side of the painting is the Virgin Mary, to whom flying angels carry a crown. Enthroned on the clouds at the top of the image is God the Father. Three kneeling figures represent the central motif and most conspicuous element in the image. Clearly recognizable on the left-hand side is the person of John the Evangelist, who is almost always depicted, as in this image, with short, curly hair and wearing claret-colored clothing. John the Evangelist may have been the patron saint of Johan Hütter. Kneeling before Saint John with hands clasped in prayer, Hütter is likely depicted as realistically as he could have been in an early sixteenth-century painting. Next to Hütter kneels another, disproportionally small male figure, obviously his son, who may have already been dead. This painting originates from around the year 1520.

The reader may ask: what was so surprising about these works on display at the gallery?

It is well-known that the late Gothic style, which emerged in Central Europe in the years 1440–1470 and flourished for more than a century, constituted an organic component of art in Hungary. Why is it not natural that church interiors in Central Europe should be abundantly adorned with winged altarpieces, statues and paintings near the end of this period?

The answer is simple: because these art treasures did not fit the generally accepted historical picture of the Reformation. The Hungarian National Gallery opened its permanent exhibitions in 1979, when we still thought that the Reformation became part of the agenda of history as a result of the decline of the medieval Roman church.

According to the prevailing concept in the late 1970s, the people had turned away from the late medieval church. The spiritual needs of the laity were not satisfied by a clergy that lived in a manner unworthy of its calling, while the dissolute life of monks scandalized the people. Conditions within the church cried out for renewal and reform. One of my unforgettable memories from this time was reading the introduction to a source publication in which the Jesuit author scourged the scandalous conditions of the old church using such scathing words that I initially thought it was a sixteenth-century text.

The unambiguous and positive judgment throughout Europe of the Reformation as a force challenging a decadent old church originated in the middle of the nineteenth century. It took shape under the influence of Darwin's theory of evolution or maybe emerged within the generally optimistic evolutionist atmosphere of nineteenth-century scholarship. This evolutionist approach has made the Reformation an important phase of European economic, social and cultural development. Friedrich Engels regarded the Reformation as the first early capitalist revolution, while Leopold Ranke believed it initiated the spread of vernacular culture.

Ranke exercised a greater direct impact than Engels on historiography regarding the Reformation. One of the possible reasons for this is that Engels formulated his thesis as part of a complex conception bearing firm political and ideological connotations, whereas Ranke presents a simple, unambiguous and seemingly unassailable argument in support of the Reformation. Ranke contended that the Reformation had placed the vernacular Bible into the hands of the people, thus permitting independent reading and interpretation. This laid the foundation for the connection between the Reformation and the appearance of the modern individual. Leopold Ranke's postulates regarding the Reformation became so widely accepted that it was not proper to question them in the writing of history.

Engels' thesis on the Reformation constituted a component of Marxist historiography until the middle of the 1980s, while that of Ranke exercised an impact that transcended various schools of thought and historiographic trends. Those who counted as serious researchers could hardly write about the Reformation from another perspective. Catholic authors either avoided the subject or embraced the philosophy of Joseph Lortz, one of the greatest Catholic church historians of the twentieth century, who published an influential two-volume monograph on the Reformation, and attributed Martin Luther's protest against the Catholic Church to the Holy See's negligence and theologically assailable deeds and decisions. However, only Protestant authors such as Max Weber, Christopher Hill and László Makkai claimed that the most important elements of Europe's cultural and economic development were products of the Reformation.

The situation has changed significantly in this regard. I once hoped that a historical narrative of the Reformation would emerge that was devoid of confessional prejudice. My hopes have not been realized. Time and time again I have encountered works that carefully register the religious affiliation of those with whom the author agrees or disagrees. The possible divergences in these disagreements result from the fact that the consensus surrounding the posited interrelationship between the Reformation and the radical increase of popular culture has collapsed.

The transformation began with polemics that took place within the journal *Past and Present* in the early 1980s. American historians Richard Gawthrop and Gerald Strauss launched the initial attack against Ranke's fundamental proposition that the Reformation had placed the Bible into the hands of the people. They asserted that regardless of the objectives of the Reformation, it could not have enabled people to read the Bible because most people were illiterate. These historians incidentally attacked the proposed link between the Reformation and the development of schooling that was generally accepted at the time, concluding that the destruction of monastic schools, libraries and monasteries in the sixteenth century represented an enormous cultural blow for England.

This reasoning provoked significant debate and, in the end, positively influenced the study of both the Reformation and the cultural and social conditions of other historical periods. Literacy research—the study of the incidence and proficiency of the ability to read and write in a given era—began as a direct result of this contention. It was for a long time a complex, independent field and branch of study within the social sciences. The challenge of the thesis regarding the Reformation's achievements in the field of popular Bible reading, in addition to other conceptual changes to cultural history and historical anthropology, led indirectly to a new understanding of the relationship between knowledge mediated via writing and that transmitted orally. To greatly simplify the situation: the consensus on the direct relationship between the Reformation and the increase in the people's overall knowledge has dissolved.

Another debate also originated from a thesis by Ranke, namely that surrounding the relationship between the Reformation and the secularization of culture. This polemic resulted in the assertion that modern scientific scholarship developed as a consequence of the Reformation, which not only liberated the individual, but also produced the Puritan movement to which the outstanding figures of the scientific revolution, including Sir Isaac Newton and other members of the Royal Society, belonged. I have permitted myself to make this simplification, because the debate surrounded very concrete, simple facts. Namely, were those who founded the Royal Society truly Puritans? And was Newton's affiliation with Puritanism confined to the fact that his mother belonged to a Puritan congregation?

No independent branch of the social sciences emerged from these polemics. However, they did contribute significantly to the transformation of the historians' frame of mind. By transformation here I mean that belief in the grand explanations of the course of history began to waver. The reasons for this were complex: the political shifts of the 1980s played a role, as did the connection of various social science disciplines to historiography. The Hungarian historian Ignác Romsics diagnosed a similar historiographical situation at the turn of the twentieth century. He cited a proclamation of the "new historiography" from the period, which stated that historical scholarship would cast off its previous limitations and

> will utilize all those discoveries that anthropologists, economists, psychologists and sociologists have made and which in the course of the past fifty years have revolutionized our notions regarding the origin, development and outlook of our species.

The "new historiography" of the period led to epistemological skepticism. Today there is again a new historiography, though we do not usually mention it as a concept. The nearly ten-year-old proclamation cited above could be repeated word-for-word, though with Einstein's theory of relativity in the place of Darwin's conclusion regarding the origin of species. And from the relativization of things arose skepticism, although perhaps an even more characteristic consequence was that the transformational intentions of the final decades of the twentieth century, under the influence of broadly defined present political movements, brought the recognition of simultaneously occurring phenomena. I have the feeling that the process began far from the domain of historiography in the field of anthropology. If I wanted to connect the beginning of this process with a specific time, I would choose the year 1949. This was the year in which Margaret Mead's book *Male and Female* was published for the first time. This book, which was published many times and appeared in Hungarian in 2003, was received with bewilderment. Based on observations regarding various, so-called primitive cultures, Mead provided guidance to the post-war generation of North American civilization that was in a state of confusion, particularly, according to the author, with regard to sexual relations. With no little malice, some wrote that Mead had to find for herself a new area of study after losing her opportunity to do anthropological fieldwork as a result of the collapse of the colonial empires.

There was really something rather absurd about placing those who lived a foraging lifestyle alongside those who used the most advanced technologies. I nevertheless believe that this much-debated act resulted in the broad acceptance within the social sciences of an anti-evolutionary approach, which considers human nature to be constant. According to the sociologist Talcott Parsons, development became a "jealous god" because it concealed the harmony of simultaneous historical phenomena. As Reinhart Koselleck put it, the presumption of development serves to disguise the interrelations of historical events and actions.

I find this concept to be extremely appealing, though I cannot comment on it from a theoretical perspective. I am not, as the reader has undoubtedly already perceived, a person of abstract thoughts. This is why I utilize practical consequences in order to illustrate the causes of my sympathy for this concept. According to the perspective arising from anti-evolutionism, history is global because it takes place within a single, universal sphere and it has no measurable absolute values. This means that various cultures of the past and present cannot be ranked according to their value based on some principle. That is, in a cultural sense there is no such thing as "better" or "worse." There is only "other."

I also find it very appealing that the global historical approach rejects the paternalistic term "developing country." It rejects this expression because the concept of "developing" presumes the future simultaneity of that which is today "developing" and that which is today "developed," whereas we have no idea what the future will bring. More precisely: we have no idea what it will bring unless we believe that an immanent force is directing the history of humanity toward some defined objective. This concept is of little use in current political discourse because it implicitly rejects the superiority of the "West." I am curious how recent political changes will affect the evolutionary view.

It is interesting that the person who articulated the most scholarly and vivid objection to the notion of "Western" superiority—Erik H. Erikson—was himself not only part of the Western scholarly world, but dealt specifically with the comparison of "Western" and non-Western civilizations. His book examining the youth of Martin Luther often appears on the syllabi of courses taught at universities. Much of Erikson's work is devoted to the study of Native Americans and to the white Americans who embody the "West." In one of his ponderous volumes, Erikson characterizes the claim that the West is "more developed" to be "childish" because only children instinctively feel that they are better than anyone else.

I agree with the view summarized in Erikson's opinion. However, I know that this perspective is far from generally accepted. On the contrary, there is an immense corpus of literature dealing with "backwardness" compared to "Europe." In this instance, the designation "Europe" refers to Northern-Northwestern Europe and North America, and "backwardness" to the fact that people in the larger part of the world live within other cultural, economic and social conditions and maintain other types of personal relationships, though are headed in the direction of Europe. Let a single group of facts serve here as a telling example. Jacques Le Goff, who was one of the greatest figures in modern historiography, edited a series of books published in many languages and in large quantity under the title *The Making of Europe* not so long ago. In 1995, Aron Gurevich's book from this series was published. The latter, according to the intention of the author and the objective of the series, examines how Europe became "the unified space of a developing universal process." And Gurevich, the luminary of Russian scholarship in those years, sees the future of his homeland in the adoption of "fundamental European values." That is, Europe represents the ideal to be reached.

I do not want to address the question of the degree to which "Europe"—seen from an evolutionary perspective—is within reach for the world. Everybody knows the kind of environmental pollution that results from the fact that high-technology civilizations function in a tiny part of the globe. What would happen if air conditioning were installed in every home in China? Or what would be the consequences of family relationships in which every family member in the world traveled in a separate car? Many have urged the West to practice technological self-restraint, though so far with a recognized lack of success. Though even if they were successful, on what grounds could one demand that the presently "backward" people of the world omit the multi-car, highly mobile, temperature-controlled, extravagant civilizational phase?

Here I have apparently strayed far from the history of the Reformation. Actually I have the feeling that I am plying the depths of related problems. Because it is from here that some grave dilemmas, which those who these days deal with the Reformation must face, are most clearly perceptible. Should he or she regard the Reformation as one of the important stages in European development? To do so is possible since Eurocentric historiography has remained virulent. In this case, it must be claimed that compared to the traditional church, the churches that emerged from the Reformation are more "developed"—a word that has been coded in our consciousness to be a synonym for "better." I, for one, do not gladly rank either churches or church teachings. Should my opinion therefore be that the Reformation represented an event that took place within a single, unified global historical space and in a relative sense involved very few people? And should I seek to identify the other global events and actions that were interrelated with the Reformation? This procedure is sometimes considered to be global historiography. In connection with this, the widespread disappointment surrounding the volume of essays that Reinhart Koselleck published in 2000 was very revealing. Many expected him, who for the previous three decades had written about the global historical perspective, to produce a history that presented the events of the world within a comprehensive narrative. However, the essays in Koselleck's book were again just theoretical reflections and were the subject of derisive criticism.

I have not looked to find out if the father of the global historical approach responded to the attacks on his book, though I am unequivocal in my belief that global history cannot be written as a history of events unless the historian has an extremely broad knowledge of languages—and even in this case it might not be worthwhile. It would result in the same thing as that which today we produce in the name of world history. After promising introductions, these works present the histories of various countries organized, at best, around identical themes. However, it is possible to examine certain phenomena from a global perspective. I do not regard the fact that the demand for global history has appeared most decisively within gender studies to be accidental. The relationship between genders is indeed universal: every society in the world has been constructed from female and male members.

The study of emotions is similarly a good theme. It can be researched in every culture and at every time. For example, Hans Medick and David Sabean, who are among the most inventive historians of the present day, have been pursuing such study without ostentatiously emphasizing globalism. The volume of studies that Medick and Sabean published several years ago regarding the interconnection between interest and emotion represents one of the classic works of today's new historiography. They have engaged in a self-evident manner in projects dealing with gender and family as well. At the same time, one can see also ventures organized more closely to chronology. The Internationaal Instituut voor Sociale Geschiedenis, for instance, has undertaken a project to write the global history of textile workers from 1650 to 2000. The results appeared in 2010.

In the end, it would be justified to examine the Reformation as an individual manifestation of a universal phenomenon. In order to do this, the concept of the Reformation must be clarified. We are at the moment very far from having achieved such clarity—there was not even agreement regarding the concept of the Reformation at the very beginning of its modern thematization. Engels considered the German Peasants' War and associated anti-feudal ideology to be part of the Reformation, while Ranke objected in most strenuous fashion to the posited connection between the peasant uprising and the Reformation as he interpreted it. The situation remains essentially unchanged today. It is only a slight exaggeration to claim: everybody maintains a different understanding of what the Reformation means.

The various definitions of the Reformation contain a single more or less common element: that it started with the publication of Martin Luther's ninety-five theses on indulgences in 1517. Beyond this, it is possible to portray the Reformation as a revolution, as Peter Blickle, one of the greatest recent specialists on the movement, did in his 1998 book. Referring to postmodernism, Blickle has noted ironically that he deconstructed his own scholarship in this work, and he is going on with the revolution concept. Reformation historians have argued about it, and their differences of opinion were not connected to Marxist theory. Bob Scribner, perhaps the most versatile and inventive historian of the Reformation, somewhat earlier advanced the idea that the Reformation deceived simple people because it did not represent their interests, but those of the intellectual élite and, perhaps, of the political élite as well. Many scholars espoused Scribner's viewpoint, which a few decades ago would have been regarded as sacrilege. Or what could have represented a more solid fact than that the Reformation rejected the teachings of the Roman church? Today, Heinz Schilling's notion of the process of confessionalization, which indicates that Catholicism itself is a product of the Reformation, has also become an established idea. And the church schism? Everybody previously saw this as the most important, or at least one of the most important, consequences of the Reformation. In her 2003 book, Christine Peters portrayed the Reformation as a gentle transformation of traditional religion. And she makes her claim with regard to England, where a series of laws prescribed the suppression, restoration and renewed suppression of the Roman Catholic Church.

I am therefore unsure of the precise category into which this multifaceted Reformation can be properly placed. The choice is still free. The Reformation has no generally accepted content. Facts cannot, however, be ignored and, furthermore, it is fortunate if the historian, as scientific researchers in general, states the subject of his or her investigations and the questions which he or she is seeking to answer. In this way, the historian is restricting his or her own freedom, whether he or she likes it or not.

This work will examine the Reformation as it took place in historical Hungary. It is not possible to confine it to the events that took place on the current territory of the country because the lives and consciousness of its sixteenth-century inhabitants were based in the domain of common history that had emerged in the medieval Kingdom of Hungary. It is important to take this fact into consideration when studying the Reformation in Hungary, particularly in order to understand that people of various ethnicities and religions inhabited this common space. At the turn of the sixteenth century most of them were Hungarian and Roman Catholic; the German-speaking peoples were also Catholic, while the Romanians living in Transylvania and the various Slavic peoples living primarily in the northern and southwestern part of the country were members of the Eastern Orthodox Church. This raises the first and perhaps most important question: how did the coexistence of the Roman and Eastern churches and religions influence the reception of the Reformation in Hungary?

Subsequent questions are the result of the present-day status of historiography and my personal interest. To look for the revolutionary character of the Reformation in Hungary is impossible. No social movement mobilizing immense forces emerged in Hungary after the peasant war of 1514. The possibility of research, however, into acculturation seems not to be absurd, since highly educated intellectuals championed the teachings of Martin Luther with support from powerful and in many cases very well-educated lords. The question is, who was the initiator: did the élite rise in opposition to the knowledge of the simple man or did the latter demand new knowledge? Power was certainly not in the hands of the "poor community," as the ordinary people were called at the time. But did the Reformation provide them with more power, or make them even more vulnerable than they had been previously?

Finally, we know for certain that the church organizations of the various denominations came into existence. Uncertainty surrounds social and cultural differentiation: who were closer to one another, the Catholic lord and the Catholic peasant, the Protestant lord and the Protestant peasant, or the Catholic and Protestant lords and the Catholic and Protestant peasants? The division of the medieval Kingdom of Hungary into three different state configurations beginning in the middle of the sixteenth century further complicates the situation. The Habsburg king, the national prince and the Ottoman Turkish sultan all ruled within the common historical space. With the exception of a brief period of just a few years, none of them was the member of a Protestant denomination. Nevertheless, by the end of the sixteenth century, the large majority of the inhabitants of Hungary became adherents of confessions that had grown out of the Reformation. How did this happen? Was there any external pressure in it?

I place the time frame of this narrative or meditation between 1444 and 1590. The former year was that in which a document was dated that provides indisputable data showing that patrons in Hungary exercised patronage over the churches on their lands without regard to their religious affiliation. The latter year was that in which the full Hungarian translation of the Bible was first published, in the small village of Vizsoly. I selected this event because the translation of the entire Bible represented the greatest intellectual achievement of the reformers in Hungary—one that also points to the future. The text, composed under the leadership of the parish preacher Gáspár Károlyi, established the fundamental standards of the Hungarian language that have remained valid until the present day. In addition, the time between the middle of the fifteenth century and the end of the sixteenth is the period in which I feel myself intellectually comfortable.

The train of thought of my essay will be meandering rather than linear. I begin from afar because I presume that the Reformation represented a significant change, and changes cannot be understood properly when examined in themselves. I began writing under the presumption that I knew the ending of the story. However, it turned out that many things were completely different than I had previously thought. Perhaps I have followed a line of thinking that departs from the previous ones. I will present to the reader this meandering path.

Before I begin, I would like to return to the theme of art treasures. I am not aware of the personal reflections or motives that have led others to adopt an interpretation of the Reformation that represents an almost perfect departure from that which prevailed previously. The surprise I had at the Hungarian National Gallery exercised an enormous impact on me. This could be because as a historian I have become accustomed to intellectual experiences acquired via reading and thus the visual sensation of the exhibition shocked me. I could have obtained information regarding the date of origin of the works of art from books and I certainly had gained knowledge regarding them in this traditional manner. However, it is one thing to know the facts of art history, and another altogether to marvel at treasures of art that long ago represented the means of exercising piety for people who have become close to me as a result of my research.

This surprise was primarily a personal experience, though it also led to my recognition that there was something wrong with the explanation for the Reformation that I had learned. I had previously found plausible the frequently cited contempt and estrangement of the faithful of the old church before I suddenly realized: the works of art standing before me are tokens of an extremely vivid piety. It is hard to determine if this traditional piety at the time of the Reformation was more vibrant than that of the previous ages. I doubt that comparisons of this nature are feasible or worthwhile. I will not even make an attempt to make such a comparison. I will simply state the conclusion that no matter how we regard the Reformation, it took place during an age in which there was an intensive interaction between the believers and the church.

I am not alone in this opinion. Lajos Pásztor, an outstanding though long-forgotten historian who dealt with piety in the decades before the 1526 Battle of Mohács, described the same thing, though only in indirect connection to the Reformation in Hungary. Pásztor's fundamental proposition was that

> The fourteenth and fifteenth centuries not only brought a deepening of piety, but also enhanced knowledge and culture, elevating them into the broadest segments of society and the people.

Pásztor's book, which did not polemicize, was published in 1940, but from the perspective of the prevailing Reformation discourse, it claimed that the Reformation was unnecessary in Hungary because all the inferred religious consequences of it had already taken place during one of the rich periods in Hungarian church history. Pásztor's opinion had little impact during his own era.

Seen from today's perspective, Lajos Pásztor's book can be regarded as a series of postmodern, microhistorical analyses. His work provides detailed descriptions of piety manifested in active, living deed within the context of monastic life, lay confraternities, pilgrimages and church building. Pásztor arrived to the recognition of living devotion not through sudden insight, but through scholarly research. His assertion that religious life had undergone transformation in Hungary prior to the Reformation can also be correct, even if I am uncertain about it. There is no means for comparing the intensity of pieties through time. In spite of this, there is no doubt that before the Reformation parishioners maintained a close relationship with the church and they took an interest in matters of religion.

I am presently looking at how the Reformation evolved from this perspective, from the premise that relations between the congregation and the church were healthy. I have already stated my research questions. They can be summarized briefly as follows: what did the Reformation mean for the simple man and woman in Hungary?

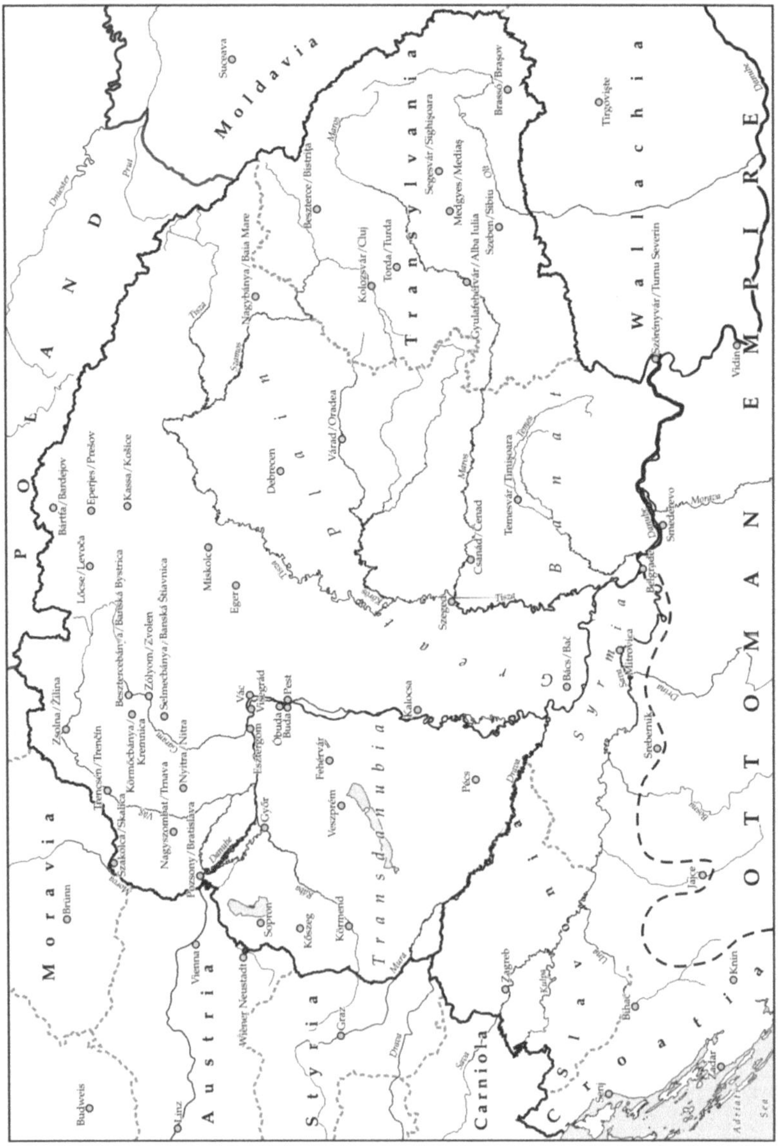

Fig. 2. Map. The Kingdom of Hungary in the Early Sixteenth Century

2 The Coexistence of Languages and Churches

Hungarian and Other Vernaculars

In this chapter I would like to describe how the inhabitants of Reformation-era Hungary tolerated each other's languages at all levels of society, and that the simultaneous presence of two religions—the Western Latin and the Eastern Orthodox—did not cause conflict. From an evolutionary standpoint this would not be surprising. It is common knowledge that the history of European development examines within the context of nation building the emergence of the need to forge cultural unity, which includes a consciousness regarding the use of the native language and religious affiliation as well. However, the peoples of Hungary did not constitute nations in the modern sense of the term at the turn of the sixteenth century. Consequently, there could not have existed between them linguistic or cultural antagonism.

I would not at all dispute the nonexistence of nations in Hungary at this time. I have not previously engaged in contemplations of the philosophy of history, nor will I now. I would simply emphasize that my research experience has shown that medieval people were very attached to their native languages and the cultural practices connected to their religious affiliation.

I believe that the fact that the kings and queens of Hungary learned the Hungarian language provides conspicuous proof of the importance of the mother tongue. This was a long-established practice by the time of the Reformation: since the death of the last Árpád-dynasty king, Andrew III, in 1301, the kings of Hungary had, with only two exceptions, not spoken Hungarian as their native language but they had to learn it. Even King Sigismund of Luxembourg, who became Holy Roman Emperor in 1411, knew Hungarian and, if needed, used the language as well, as Elemér Mályusz indisputably proved. This means that the most powerful sovereign in Europe was not above speaking in the Hungarian language just as any Hungarian peasant would. The nobility did not develop its own language in Hungary—the linguistic separation between the powerful and the people did not take place. This was a peculiar situation that diverged from the situation in countries to both the West and East of Hungary, including the Romanian voivodeships. I have not yet discovered the reason for this peculiarity.

I do not even regard it to be completely understandable. In seeking the reasons for which the rulers of Hungary learned the Hungarian language, I stumbled upon the odd circumstance that Hungarian aristocrats used the power of the mother tongue only against the monarchs. The kings and queens had to learn Hungarian, though the aristocracy of Hungary not only acknowledged the existence of various languages, but learned each other's languages as well. Or it might be more precise to write that the aristocrats of Hungary spoke the several languages used in the country. I believe this unambiguous wording to be warranted due to my uncertainty regarding the issue of the aristocracy's native language. Earlier, when I read in a letter dating from the early sixteenth century that the approximately three-year-old daughter of Palatine György Thurzó addressed her father as *Pane apka*, I concluded that the native language of the family was Slovak. I assumed that the child was speaking in her native tongue. However, after doing more research on the aristocracy of Hungary, I now conclude that a Slovak servant most likely took care of the little girl, thus the little girls also spoke Slovak and in the given circumstance used this language to address her father, though she could have just as well spoken to him in Hungarian. Thurzó and his wife, Erzsébet Czobor, conducted their correspondence in Hungarian and if I had not encountered the Slovak-language quotation in the otherwise Hungarian-language letter, I would have naturally considered Hungarian to be the native language of the Thurzós.

I do not want to overcomplicate the issue of the native language of the aristocracy in Hungary, though I cannot resist the opportunity to draw a conclusion from the case of the Thurzós mentioned above. The origin of the family can be traced to Austria. Johannes Thurzó, once the mayor of Kraków, moved among them to Hungary. One member of the family—Alexius Thurzó—asked a German-speaking Transylvanian Saxon scholar to serve as a tutor for his daughters in the 1540s. Some time before that he wrote the first Hungarian-language love letter that has been preserved. Kata Zrínyi, the daughter of the hero of Szigetvár, Miklós Zrínyi, married into the Thurzó family. We know that she grew up in a Croatian-language environment. Nonetheless, she conducted her correspondence in Hungarian as an adult. What was the native language of this group of people? If they were still alive, it would be possible to ask them about the language and ethnic group with which they identified. However, since this is not possible, I will refer to Tibor Klaniczay, one of the greatest specialists on the era of the Reformation in Hungary. Klaniczay asserted that the people of Hungary, including both the aristocracy and the intellectuals, were imbued with "*Hungarus* consciousness." That is, they felt themselves to be the inhabitants of Hungary—a sentiment that included not only the use of their own mother tongue, but command of the Hungarian language as well.

Thus the aristocrats and the intellectuals—though I will not write about the latter in this train of thought—of Hungary knew Hungarian. However, this does not in any sense mean that they had assimilated. They had not assimilated by learning the Hungarian language, just as the foreign sovereigns who learned Hungarian obviously did not regard themselves to be Hungarian for this reason. I could not define the concept of "native language" under such circumstances, but whatever it was, they did not relinquish it for Hungarian. I can cite, for example, the sixteenth-century correspondence between two magnates, Ferenc Batthyány and György Zrínyi, conducted in Latin, Hungarian and Croatian. I have no idea which of the latter languages was their vernacular. The only certainty is that neither of them forced the other to use his own. The number of such cases is nearly innumerable.

I will now make a big leap, from the lords to the tenants. I omit the burghers, who most often used their German native language. This is not surprising: they were the free citizens of free cities. But the tenant peasants? No one claims that they were free in the late fifteenth and early sixteenth centuries. At the same time, no lord, authority, county or state interfered in the issue of their language use. Nobody forced their subjects to learn the language of the majority.

Much data—as well as the non-existence of data—verifies this relationship, which could be deemed tolerant using the language of today, between the peasantry and choice of language. There is no information suggesting that officials of the manors demanded that tenants use the Hungarian language. In fact, there is indirect data proving just the opposite. None of the complaints connected to the 1437 large peasant revolt led by Antal Budai Nagy were related to language. I believe this to be significant because a large proportion of the rebels had Romanian as their mother tongue. Their dissatisfaction was nourished from several fonts, but the inability to use the Romanian language freely was not among them.

With regard to the conspicuous lack of language-related complaints from Romanians in 1437, one could say that the consciousness of language had not yet reached the level at this period that would have enabled them to perceive attacks on their mother tongue, even if such attacks had taken place. Simple facts tell another story. Romanians participated in the revolt emphatically as Romanians. According to the Latin text of the agreement signed with the lords before the Kolozsmonostor convent, the participants in the uprising were *hungari* and *volahi*, that is, Hungarians and Romanians in the words used at that time. This is what appears also in the charter pertaining to the first agreement as well as the convent's record of the affair. The second agreement reached after much controversy mentions captain *Michael Volachus de Wyragosberek* in prominent position among the peasant leaders. That is, a Romanian named Michael from the village of Virágosberek (Floreşti, Romania) was one of the leaders of the movement.

It is certain that the peasants who participated in this fifteenth-century uprising were consciously Hungarian or Romanian. Their agreement with the lords was inscribed using the standard procedure at the time, that is, according to verbal statements that the parties made before the authorities. The peasants referred to themselves as Hungarian or Romanian and captain Michael from Virágosberek himself stated his name together with the definition of himself as Romanian. The peasants who took part in the revolt clearly made a distinction between the Hungarian and the Romanian mother tongue. The Romanians would have obviously complained if they had been regarded as Hungarians and forced to speak the Hungarian language. They apparently maintained no such grievances. They could not have even done so. All available data shows that the landowners and the manorial officials adapted to the language of the peasants.

This linguistic adaptation is reflected above all in the names of the peasants used in manorial documents from the period. There are many records containing such names, which manorial officials frequently specify are derived from verbal information from the peasants. These documents reveal that the representatives of the lords spoke with the tenants in their vernacular. That becomes evident when native-language manorial surveys in Hungarian, German or various Slavic languages began to be written beginning around the middle of the sixteenth century. As one might expect, I know of no such registers in the Romanian or Rusyn languages. During this period, both languages were written using Cyrillic script, which not only manorial stewards, but Eastern Orthodox priests generally could not write. Romanian or Rusyn names were recorded in documents, most of them written in Hungarian, based on their sound.

The adaptation of manorial stewards to the language of the tenants is demonstrated most clearly in Latin manorial surveys (*urbaria*) originating from the period before the emergence of native languages on the landed estates. The Latin texts of these registers were written according to information that the peasants provided in their native languages. This mother-tongue form of self-definition speaks loudest in the names of women appearing in the Latin *urbaria.* Since the Latin language contains no construction to express the female family name, it would have been logical to simply omit the unnecessary derivative. However, this is not what happened. Maria Schreyfogelin, the daughter or wife of a German man with the family name Schreyfogel, for example, was not registered in the Latin manorial survey as Maria Schreyfogel, but just as the German-speaking tenant providing the information for the documents pronounced her name: Maria Schreyfogelin. Moreover, the Christian names of various Slavic peoples were never translated into Latin. Most of these Slavs bore the names of Byzantine saints—Anastasia, Priscilla, Ludmila, Greško, Şerban and Vitus—that had no equivalent in Latin. Thus the names provided in the Slavic mother tongue remained in their original form in the documents. Slavic family names in the feminine form were also unaltered. Thus widow Sukniczko was registered as Sukniczkowa, with the Latin word for widow—*relicta*—also indicated. Although use of the latter word was standard in Latin documents, some form of the word *widowa* was used to designate widows in regions with a large number of people who spoke some Slavic language as their native tongue.

In the end, I found no evidence of acts of violence related to language. At the same time, I am aware that those about whom I am writing were mortals. They lived in accordance with both the fundamentally peaceful natures that anthropologists have ascribed to humans and their general human weaknesses. I also know that the Hungarian expression "the *Tót* [slang for "Slovak"] is not a human being," which one might regard as a product of nineteenth-century nationalism, already existed in the fifteenth century, when it appeared in Hungarian in a Latin-language chronicle in reference to rebellious peasants. Standing at the other end of the social spectrum was Miklós Oláh, who began his career as a royal secretary before becoming a member of the court of Queen Mary of Hungary and later rising to the headship of the Catholic Church in Hungary. Oláh, an outstanding humanist who corresponded with Erasmus, was subjected to a series of pasquinades ridiculing his Romanian origin. Gábor Almási has drawn my attention to this phenomenon. It would obviously be possible to find other such data. However, historiography cannot focus separately on every single individual.

Two Churches before the Reformation

The coexistence of the churches developed similarly to that of languages. During the rule of the Árpád dynasty there had been politically tinged conflict between the adherents of the Roman and Byzantine churches, although by the end of the Middle Ages this discord had long since passed. A large majority of the landowners were Latin Christians, though there were great families of Eastern Orthodox faith even in the middle of the sixteenth century. There is no data showing the number or proportion of Eastern Orthodox among either the higher or lower social strata. The majority of inhabitants belonging to any social strata was certainly Latin Christian, while the majority of Eastern Orthodox were peasants.

There is no indication that members of either denomination bothered those of the other despite the obvious differences between them. Evident disparities emerged in church teachings, though it is unnecessary to record them here because we know very little regarding the degree to which simple people were aware of the nuances of church teachings. There is no point in brooding about the issue of whether they ever meditated about the fact that their relationship with the saints and with the Virgin Mary was normatively different. However, ordinary people must have perceived visual differences between the two religions. In this regard, one must not think of church interiors, because the faithful of each denomination likely did not attend the religious services of the other. What they saw were each other's processions, those of the Latin Christians with their portraits of saints and portable statues and those of the Eastern Orthodox with their icons. The piety of Eastern Christianity differed from their Western counterparts in their lack of three-dimensional representations and lifelike paintings. Thus those who witnessed religious processions could immediately determine the church to which they belonged.

The relationship of clergymen with the faithful, which was reflected in both their appearance and social status, represented a significant difference between the Latin and the Eastern Orthodox church as well. It was clearly perceptible without any knowledge of theological teachings. Latin priests were expected to be unmarried, to be clean-shaven, to tonsure their hair and to wear priestly vestments while the Orthodox had no such prescriptions. Parishioners could see the difference even if many Roman clergymen obviously neglected the rules. They could also see the difference in the way that Orthodox priests and their families mingled with the members of their congregations—whom they resembled not merely in appearance—and the hidden and irregular sexual relations of Roman priests who strove to avoid the grace of children if possible. However, many Latin priests must have lived as they were expected to live, thus differentiating themselves even more from their Orthodox counterparts.

The difference in social status between the clergy of the two churches manifested itself in the fact that the Orthodox usually lived on tenant plots, whereas the Roman priests only very rarely, if ever, did. In my decades of research, I have not yet encountered a Latin clergyman living on tenant holding. In Orthodox villages residing on tenant plots was the norm for the *batykó*, *kalugyer* or *pop*, as their priests were called. Landlords differentiated those priests from tenants at most places by exempting them from the customary liabilities of the subjects. Sometimes they had to provide the lord with a small so-called "gift," candles, straps and the like. Thus the distinct, albeit serf-like, social status of Orthodox priests was acknowledged. Latin priests, contrarily, were not only exempted from service and liability, but often received some sort of income from the lord. The faithful certainly noticed this difference, if in no other way than in the disparity between the material circumstances of Latin and Greek priests.

In addition to the disparate manifestations of piety between the two religions and the differences in the lifestyle of their priests, the members of the two Christian churches maintained distinctly dissimilar customs. This divergence was most conspicuous with regard to marriage. Although elopement—entering into conjugal relations without the permission of the family—was customary among all peoples, officially recognized marriage differed between Roman and Eastern Christians.

Church weddings were considered standard among Latin Christians in Hungary during the Reformation era. I consider this to be almost incomprehensible because tradition did not call for church wedding ceremonies. At the time of a synod decree issued at the beginning of the twelfth century regarding the conduct of weddings "in the presence of the church" (*in facie ecclesie*)—a decree that may never have been codified—weddings that could be called private-law marriages were common practice. That is, the families of the partners came to a private agreement and made the fact of the union public in a ceremonial manner of some type that likely included a rite of pagan origin. Nevertheless, the synod decree was not reissued and whether codified or not, it is certain that no law was adopted after the early twelfth century regarding obligatory church weddings. On the other hand, laws were passed concerning other marriage-related issues such as inheritance that considered church wedding ceremonies to be natural.

Church weddings appear to have become a social norm among Latin Christians in Hungary to the extent that the marriage partners were either truly married in a church or claimed to have been married in a church in order to comply with well-known official norms. However, to make such a false claim was extremely risky, threatening both the inheritance of the offspring as well as the marriage itself, which could be invalidated if reported to be irregular. It is likely that only marginalized Latin Christian couples failed to hold church weddings. In any case, church regulations enacted in the sixteenth century, just as the synod decree issued three hundred years earlier, describe the standard wedding ceremony and prescribe no punishment for those not held in churches. This suggests that failure to observe the standard wedding procedure was not common. Secret marriage was subject to penalty and priests were forbidden by church authorities to officiate them. The reason for declaring that at synods repeatedly has a single explanation: secret marriages happened in churches, with priests celebrating them. Sources show that the main point, as regards clandestine marriages in the sixteenth century, was not the presence or absence of the priest but the knowledge about the ceremony of the congregation. Church weddings were considered to be perfectly regular if the community became aware of them. Let us add: not only became aware of them, but approved them as well. Church authorities insisted upon making the weddings public so that possible impediments to the marriage would come to light or that the nonexistence of such impediments would become certain.

The custom of church weddings did not develop among the Eastern Orthodox by the sixteenth century, although the much-cited synod decree, before the Great Schism, pertained to members of this church as well. Eve Levine, who wrote on sexuality in Slavic countries and examined the regulation of marriage as well, asserts that not even the joint effort of the state and the church managed to eliminate the old customs by this time. These traditions remained even more entrenched in Hungary, where the large majority of Orthodox lived on the estates of Latin Christian landowners. The lords simply acknowledged the customs of the Orthodox communities. Neither did they attempt to force them to conduct church weddings nor did they object to either husband- or wife-initiated dissolution of their marriages. At the very most, fines were imposed on the party initiating the divorce on some estates.

Orthodox Christians were not forced to observe Roman canon law, just as they were not subjected to attempts to convert them or to change their religious practices. This fact can be demonstrated most clearly in the case of the Romanians who moved to Transylvania in ever greater numbers at the end of the thirteenth century. Landowners invited them to move to this region of Hungary to serve as soldiers or farmers. And although sources show that the majority of landowners were Latin Christians, the notion of forcing the Orthodox Romanians to change their religion did not even occur to them. The Romanians who thus moved to Transylvania requested and received permission to build Orthodox churches and were able to practice their religion without any external interference until the first decades of the sixteenth century.

Landowners were not interested in interfering in the religious affairs of their tenants, because church affiliation exercised no impact on the rights or obligations of the latter. The landowner served as the patron of both Roman and Orthodox churches. According to canon-law specialists, patronage did not proceed from land ownership. They refer to the fact that royal or private charters mention the transfer of ownership and of patronage often separately. The precise source of patronage has not yet been determined. In practice, by the beginning of the sixteenth century it had come to constitute the strongest element of seigneurial power.

The Roman church attempted to curtail it by making the nomination of parish priests contingent upon episcopal approval. However, the patrons insisted on maintaining their right to appoint parish priests. This dispute reached the Diet in 1504, ending with the victory of the patrons. In this year, an act was passed in which the king and the estates declared that bishops had no right to interfere in the patron's right to elect the parish priest. The law furthermore stated that the obligation of the relevant congregation to pay tithes would be suspended in the event that a bishop installed a priest to a parish against the wishes of the landowner. No such conflict could have emerged between the Orthodox church and the landowners for two reasons: first, the Orthodox church had no representation in the Diet; and second—and more significantly—the residence of Orthodox priests on tenant plots. As plots could be assigned only by landowners, the appointment of Orthodox priests was naturally contingent upon seigneurial approval.

It is also certain that the assertion of the right of patronage did not depend on the religious affiliation of the landowner or the faithful. The transfer of patronage over Eastern Orthodox churches is mentioned separately in donation charters, just as it is for Roman churches. Since both Orthodox and Roman churches could exist on a single estate, the landowner, regardless of his religious affiliation, received patronage over the churches of both denominations. An extremely clear case of this is connected to the fifteenth-century military and political leader János Hunyadi. Based on the justification that he had financed his military campaigns against the Turks using his own wealth, Hunyadi claimed many estates. According to one of the donation charters, he received some of these estates from one of his allies, the Serbian Despot Đurađ Branković, who was also the Lord of Albania.

Despot Đurađ was, through his extensive kinship and an enormous amount of land in the country, a member of the Hungarian aristocracy. When he transferred all his estates in Hungary to Hunyadi in 1444, these included holdings in the purely Hungarian-inhabited city of Debrecen and the primarily Rusyn- and Romanian-inhabited Orthodox regions around the Munkács (Mukachevo, Ukraine) and Világos (Şiria, Romania) castles. Branković spoke Serbian as his native language, while Hunyadi spoke Romanian. Branković was Orthodox, Hunyadi at that time conspicuously followed the Roman church. None of these facts played any role in the transfer of property from Branković to Hunyadi. The relevant charter states that the estates would be transferred to Hunyadi along with the "Christian and Vlach" churches. The Eastern Orthodox Branković obviously regarded himself to be just as Christian as the Roman Christian Hunyadi, though he used the customary terminology differentiating churches belonging to Western and Eastern Christianity.

Seen from our modern perspective, Branković indirectly declared himself to be a non-Christian. However, people living at that time looked at things differently. Although they obviously noticed disparities in language and religion and thought them to be important, under normal conditions nobody derived benefit or suffered disadvantage as a result of these differences. The distribution of power depended neither on native language nor on religion. At an everyday level, the mother tongue and religion of the landlord did not matter to the people living on his estates and vice versa.

Neither side bothered the other on the basis of language or religion, although the people living in Hungary at the end of the Middle Ages cannot be said to have been particularly peaceful by nature. The peasants conducted cruel uprisings that the lords brutally suppressed. The events of the 1514 peasant revolt that took place in Hungary under the leadership of György Dózsa are a reflection of many conditions; peaceful coexistence between lord and peasant is certainly not among them.

Attempts to redistribute power provoked upheaval, though before the Reformation neither language nor religion represented factors related to power and did not arouse agitation. More precisely: it was not a social custom that they should do so.

ASPASIA
ASZSZONY DOLGA
ÉS AZ IO ERKŐLCZŰ ASZ-
SZONYOKNAC TŰ-
kőre.

Az Lucretia notayára.

Iane, tuæ Aspasiam memorari Forro puellæ
Nicoleos Figula de gente Bogathius optat.

NYOMTATTOT COLOS-
uárat az ò Várban. 1591.
Esztendőben.

Fig. 3. Bogáti Fazekas Miklós, *Aspasia aszszony dolga és az io erkölczü aszszonyoknac tüköre*, Colosuarat, 1591. Front Page

3 Some Facts about Domination

The Poor Community

Disturbances in the flow of authority arose from the side of the common man, entailing the defense of power against their penetration attempts. I struggle with terminological difficulties as I write this. The generic term *gemeiner Mann* had at the time of the Reformation in the country of its origin, Germany, several contents, one of which was to describe the individual social and intellectual troublemaker. The *gemeiner Mann* was a protagonist of the German Peasants' War and it also appeared in contemporary literature. Many researchers believe that he entered the pages of literary fiction from the reality of the peasant war.

In Hungarian, the word *közember* could be regarded as the equivalent of *gemeiner Mann*, though it was not used in Hungary to designate such troublemakers during the Reformation period even though such people existed in the country. For the time being, I will refer to such people using the term "simple man." Mihály Balázs, an expert on early Unitarianism, proved their unquestionable existence. He examined the most common literary genre pertaining to the existence of the troublemaker, the so-called Reformation dialogues. Balázs determined that the version of this genre that appeared in Hungary proceeded from the same broad social and linguistic base as the original Reformation dialogues in Germany. He concluded, furthermore, that the Reformation dialogues in Hungary utilized the same motifs in order to introduce the simple man who interfered in the debates of scholars or outwitted the authorities as were used throughout the rest of Europe.

Why did the term *gemeiner Mann* come into usage in Germany, whereas no such common expression emerged in Hungary? I think that the formal explanation for this might be that whereas the simple man who disturbed the well-arranged order of things elsewhere in Europe was most often a mason or a peasant, in Hungary he was generally a village judge. According to the authors of Reformation dialogues in Hungary, village judges identified by name, sometimes together with masons or peasants, expressed the correct opinion and made the voice of the people heard vis-à-vis the cunning enemy, a learned or socially influential person.

In terms of content, this means that the judge appears as the chosen representative of the simple people. One could also depict this as the ordinary man acting collectively in the role of troublemaker. The term that was used in Hungary instead of *gemeiner Mann—község* ("community" or "congregation")—reflects this collective character. I do not know if the divergent outlook of those who composed literature or the divergent behavior of those described in literature explains this difference. I raise the latter possibility because, beyond confusing the dialogues, the poor community acted earlier than the *gemeiner Mann*. The people who personified the German term brought their displeasure with the existing order to the attention of its representatives via the German Peasants' War, following Luther's countenance. Those who embodied the Hungarian term did the same thing via the 1514 Dózsa revolt, in other words a decade earlier. Since Dózsa's peasant war became a taboo right after the events, it inflicted a collective wound upon Hungarian society. The name of the participants was "crusader." And nobody spoke of them thereafter.

The word "community," commonly expanded to "poor community" to express the sympathy of the representatives of the Reformation, came to collectively define the simple people in Hungary. In contrast to them stood the "princes," whom in the words of Gáspár Károlyi,

> Flay the poor community, eviscerate it, disfigure its corpse as a senseless beast fit for butchery. If they want gold or silver, they open their throat wide so they can take from the poor person what he has.

The term "poor community" was, accordingly, very complicated and designated a very complex social formula. It is flayed but gold and silver can be taken from it. The "poor community" was not necessarily poor, otherwise it would not have possessed gold and silver. However, it was not necessarily rich either, otherwise it would not have been flayed. The "poor community" in Hungary is thus just as complex as the *gemeiner Mann* in Germany. Many researchers are trying to determine the social group specified according to the latter term. Does it indicate both rural and urban people? If so, then what position of rural or urban life? Wealthy? Eking out a meager existence? There are major debates regarding these questions within both German and Anglo-Saxon historiography, the latter of which uses the expression "common man" to designate the troublemaking *gemeiner Mann*.

Endless debates could be initiated regarding the Hungarian term as well. However, I will not proceed in this direction now. I would simply note: I am interested in the rural "poor community." From the term "prince" used by Gáspár Károlyi and other reformers I have chosen the landowners. I am dealing with the community living under the authority of the landowner. Based on the work of Tibor Klaniczay and László Makkai, those living in the market towns are generally separated from those living in the villages. My research experience suggests that no significant difference can be made. The landowning prince ruled over the market-town community just as he did over the village. I only deal with city dwellers, whose prince was the king himself, in instances in which sources do not permit separation. This will be the situation in the case of lay preachers, whose rural or urban background is impossible to ascertain.

With regard to the importance of urban poor community, let it suffice to say that most of the beautiful ecclesiastical treasures described in the introduction were originally located in urban churches, which to this day contain works of similarly great value. Representatives of the urban poor community, the judges and the elected magistrate, took care of the construction and maintenance of churches. I find an incident that took place in Kassa to be revealing. When certain people appeared in the predominantly Lutheran city with the teachings of Calvin, it was not their teaching that caused the greatest indignation, but their removal of embellishments from one of Kassa's churches. The city magistrate took immediate action against them. People had become attached to the old, magnificent interior of the church. One of the reasons that cities in Hungary remained Lutheran in contrast to their counterparts in Western Europe might have been that very few changes needed to be made to their originally Roman churches.

The Simple-minded

I thought for a while about using the word *simple-minded*, *együgyű* in Hungarian, to refer to the common man. In the end I rejected this possibility for two reasons, one related to the behavior of certain contemporaries of the Reformation and one connected to the opinion of certain historians who deal with the Reformation. I will briefly describe both of these reasons, because they are characteristic of the era and the historiography regarding it equally.

With regard to the Reformation age, I noticed the odd phenomenon that there was great interest in the community from contrasting directions. It could be interpreted as an attempt to voluntarily distribute power. One of these sources of interest originated in the studies of humanist scholars, the other emerged from the halls of the papal state. The humanists wanted to extend the power of knowledge to the common man, while papal officials wanted to share with them the power of the church's secrets. These objectives were founded upon the same spiritual need of the community and can thus only formally be separated from one another. And in fact, both of them were realized.

Seen from the perspective of the current media-centered world, it is hard to imagine a time when scholars did not want to reach the largest possible audience. In reality, scholars were long reluctant to leave their ivory towers for the real world and did not come into contact with the simple people until around the time of the Reformation. This is when they discovered them as an audience. Or, perhaps, this is when interest in learning awoke in the simple people. There are debates among historians regarding whether the desire to communicate or the receptiveness to learning emerged first. There is, however, agreement among them regarding the importance of the new medium of the age—the printed book—in this process.

Amid the cultural circumstances in which we presently live, more than a few people are concerned about the survival of the galaxy that Johann Gutenberg constructed just in the middle of the fifteenth century. The Bible was naturally the first book that he printed, and then the printed letter was subsequently used for many purposes. I do not consider it to be a coincidence that science and the church simultaneously recognized the possible benefits and threats of connecting the new medium with the new audience. The Fifth Lateran Council issued a decree in 1514 making the permission from local bishops a requisite for the printing of any book. The justification for this decree was that reading had produced much "scandal" and that the spread of further such deviancy must be prevented. On the other hand, the prince of the humanists, Erasmus, wrote in his famous *Paraclesis* published for the first time in 1516 that the Christian religion cannot be defended by preventing the people from becoming familiar with it:

> Indeed, I disagree very much with those who are unwilling that Holy Scripture, translated into the vulgar tongue, be read by the uneducated, as if Christ taught such intricate doctrines that they could scarcely be understood by very few theologians, or as if the strength of the Christian religion consisted in men's ignorance of it.

The *unlearned* of Erasmus, *populus* in the Latin original, became in the first Hungarian translation by Gábor Pesti *együgyű*. That means that it could be applied to the community as an authentic term. Contemporaries, however, seem not to have appreciated it. They, as far as I can tell, did not take over the use of *együgyű* in this sense. I left it as well. Further, its connotations in modern public discourse are excessively negative. I fear that use of the word *együgyű* or *the simple-minded* would give the impression that I disdain the relationship between the Roman church and the uneducated people about whom I shall hereafter write.

The interest of the papal state in the community and the recognition of its intellectual and spiritual needs led—along a winding path—to the sale of indulgences for money. I do not want to write in detail about indulgences because the teaching pertaining to it is incomprehensible for today's laypeople and the reader who is familiar with Roman Catholic theology will know it anyway. With regard to the simple people, the most important thing to know is that the price of indulgences counted as an offertory, a pious donation. The pope originally tied the payment of such money to auricular confession and participation in the sacrifice of the Holy Mass. Those who paid for indulgences received a voucher known popularly as an indulgence slip that could be used to provide proof that such a remission of sins had been obtained. However, certain sellers of indulgences simplified the procedure, issuing indulgence slips in exchange for money only. In this way, simple people got the impression that it was possible to obtain indulgence without having a share of divine grace mediated in the sacraments.

The matter of those who sold indulgences "fraudulently" became the subject of official interest in a place as far from the center of Latin Christianity as Veszprém, Hungary. In 1515, Bishop of Veszprém Péter Beriszló and many secular dignitaries summoned a diocesan synod. The text of the decrees adopted at the end of this synod represents an important source among the few historical documents that originate from late medieval Hungary. This document was long only partially known from a fragmentary eighteenth-century manuscript that contained many retroactive insertions. Gedeon Borsa discovered the document in its full original form a couple of decades ago and László Solymosi published its critical edition in 1997. This document offers the reader extraordinarily useful information.

The fact that clerical officials in the region of Veszprém dealt with the matter of possible abuses connected to the matter of indulgences, and that they issued a decree intended to prevent such abuses, reflects both widespread interest in the indulgences and the frequency of corrupt practices surrounding them. From this point it would be possible to follow a clear logical progression, in the manner of traditional historiography, toward the corruption of the Roman church.

However, it is also clear that those who purchased indulgences for money were pious members of the church. The sale of indulgences together with the abuses satisfied their needs. One cannot make money from something for which there is no demand and the sale of indulgences proved to be big business. The extent of its profitability around the time of the Reformation can be seen in the fact that the most successful banking dynasty in European history, the Fugger family that flourished financially in the early sixteenth century, became heavily involved in this business.

In fact, what took place was that people dressed in priestly vestments appeared at various locations and claimed that in exchange for a bigger or smaller pious donation they could curtail the period of purgatory—or perhaps even eliminate it altogether. And the believers—not all, but many of them—offered donations for this favor. How could they have known that if they simply paid for the indulgence without participating in the sacrament of penance and of the Eucharist that it would be invalid? Some sellers of indulgences cheated their customers. The reason they could do so was that the faithful trusted priests and would pay someone who bore the external markings of the clergy. Rome's calculations proved correct: the reason it happened this way was that church superiors assessed the demand correctly. People were genuinely willing to make material sacrifices in order to obtain the mediation of the church.

Luther, who originally believed in indulgences, was a loyal son of the church and the abuses incensed him. As everybody knows, he composed his famous ninety-five theses in his anger against the sale of indulgences.

Here I have reached a sensitive issue. I hope that I have argued with persuasive logic that the humanists and the church correctly recognized the intellectual and religious interests of the community. However, I know that there are serious scholars throughout Europe who maintain the opposite opinion. The "profound ignorance" of simple people at the time of the Reformation is a historical platitude. This has been stated regarding the German people just as it has about the Icelandic people, the Polish people and the Hungarian people. In Hungary, church historian and Reformed Bishop Imre Révész wrote in the most scathing terms about this issue, asserting that the Reformation did nothing to change the "total lack of education" among the lower strata of society.

The lack of sources from the late fifteenth and early sixteenth centuries makes it difficult to counter this opinion with straightforward facts. Moreover, much depends on what one regards as knowledge and education. Do we regard only those who are literate and perhaps even have a big library as educated, or do we also include those who were illiterate though maneuver successfully in the world around him or her? With regard to this topic, I agree with Robert Redfield and his school. According to them, purposeful human activity is a reflection not only of education, but presumes scientific thinking because it is built upon a firm belief in the power of reason.

In fact, I could merely claim that everything is a question of opinion and historical outlook. I will not do this. In the course of my research, I have identified with the poor community to a degree that is impermissible to the historian. I have difficulty tolerating discourse regarding simple-mindedness when this expression is used in its everyday meaning. And I have conducted research only in Hungary, thus I have no insight regarding the education of simple people elsewhere. With regard to Hungary, there was an important sequence of events that provides proof of the community's degree of knowledge.

I am thinking of the 1514 Dózsa rebellion. Data regarding the uprising sheds light upon the ideas that impelled the simple people to take action and which those who knew precisely what their community understood used to mobilize the masses. The reasoning behind the revolt provides a reflection of the culture of the peasants. This also fits into the present train of thought because the fact and outcome of 1514 determined the social disposition of the sixteenth century. Those people who either accepted or rejected the teachings of the Reformation lived according to the lessons learned from the rebellion.

Fig. 4. Stephanus Taurinus, *Stauromachia,* Vindobonae, 1519. Front Page, the execution of the peasant leader György Dózsa

4 Peasant Rebellion in 1514

Fight for Freedom

Jenő Szűcs, who moved through history with brilliant empathetic power, concluded that the Dózsa rebellion was aimed at achieving freedom. Here freedom has a very general meaning. It does not, therefore, mean that the peasants wanted to obtain freedom from one or more seigneurial burdens. Individual peasants or peasant communities frequently achieved freedom from obligations through agreement, not through battle. The deal concluded between several villages on the Németújvár (Güssing, Austria) estate and landowner Lőrinc Újlaki represents a good example of such agreements. In this instance, Újlaki exempted the inhabitants of these villages from the obligation to perform manual labor, presumably in exchange for a large sum of money. Their freedom was proclaimed in a charter. We do not know the date of this charter, though taking into account Újlaki's career, one may presume that it was issued before 1493. Later documents reveal that the "freedom" that "Prince Lőrinc" accorded to a group of villages on his estates remained valid for centuries and persisted through changes in ownership of the lands.

As to the Dózsa uprising, Szűcs managed to separate much diversionary data from the social-philosophical freedom contained in the demands of the rebels. Since he worked with peasants and simple intellectuals who had intermingled with them, he did not presume the existence of theoretical reasoning behind their notion of freedom. Szűcs concluded that György Dózsa, who, like many of his fellow rebels, likely belonged to the *Székely* subgroup of the Hungarian people, acted under the influence of the ideal of *Székely* freedom.

The Dózsa rebellion previously appeared in Hungarian historiography as a desperate action of the woefully oppressed and aggrieved peasantry. According to Szűcs, the revolt represented an effort of a rather broad, prosperous segment of the peasantry to attain their share of power. The origins of the uprising can be traced to events that can be characterized as "interesting" in the most vulgar sense of the word. Tamás Bakócz, Archbishop of Esztergom, whom contemporaries nicknamed "Wheelmaking Tamás" because his father was indeed a wheelwright, decided in 1513 that he would culminate his incomparable ascent within the ecclesiastical hierarchy by attaining the papacy. He had three orders of finery made for his household, loaded gold tableware onto ten wagons and made a majestic entry into Rome by horse and carriage. Throngs greeted Bakócz wherever he went in the city, though the College of Cardinals did not elect him pope, but instead chose Giovanni, a member of the banking family of the Medici that had long ruled over the Republic of Florence. Medici took the papal name Leo X, and in the writings of Luther he quickly became known as Antichrist.

Bakócz did not, however, leave Rome empty-handed. Pope Leo X compensated his defeated rival by appointing him to serve as the highest-ranking papal legate to an enormous territory stretching from Denmark to Wallachia and according him leadership of the crusade against the "infidel" Turks. Pope Leo X invoked the authority he had received from Christ to promise salvation and eternal life in the company of angels to all of those who participated in the Bakócz-led crusade in person. The pope made the same promises to monastic communities and laymen who provided a certain number of soldiers for the crusade as well as priests who made the call for war, those who provided donations for the campaign against the Turks as well as doctors, food suppliers and anybody else who participated directly or indirectly in the military operation. Pope Leo proclaimed eternal damnation with equal zeal upon all those who refused to join or otherwise assist the crusade. The relevant papal bull repeats in every possible place that the previous promises and threats apply to all Christian faithful regardless of gender.

I ask the reader to keep the previous fact in mind. We will return to the issue of believers of both sexes when examining the Reformation itself. With regard to the concept of the church, I consider the following fact to be important: women were unambiguously members of it. The fact that Pope Leo X emphatically counted upon women to participate in the crusade against the Turks in the explicitly male-dominated world of the early sixteenth century provides evidence supporting this understanding. If I am interpreting the text of the papal bull correctly, it applied equally to nuns, canteen women and aristocratic ladies.

An important element in this train of thought regarding the Dózsa rebellion is that the pope opened the possibility of participation in the crusade to all the Christian faithful and promised eternal salvation to all those who took part in it. One could state cynically that the offer of redemption substituted that of material benefit. In light of events it became clear that to contemporaries, or at least to many of them, the plenary remission of sins and eternal life were worth more than money. Tamás Bakócz proclaimed the papal bull in Hungary on April 9, 1514, along with the promise of salvation, appointed Dózsa to the leadership an April 24, and on May 9–10 the army started operations.

The participants in the crusade assembled slowly at first, then began to convene at the designated gathering places with increasing speed. The arrival of the crusaders depended primarily on the swiftness with which Franciscan friars whom Bakócz had called upon to levy recruits disseminated the pledge of salvation. The lords greeted the news of the crusade with little enthusiasm, while they regarded clergymen engaged in widespread recruitment with downright indignation. Already at the end of April 1514, lords complained that fraudulent preachers were calling people to enlist in the crusade with "sacrilegious audacity and baneful temerity," holding assemblies and generally inciting people to disobedience toward their superiors. We are unaware of the grounds upon which they regarded those engaged in the recruitment of participants in the military campaign to be fraudulent. One can only suspect that preachers acting under official sanction sought to punish those who had failed to provide the crusade with a sufficient number of soldiers in spite of the papal summons.

In any case, the complaints of the nobility alarmed Bakócz, who on May 15, 1514 suspended the public proclamation of the crusade by claiming that he had discovered that certain excommunicated friars and secular priests had been sowing the "cockles" of discord on the pretext of recruiting people to participate in the campaign. Bakócz used in the Latin text the word *zizania*, a term meaning field weed. It had been long used by the church to designate "straying" from its official teachings.

Bakócz's order arrived too late and could not prevent the crusade against the Turks from turning into a rebellion against the lords. At first sight, the arguments that sustained the uprising appear, absurdly, to have remained within the framework that the pope had provided. They were based on the teachings of the church, or more precisely, they utilized the concepts of the church. Only the identity of the enemy had been changed. The "infidel" lords and anybody else who actively opposed or refused to support the peasants had substituted the "infidel" Turks. Now the former faced the threat of eternal damnation, though this time via the volition of the rebel leaders rather than that of the pope. This transformation reached the point at which one of the leaders of the movement, the priest Ambrus, took upon himself the right to consecrate the army. The source of this information is György Szerémi, a contemporary chronicler, who although not a participant in the uprising, sympathized with the peasants.

According to Jenő Szűcs, priest Ambrus's act reveals that the notion of an army consecrated by its own priests and performing a divine mission existed throughout the time of the uprising. He arrived at this conclusion by examining contemporary ideas, such as the social criticism of influential Franciscan preachers Osvát Laskai and Pelbárt Temesvári, as well as the spiritual heresy of certain Franciscan friars or entire Franciscan cloisters that church authorities had so frequently condemned. I have summarized Jenő Szűcs's train of thought in very rudimentary form, though the reader can see that his reasoning is perfectly persuasive.

Seen from another perspective—that of the actions of the participants in the uprising—the ideas of the Dózsa rebellion show that the peasants understood the language of the church. This was the language that had to be used to communicate with the peasants, because this is the one they had learned from the pulpit, during confession and within their spiritual-intellectual environment. Gabriella Erdélyi examined the theological knowledge of the laity in connection to a much smaller affair that took place at roughly the same time as the Dózsa rebellion and concluded that on the part of the faithful there was a huge lay demand for the clergy and the church liturgies performed by them. People were familiar with church teachings to the extent that they explained their acts of negligence by citing official dogma. For example, if they failed to partake in Holy Communion at the prescribed time, at Easter, they claimed that they had maintained hostilities with some of their neighbors and did not want to partake of this sacrament in conscious sin before reconciliation.

I call this education. Because a person who successfully orients himself or herself within the intellectual world that surrounds him or her can be said to be educated. I must add that this is a question of perspective—how we evaluate the behavior of the official representatives and unofficial propagators of ideas. The pope could be the exploiter of the presumed and actual knowledge of the simple people as well as a recipient of common knowledge and faith. The clerical leaders of the uprising could be exploiters, users or teachers. They were certainly aware that they were building upon existing knowledge.

The brutal suppression of the uprising that itself had devolved into brutality also took place in the language of the church. It is commonly known that Dózsa was burned alive and many of his followers were executed. The details of the public execution are more or less familiar facts. However, we do not usually write about the reality that the objective of the post-rebellion reprisals was to kill the leaders of the uprising in both body and spirit. They did not receive the sacraments of confession and extreme unction and thus lost their Christian character. Szerémi's narratives indicate that György Dózsa considered himself until the last moment to be a member of the church. He allegedly made the following statement during his quietly endured, humiliating execution: "I have always thirsted for this on behalf of the pagans and now I am suffering it from my brothers." Dózsa was speaking the language of the church, and those who not long after the execution began to make pilgrimages to the site of his execution were using it in their act as well.

Lesson for the Lords

Hungary's Diet convened a few months after the post-rebellion reprisals. Its members made decisions based on their continued quest for vengeance. With reference to Tamás Bakócz's responsibility for the uprising, they proclaimed that the king should never again appoint a prelate of peasant origin. They also adopted the well-known law stipulating that tenants could not move off from the plot on which they lived. However, a loophole was built into this law, which was subsequently amended on several occasions and thus practically annulled. The lords of Hungary were realists. What would their power be worth if they were unable to entice the serfs who provided them with both money and produce away from one another?

Jurist and statesman István Werbőczy, who was not particularly popular among his contemporaries and gained an explicitly antipathetic reputation in the eyes of posterity, described the generally valid lesson to be learned from the Dózsa rebellion. He was an educated and philosophically informed man. Thus perhaps even the principle of natural law occurred to him in the course of his composition. Werbőczy concluded that all traitors who took part in the rebellion should be executed, though this would be impossible because it would lead to the disappearance of the peasantry without which the nobility would be worth little. This is what Werbőczy wrote into the proposed law that the majority of the Diet of Hungary subsequently adopted. Philosophical considerations likely did not emerge in the minds of the Diet's participants. They visited the Diet not to engage in philosophical deliberations, but to debate with the king, with one another, the great lords with lesser ones, and to pass legislation. Members of the Diet enlisted a jurist to draft the proposed law, which became definitive when the majority of the body approved it. This was what custom dictated as the introduction of the law in question in 1514 clearly indicates.

The nobility is worth little without the peasantry—this was the practically unanimous opinion of the lords who gathered in deliberation following the Dózsa rebellion. They had reached this opinion at the price of bitter experience and continued to adhere to it for a long time afterwards. Ever since the beginning of my career as a historian, I have had the feeling that during the period with which I am familiar—roughly the sixteenth and seventeenth centuries—the lords were afraid of the peasants. Although I do not wish to present here all of my fleeting impressions in this regard, I would like to highlight the most important one of them: the landowners in Hungary did not interfere in many issues in which their counterparts elsewhere did interfere.

I would put the most important element in self-identity—the name—in the first position in terms of the non-interference of landowners. Researchers in the countries neighboring Hungary maintain that peasants received their names from ecclesiastical or secular authorities. That is, superior powers determined the name that would represent them in parish registers, tax registers and other documents. There is no evidence that authorities of any type interfered in the naming of peasants in Hungary. I minutely described in the previous chapter the data regarding the use of mother tongues that are relevant to the present issue. To this I add: in another work I examined the use of names among the tenants and discovered that in Hungary communities of all native languages either gave their members names or permitted them to select their own family names.

I would rank marriage in second position in terms of landowner non-interference. In other countries, peasants either had to obtain permits to marry or were required to marry. There is no evidence of either such practice in Hungary. They were not forced to marry despite the common law stipulating that only married tenants had to perform feudal duties. I am aware of some exceptions to the regulation but I have never found any data suggesting that landowners ever forced peasants to marry. The peasant man selected his wife according to the norms of his local social environment. Unmarried women and widows entered into marriage in the same way. The landowner did not even interfere in the marriages of those who owned tenant plots despite the fact that the inheritance of their descendants entailed innumerable possible complications.

Another conspicuous consequence of the non-interference of the landowners in Hungary was the undisturbed authority of tenants over their children. Elsewhere, the unmarried sons and daughters of tenant peasants had to perform domestic service for the lord and were required to work on his manor until a certain age. I do not remember ever encountering in the course of my research evidence that the possible desire of a son of a tenant to study represented a source of conflict with the lord. The fact that the children of the subjects were not obliged to work as seigneurial servants does not mean that they could not do so. In my examination of the dreadful case of Countess Erzsébet Báthory, I noticed that people offered the services of their daughters to her court even after it had gained a reputation for cruelty. Power was a great attractive force then just as it is now. But the desire to learn or obtain higher social status through learning was great as well at that time. By the end of the Middle Ages, many children of peasants studied at universities abroad. As long as families satisfied their obligations connected to the tenant holdings, landowners took no interest in their children attending nearby or distant schools. Some landowners occasionally even provided financial support for it.

Finally, I would rank the issue of the system of serfdom in last place even though it is not the least important. According to many historians, the system of perpetual serfdom came into being in Hungary after 1514, which meant that peasants lived under permanent constraint and were at the complete mercy of the lord. The facts that I have presented regarding the non-interference of lords reflect the degree to which I do not agree with this notion. I believe that the traditional opinion of hereditary serfdom can be looked at as the legacy of the rural community studies movement vivid in 1930s-Hungary. The horrible findings of village researchers had a huge social resonance. It is understandable: indeed, industrialization carried out in a wretched way resulted in extreme poverty and the peasants' humiliation at that time. It was plausible to assume that the ancestors of these people, the serfs, lived similar lives.

Jenő Szűcs had the courage to assert that the war for freedom associated with the name of György Dózsa was unique among peasant movements of the Late Middle Ages. Using this assertion as support, I would dare to say that the serfs in Hungary were not identical to those who lived elsewhere. Whereas some version of the word "servant, serving" is used everywhere else, from England to Russia, to describe the peasant living under seigneurial authority, in Hungary the word *jobbágy* referring to that social stratum, originally was equal with "noble" or "high-born." At the beginning of the Middle Ages, until the fourteenth century, people referred to as *jobbágy* were distinguished lords, the *jobbágy* of the king.

I regard the work that Jenő Szűcs and Pál Engel did on the origin of the lord-serf relationship to be significant. Szűcs framed his opinion regarding the origin of the serfs in Hungary with enormous erudition and familiarity with the text of almost all medieval charters. He wrote that landowners began to engage the services of people who had originally been servants via individual contract as serfs. Engel essentially continued Szűcs's train of thought. Citing the instinct he had acquired in the course of four decades of history writing, he formulated a new concept regarding the origin of the word *jobbágy*. Previously this word had been traced to the adjective *jó*, or "good." Engel, contrarily, identified the adjective *jó* with the ancient Hungarian *szabad*, or "free." This, in his opinion, is how the word *iobagio*, which meant "lord" in the Early Middle Ages, transformed into the word *iobagio* meaning "serf." The first was the free man of the king, the second the free man of the landlord.

The year 1514 certainly represented an important station in this change, though it did not transform the essence of the landowner-serf relationship. The serf in Hungary was likely more vulnerable in economic terms, though less beholden in personal terms, than those in other countries. István Szabó, who knew more about the peasantry than anybody else, asserted that the degree of economic vulnerability and personal constraint was not uniform in all places. András Kubinyi later confirmed this assertion. Landowners in Hungary thus apparently encountered less resistance in their exertion of economic power than they did in their effort to restrict individual rights. Historians expose the state of affairs by investigating sources; landowners of the time learned it via experience.

Lesson for the Peasants

The peasants changed tactics after losing the war for freedom. They naturally did not have a diet, but acted as if they had made a collective decision. Although it is naturally impossible to make such an assumption, I must note that events that occurred at this time, not only those that took place among the peasants, often give the modern observer the impression that information and ideas flowed through the social tissue with breathtaking speed as through capillaries.

In accordance with their new tactics, the peasants discarded the weapon of open resistance and turned their focus toward exploitation of gaps in the system of servitude. Their new attitude resembled those which J. C. Scott and many others in his footsteps have characterized as the "weapons of the weak" or "everyday resistance." Among peasants, however, in Hungary it entailed none of the feigned ignorance that Scott described as "Schweikian or Brechtian" maneuvres. Instead of that, the peasants' attitudes in Hungary reflect a refined sense of power relations and the nature of the social system. Sources reveal people who were aware of all the nuances of lord-peasant relations and the administration of the enormous estates. They used this knowledge to their own advantage.

The fundamental recognition or social experience of the peasants was that the tenant-lord relationship was based on possession of the tenant plot: that is, that the landholding of the peasant tied him or her to the lord or the lady and imposed on them the necessity to perform duties and services. It was therefore clear that freedom from the tenant plot would entail freedom from seigneurial obligations.

I know, for example, a sixteenth-century tenant from Sárospatak named Antal Kovách. At the beginning of his career, he lived on a tenant plot and performed the associated duties. He later managed to gain freedom from this holding under circumstances of which I am not aware and became a lodger, a person who was not even recorded in the manorial surveys. He simply disappeared from the *urbaria*. One might conclude based on the description of lodgers in traditional historiography that Kovách lived his life on the margins of human existence under miserable conditions. Instead, however, he developed a major commercial enterprise from his hometown stretching all the way to Vienna.

We know about Kovách's commercial undertakings because his partner in Vienna went bankrupt, and officials of the royal court asked the royal Chamber of Szepes to examine his connections to Hungary. Documents related to the subsequent investigation, to which József Bessenyei has drawn my attention, have survived among the records of the Szepes Chamber. Kovách disappeared from manorial records for several decades after relinquishing his tenant plot despite the fact that he subsisted in Sárospatak and travelled to Vienna and possibly elsewhere on occasion because he lived in somebody else's house. He may well have been the wealthiest man of the locality at the time without having to pay anything to the landlord.

The case of Antal Kovách serves as a prime example of the opportunities that existed to escape from interconnected tenant plots and service. Many people took advantage of these opportunities and developed significant economic interests as cotters. Data showing that somebody lived on a fragmentary tenant holding while maintaining a large stock of domestic animals is conspicuously common. I have, in the course of my research, encountered people living on eighth sections of a customary tenant holding who owned eight oxen while at the same time those who lived on whole holdings owned no draft animals whatsoever. In this instance, the former obviously worked the land of others for money or some other form of compensation, or perhaps utilized his animals on other types of lands which he acquired outside the tenant holdings of the given estate, while remaining liable to only minimal obligations toward the landlord arising from his fragmentary tenant holding.

The moving together or moving apart of family members also represented an effective means of escape. It is very difficult to follow such cases in available sources because estate documents seldom refer to them. The large majority of manorial surveys recording duties only display the name of the person responsible for services proceeding from the tenant plot, most often the head of family. Perhaps the scarcity of sources explains why peasant family formations have become so clear-cut in the description of historical demography.

The extraordinarily gifted historian Éva Veress developed an ingenious method of family reconstruction from this period. She could not use parish registries—the commonly used source of data for family reconstruction in other countries—in Hungary because such records have survived in the country only from a much later period. Veress therefore took the trouble to gather various types of manorial documents in order to become acquainted with individual peasants. She did so in 1965, precisely when modern scholarly debates regarding family forms began, coming to the conclusion that there were no firmly fixed family forms during the period in question. According to Veress, the structure and composition of communally producing and consuming individuals in the family varied according to the opportunities and obligations of families.

Éva Veress thoroughly examined seven villages in the regions of Hegyalja and Bodrogköz in present-day northeastern Hungary, arriving at the astonishing conclusion that during the middle of the sixteenth century, the structure of the families changed an average of four times every twenty years or so. According to Veress, this flexibility ensured the functioning of society. Clinging rigidly to a single family form would have very likely led to the destruction of the examined families. Flexibility permitted these families, peasants living in small villages, to attain a significant degree of social mobility manifesting itself in many forms, from advantageous marriages to acquiring separate plots for the old or the young of the group. It could mean, for instance, that a head of household, whether a man or a woman, was able to move together with a part of the household or with all members of it from the periphery of the villages toward the center and thus to the vicinity of major roads, which provided them with a better opportunity for commerce.

Certain peasants and peasant communities utilized the insatiable appetite of the lords for cash to their benefit. This was not a new phenomenon of the sixteenth century. I have already mentioned the pre-1493 agreement between Lőrinc Újlaki and a group of villages in which the lord granted the inhabitants of these villages an exemption from the obligation to perform manual labor in exchange for a large sum of money. Such agreements subsequently became stunningly common. I was particularly surprised by the number of landowners who obtained loans from their tenants. The guarantee of repayment was some sort of "freedom," which survived for a long period of time due to the reluctance of landowners to repay their debts. Written requests for repayment of loans that the peasants submitted to the lord via stewards of the manor often contain the response "We cannot do so." The landlords' continual need for ready cash led to the absurdity of permanent exemption for money. Sixteenth-century estates became full of "free" tenants who had gained their freedom from performing obligations for the landowner. The number of nobles living on tenant plots also increased at this time, as a result of the fact that lords gave permission to peasants to apply for nobility at the relevant royal office in exchange for money as well. Later, this propensity became the source of significant social and political tension as a result of the paradoxical phenomenon of nobles living on tenant holdings.

With regard to the train of thought that began with the Dózsa rebellion, the important thing to realize is that peasants, who were able to successfully negotiate the labyrinth of landowner-tenant relations, did not use the language of the church to assert their interests. It appears that along with that of open resistance, the peasants laid down the weapon of ideological argument as well.

5 The Beginnings of the Reformation

Luther and his contemporaries did not refer to the Reformation as such. According to his supporters, Martin Luther "brought the Gospel into the light of day," while his followers "proclaimed the Gospel" and strove to live their lives according to it. In these statements the originally Greek word "gospel" refers to "good news" and those who proclaimed and followed the Gospel referred to Luther's fundamental proposition: one can earn eternal life through divine grace "by faith alone" without the mediation of the church. Luther and other reformers subsequently formulated many other tenets. However, the essence of their message did not change: acting under the influence of Ulrich Zwingli, the Council of Zürich asked to "proclaim the Holy Gospel." John Calvin declared that God had appointed him to serve as "servant and herald of the Gospel." And Ferenc Dávid, the most original Hungarian theologian of all time, believed that it was his duty to finish the work that Luther had begun, writing: "If the whole light of the Gospel had illuminated before our eyes after such great darkness, the abundant brightness may have deprived us of our vision."

The names of the theologians cited are associated with the three major Protestant denominations—Lutheran, Reformed and Unitarian. During the sixteenth century, none of these churches regarded their teachings or their origins as the Reformation. This is not difficult to ascertain in these days of electronic data carriers. Those who lived at the time of the Reformation did not use this term to describe the activity of Luther or any subsequent religious reformers, although the Latin word *reformatio* (originally meaning improvement) had become part of the vocabulary of the church at the beginning of the fifteenth century, albeit with only limited meaning. The Council of Constance withdrew certain papal donations on the grounds of "reformation of the church." In 1514, the Fifth Lateran Council issued a papal bull regarding the "reformation of the church." People living in the sixteenth century generally used the term "reformation" to designate church reforms expected to be headed by Rome itself. Distinguished and high-ranking theologians held meetings to discuss the issue of general "reformation" at the papal state.

Sixteenth-century church reformers, or those who are today regarded as such, were therefore familiar with this meaning of the term "reformation." Before assuming the role of church organizers, all of them were faithful members of the Roman church and familiar with ecclesiastical matters. If they did not use the contemporary concept of the "reformation" to describe their own activity, they did so consciously. Martin Luther expressly rejected the concept when explaining some parts of his ninety-five theses:

> The church needs a reformation which is not the work of man, namely the pope, or of many men, namely the cardinals, both of which the most recent council has demonstrated, but it is the work of the whole world, indeed it is the work of God alone.

Zoltán Csepregi concluded in his recent examination of the use of the term "Reformation" in Hungary that it was not used under its current meaning until the beginning of the seventeenth century.

The Agents of Change

From the perspective of their adversaries, those who initially proclaimed the tenets of the Reformation under its current meaning were attempting to spread a dangerous contagion. In Hungary, the jurist and politician István Werbőczy was likely the first to describe the ideas of the reformers as such, writing in the spring of 1521 that Luther's "aberration" had brought grave illness upon the country and asking the king to eradicate "this raging plague." In the vocabulary of their rivals, the new teachings were referred to as Lutheran contagion, Lutheran contamination and Lutheran heresy. That is, as far as I can tell, the new teachings and activities to be persecuted were always connected directly to Luther's name. Interestingly, the previously mentioned Latin word *zizania* ("cockles") that Archbishop of Esztergom Tamás Bakócz had used in the text of his justification for suspending the crusade against the Ottomans was not among those used to describe Luther and his teachings. Apparently *zizania* referred only to the straying of an undefined, obscure character.

Lutheran teachings were received everywhere with great interest. In Hungary, as throughout the territories in which Roman Christianity predominated, this interest manifested itself in diverse forms ranging from sermons to discussions at the local tavern, marketplace or the church. Everywhere, in fact, where people gathered the new belief became a topic of discussion, much like how politics is a topic of conversation today. And although sermons or conversations considered suspicious by authorities were characterized as Lutheran in Hungary just as they were in Poland, England and Iceland, it is far from certain that they indeed spread the tenets of Martin Luther. We have little knowledge regarding the actual content of the public discourse in question. Recent research on the Reformation conducted in the aforementioned countries has examined fragments preserved by chance and usually in the accounts produced by the adversaries of the evangelical movement. These suggest that this discourse most often did not transmit Luther's theology.

It is easy to understand the reasons for this. I see two main causes. The first was the persistence of long-established, in some cases centuries-old, ideas that were, by Roman Catholic standards, "heretical." Some of these notions were of unidentifiable origin and sprang from the fact that those in power have always and everywhere established their own enemies. Other "heretical" notions are connected to the activity of prominent and well-known individuals. The Englishman John Wycliffe in the middle and late fourteenth century, and the Czech Jan Hus one generation later, had perhaps the greatest influence among these personalities. The official church made the interrelationship between their teachings obvious in a dreadful way. When the Council of Constance excommunicated Hus in 1415 and—ignoring the emperor's protection—had him condemned to death by burning, it also ordered that Wycliffe's body be exhumed and burned. Jan Hus was promptly burned at the stake, while Wycliffe's corpse was exhumed and burned in 1428.

Wycliffe and Hus proclaimed the truth of the Holy Scripture and salvation through personal faith against what they and their followers considered to be the sinful church. Historical scholarship considers Wycliffe and Hus to be the precursors of the Reformation, which initially seems inconceivable as a result of their distance in both time and place from Luther. However, the notion of Wycliffe and Hus as the precursors of the Reformation is nevertheless not an abstract concept of the history of theology. Martin Luther himself clearly perceived this connection. At the very beginning of his reform activity, Luther said "We are all Hussites without knowing it," and Luther emphasized his affinity with Wycliffe by publishing a manuscript produced in Wycliffe's circles in which the pope appears as Antichrist. According to the foreword to this work, Luther published it in order to demonstrate that there were personages long before him whose thoughts about the church were very similar to his.

Martin Luther's own statements therefore make it clear that the so-called evangelical teachings did not necessarily begin with him. Following this line of logic, one might presume that within a hostile context, we would likely not recognize Lutheran theology even from one of Luther's sermons. In this way, it was possible to connect all people regarded as heretics with Luther. In 1520, Pope Leo X issued an elegantly phrased bull entitled *Exsurge Domine* ("Arise O Lord") in which he threatened to excommunicate Luther and forbade the faithful from reading, praising or printing his teachings. However, this bull did not define Luther's doctrine. Nobody was therefore aware of exactly what teachings the pope had forbidden. Authorities simply referred to anything that did not please them as "Lutheran" and accusations of "Lutheranism" almost naturally gained a solid foundation.

In Hungary, where the first vernacular translation of the Bible was prepared by Hussite priests, Hussitism had exercised a significant impact and most probably persevered for a long time. Its elements, or the popular rendering of them, could appear even in tavern table talks. However, I have come across two, otherwise well-known sources, which reveal the factual familiarity of certain laymen with the teachings of Luther himself.

The first of these sources records a discussion that took place in a pub in the city of Sopron in 1524. The participants in the conversation, among them a cobbler, drank wine and debated whether God had arms, legs, eyes and ears—that is, whether he resembled man in form. The conclusion is not overly intricate: Luther's 1520 sermon on good works served as the inspiration for this conversation. Obviously Martin Luther did not personally deliver this sermon to those who discussed the issue of God's physical appearance at the tavern in Sopron, but instead somebody who had read the homily and presented it as his own. The point is that simple people became familiar with the reformer's ideas and some of them agreed with them, while others contested them. In any case, they were certainly aware of at least one of Luther's sermons.

The second of these sources also refers to an incident that took place in Sopron, though pertained to another issue. A Franciscan friar named Kristóf ostensibly preached in the town based on Luther's ninety-five theses. When interrogated about the sermon, artisans, merchants and other laymen said that the friar had declared that not only the pope, but any priest could provide complete absolution from all sins. The astounding fact surrounding this incident is that theologians from Mainz, whose expert opinion regarding the ninety-five theses a bishop requested near the end of the year 1517, made similar statements. It thus appears that simple laymen and highly trained scholars had arrived at the same opinion regarding Luther's teachings.

I do not propose that the reader conclude from the above, luckily discovered, accounts that laymen in Hungary were better informed with regard to Lutheran teachings than their counterparts in England or Iceland. The degree of information among the people was uneven everywhere, though the extent to which individuals took an interest in evangelical teachings did not depend on education or knowledge. Just as today, there is no direct connection between religious faith and knowledge. I asked several of my devout friends about the central tenets of their religion and none of them could recite them. Yet respondents participating in a scientific survey on religious practices with which I am familiar affirmed the importance of learning the teachings, though to my great disappointment the researchers made no inquiries regarding their actual degree of religious knowledge.

Here is the second reason why I am not surprised that the first generation of preachers referring to the evangelical tenets did not present strictly Lutheran ideas. If pious members of the modern church are unfamiliar with centuries-old tenets of their religion, it would be nearly ludicrous to expect people living at the time these teachings were born to have been perfectly acquainted with them. This is true even if priests were among the initial disseminators of the contagion. The latter naturally acquired their religious knowledge through a Roman Catholic education. These priests were thus compelled to fit the new teachings into their prior learning. Some were more successful than others in this task.

Itinerant preachers were among the first to transmit the new teachings in Hungary as elsewhere. Many Franciscan friars joined in. Their role in proclaiming the Gospel is easy to understand. I would remind the reader: the same friars had preached the cross a few years previously. Archbishop Bakócz entrusted them with this duty because it was a well-known fact that the mendicant Franciscans spent much time among the people, and were able to converse with simple people as a result of their shared social origin. The archbishop failed to consider the fact though that they, also, carried the seeds of spiritual heresy. Now they heard something in the teachings of Luther that was closely related to their earlier thinking and they began to talk about them in the course of their wanderings.

Unfortunately, we become familiar with individual friars preaching the new tenets only later, beginning roughly in the 1530s. We do not know whether highly educated Franciscans preached among the people at the very beginning. However, we do know that they began to do so somewhat later. One of the most influential itinerant preachers in Hungary, Mihály Sztárai, was a Franciscan educated at the highly esteemed University of Padua. Prior to Sztárai, who worked in the region of southern Hungary that was already under Ottoman rule, Konrad Cordatus and Johan Kresling of Buda were among the scholars who assumed the role of itinerant priest. Cordatus and Kresling had belonged to the entourage of Queen Mary but were forced to leave it after the wrath of the nobility turned against the court after the fall of Nándorfehérvár (Belgrade) to the Ottomans in 1521. Cordatus and Kresling thereafter began to preach the Gospel in the mining towns of upper Hungary. They must have been very successful, because their detainment on the orders of the Archbishop of Esztergom sparked a rebellion among the miners of the region. Cordatus and Kresling subsequently escaped abroad. The former became a close associate of Martin Luther, while the latter returned to Selmecbánya (Banská Štiavnica, Slovakia) after the city decided to accept the evangelical faith.

However, the itinerant preacher was typically not a learned man. Many sources assert that "laypeople of both sexes" spread the contagion. Thus both women and men were among them. Sources indicate that they preached not in churches, but before the city gate, under a big tree or in a private home. Most of them were simple people and they preached for a long period of time. We know this because some unambiguous information has survived about them. In 1548, the Diet condemned those lords who tolerated the preaching of "ignorant men, primarily masons." Hardly more than ten years later, a Roman Catholic canonical visitation record claims that certain priests characterized as heretics had originally been village judges, soldiers or peasants. In the first case, the lords who participated in the formulation of the relevant law obviously did not deny—or at least did not successfully deny—that ignorant masons were preaching on their estates. In the second case, according to the custom of church visitations, the information contained in their records derived either from a member of the relevant congregation or directly from the person in question, in this case priests who had previously been village judges, soldiers or tenants.

Other types of sources provide a similar depiction of the first evangelical preachers, describing them as simple, nameless people. György Szerémi, whom I have already cited on several occasions, was the author of the earliest such source. His slowly meandering narrative seems to suggest that "Lutheran doctrine" first appeared in Hungary in 1520 and that the spread of Lutheran ideas occurred in two phases: in the first they were "brought in" and in the second they were "publicly propagated." I find it significant that Szerémi, although he devoted only a few lines of writing to the spread of Lutheran doctrine in Hungary, felt the need to make the distinction between these two phases. I presume he had good reason to do so. Szerémi must have observed at the royal court in Buda, where he served as a royal chaplain, that "learned men and courtiers" initially talked about Luther or his works among themselves without any practical consequences. Thereafter some people, whom he does not describe in detail either because he did not know who they were or was not interested who they were, preached Luther's teaching publicly and then had to pay the penalty for doing so. According to the chronicle, two lords had a total of eleven people executed for public preaching of Luther's teachings.

These executions likely took place following the Diet's adoption of a law in 1525 prescribing the execution by burning of those who propagated Lutheran doctrine. Szerémi ends his short paragraph with the statement that Luther's teachings "nevertheless continued to spread day by day." According to the founder of modern Hungarian church history, Jenő Zoványi, those executed included some booksellers and some participants in the rebellion that erupted during the spring of 1526 as the result of the arrest of Cordatus and Kresling.

The next such source of information regarding the spread of Lutheran doctrine in Hungary is derived from the pen of András Szkhárosi Horvát, who was a preacher and very popular songwriter in the 1540s. According to Szkhárosi Horvát, the first people to diffuse the new tenets in Hungary were students, priests, children, whom he must have considered to be school pupils, and minstrels. His description resembles that of Szerémi in that both of them describe nameless people and thus do not connect the Reformation in Hungary with some well-known person, even though the preacher had already acquired greater experience and knowledge than the chronicler.

Szkhárosi Horvát conspicuously includes minstrels among the initial propagators of Lutheran ideas. Relevant literary historians uniformly regard the minstrel to have been an individual who diffused knowledge, literature and history in the form of easy-to-remember and easy-to-sing verse. One might characterize the minstrel as a wandering intellectual who held a performance at any location where he could find an audience. If Szkhárosi Horvát was speaking from experience—and there is no reason for us to presume that he did not do so —then the evangelical teachings spread not only through the mediation of itinerant preachers. They also became part of the repertoire of the minstrels who entertained the world.

Finally, I will present information from Péter Melius Juhász, who later in his life became a Reformed bishop. According to Melius Juhász, the "trading and selling peoples" of Debrecen were the first in Hungary to speak of the Gospel. In the preface of the book dedicated to them in 1561, he wrote: "you received and heard before others and you glorified and spoke to others the knowledge of God's mercy." At first reading, one might question the truth of this statement. At the same time, maybe Melius Juhász was right. Sources regarding merchants from Debrecen suggest that they were most mobile and traveled great distances. And the future Reformed bishop, who—as other members of the first and second generation of reformers in Hungary—had been born into the Roman Catholic Church; he may have heard something about the not-too-distant past.

The information from Péter Melius Juhász is important not because of the merchants of Debrecen, but as a result of his own personality. He was an exceptionally self-confident person who placed his own knowledge above that of anybody else. Melius Juhász was not reluctant to debate with church officials and those who stood at the top of the secular hierarchy. As a pastor, if he did not assert that some distinguished theologian was the first to preach the Gospel, then he surely thought this as well. One might also speculate that Melius Juhász was attempting to flatter the merchants of Debrecen. He had much for which to thank them. They supported his every step. I nevertheless claim that Péter Melius Juhász's statement represents a definitive reason to support the argument that in Hungary the community was the first to propagate the evangelical teachings. In modern terms: simple people brought the Reformation to Hungary.

Defenders of Faith

We know relatively much about the first lay preachers, since many people reported to authorities the participation of simple people of both genders in spreading the Reformation from its earliest days. Letters containing orders from King Louis II or high-ranking ecclesiastical officials to undertake investigations of such people beginning in the 1520s were based on submitted complaints and information.

The denouncers thus assumed an extremely important role. We naturally do not know what would have happened had they not turned to various authorities. But since they did so, it may appear that their actions prompted the events leading to the persecution of the new ideas. However, this was likely not the case. As with all movements that arise against the prevailing order, authorities prepared to receive such information determined their activities. They were catalysts, the accelerators of a process that had already begun. In addition, they provided Reformation studies with a great service. The protocols recording the official investigations engendered by their reports to authorities represent sources of inestimable value. Their activity was important, though we do not know their names; the royal and ecclesiastical orders state "it came to our attention" or "we learned" without citing the source. I doubt if it would be possible to gain much further information regarding the identity of the denouncers to authorities. Historians Vince Bunyitay, Rajmund Rapaics and János Karácsonyi thoroughly examined records contained in the archives of such authorities in the course of collecting material for the essential book regarding the Reformation in Hungary—*Egyháztörténelmi emlékek a Magyarországi hitujítás korából* (Church History Remembrances from the Era of Religious Renewal in Hungary). No reports from informers regarding the disseminators of Lutheran tenets likely escaped their attention.

One can thus only speculate regarding the identity of the informers. One might logically presume that they were prominent lords who maintained connections with the highest-ranking authorities. However, I would not exclude the possibility that there were simple people among them. I have already written about the facility with which peasants or peasant communities negotiated the labyrinths of power. I have no doubt that they were able to reach the highest forums with their complaints if they so desired. I also wrote about the significant impact that the papal promise of eternal life had upon them.

Let us just consider this fact: in 1514, the people were told that they would receive papal pardon of their sins if they participated directly or indirectly in the crusade against the Turks, while a few years later they heard that the conditions surrounding the absolution of sins had changed. The Dózsa rebellion took place in 1514, and Lutheran teachings appeared seven years later in 1521. During the peasant war, it had become clear that the simple man understood the language of the church and was capable of using it against the lords. Beginning in 1521, they were prompted to learn a new language. However, no passing of generations had occurred in the meantime. The very same community listened to the teachings of the Gospel that had not long previously heard sermons regarding liberation from purgatory.

It was easy to explain the reception of the Reformation from the traditional perspective. According to that approach, the representatives of the Roman Catholic Church neglected the simple people and appalled them with their behavior; then along came the preachers of the new faith and embraced those who languished in total ignorance. The interest naturally turned toward them. However, if we consider that the people were aware of the teachings of the church and that, in fact, they were not neglected, but a crusade had been proclaimed based explicitly on their intensive need for the church, the situation becomes more complex.

During the lives of the great people who became reformers, scholars conducted careful analysis of the process that led from the prevailing teachings of the Roman church to the recognition of the teaching of grace gained through divine will. In November 1509, Luther himself climbed the *Scala Pilati* on his knees, kissing its stones along the way, because he believed that he could thus gain plenary indulgence and curtail his time in purgatory. Only eight years later did he publicize his teaching that salvation could not be achieved in this way. Luther is presumed to have reached this conclusion via visions, mystical experiences and a long process of thought. But what about the simple people? They did not have the opportunity to engage in lengthy reflection. One day they were under the impression that they could move closer to salvation by praying before the statues of saints, then the next day somebody came along who told them that the intervention of saints was unnecessary. In her examination of foreign pilgrimages, Enikő Csukovits concluded that the greatest number of late medieval pilgrims came from the areas in which the Reformation gained its initial footholds. How can this be explained?

Under the premise of an intensive lay piety in close interaction with official religion, it is easier to understand the informer than those who accepted the new teachings. According to the informer-as-catalyst model, I would assert that the new faith did not affect those who provided the authorities with information regarding its propagators. The informer embodied the person who remained loyal to the traditional church. Surely not all believers became denouncers, but there is an unambiguous fact suggesting that true concern for the fate of the old church could have been the primary motive for reporting propagators of Lutheran ideas to the authorities: informers did not use the charge in their reports that alleged Lutherans had previously also participated in the Dózsa rebellion.

Records of official investigations contain both confessions and denials regarding the propagation of heresy. These records are full of circumstantial evidence. For example, that a witness suspected that students staying at an inn had broken the Lenten fast because butter had disappeared from a certain dish. This witness speculated that the students and, perhaps, the innkeeper had secretly eaten the butter. Some of the reports deal with more significant incidents. For example, that "those who can read" recited Lutheran writings in a tavern as the others listened. However, none of the witnesses indicated in these reports even mentioned the Dózsa rebellion, whereas the accusation of participating in the peasant uprising would have significantly aggravated malignant charges of heresy.

When I began reading the investigation records, I was convinced that they would contain many references to the Dózsa rebellion. To my great surprise, they did not even refer to the uprising, although it is highly improbable that the two events—the nearly simultaneous uprising and beginning of the Reformation—did not involve people who participated in both, either as sympathizers or antagonists. I once wrote that had the Dózsa rebellion taken place following the appearance of the Reformation, everybody would have characterized the former as a consequence of the latter. I now know that the two events stood in direct contrast to one another. One was based on belief in the teachings of the traditional Roman church, while the other was founded upon their rejection. Living through both the Dózsa rebellion and the beginning of the Reformation within such a short period of time must have been an immense shock for both individuals and the society at large.

I am not surprised that some people did not embrace the new faith, but instead were concerned about the future of the old one. I have inserted this passage regarding them in order to emphasize the dynamic manner in which the Reformation was received. I hope that the reader perceived already in the previous chapter that I have repeatedly written about debated ideas. Simple laymen did not merely accept without hesitation that which they heard during the evangelical preaching or when listening to the reading out loud of a text written in that spirit. Instead, although sources from Hungary during this era are rather scarce, it becomes clear that some people accepted the new teachings, while others rejected them.

In the process of receiving the Reformation, religion was essentially secularized, becoming a topic of everyday conversation. I find this to be important because it introduced a new element into the range of tasks incumbent upon the simple people: in addition to the skill of negotiating the labyrinths of power, they had to find their own way in religious terms as well. Until then, they had received unambiguous information about everything. They knew what deeds would bring them closer to salvation, when to make a sacramental confession and about what they should confess, how to receive the sacraments, and who served as the mediators between them and God. According to church historians, by the end of the Middle Ages they even knew the precise saint to whom they needed to pray in order to cure a given illness.

The shock of the Reformation in Hungary was perhaps smaller than in countries in which a single religion had previously predominated and everyone had thus sought salvation of the soul in the same way. In Hungary, the Roman and Eastern Orthodox Churches had existed side by side, but the idea of crossover did not even emerge in the minds of people. We know of no religious disputations between laymen affiliated with the two churches. The new evangelical teachings, however, prompted people to question deeply ingrained, customary knowledge. They were forced to think about things that had previously been well-known, indisputable facts.

The nature of the manner in which people received the Reformation remains hidden if we forget about those who rejected it. If we fail to remember them it could be assumed that an ever greater number of lay people became followers of the Reformation without thinking, perhaps even without the capacity for independent thought. With the lay defenders of faith in the background we can be sure of the contrary.

Entering the Churches

The Reformation entered the churches without female preachers. We do not know whether female preachers who were active at the beginning of the Reformation were regarded as regular priests and administered sacraments or if they merely spoke publicly of the Gospel. The principle of a female clergy could have been deduced from Martin Luther's initial teachings. Luther formulated and published his thesis of the priesthood of all believers around the end of the year 1520.

The teaching of universal priesthood stipulated that all believers could preach the Gospel and conduct liturgical and pastoral activities that had previously been the exclusive right of the clergy. According to the thesis, the congregation would decide whether these people were acting according to Holy Scripture or not. The concept of "all believers" logically implies both men and women. However, it is unclear whether Luther regarded women as servants of the congregation. It is also unclear whether the women who propagated the teachings of Luther were aware of his thesis on priesthood.

Here I would remind the reader of the bull that Pope Leo X issued to Cardinal Bakócz: this document designated women as possible participants in the crusade against the Ottoman Turks in every possible context. I would also draw attention to the well-known fact that in the Roman Catholic Church both male and female cloisters existed and exist today. I do not want to dwell at length on this issue because it would require considerable research. It would be important to better understand the relationship between women, or certain conspicuously pious women, and Catholicism. And it would be worthwhile to further investigate whether women largely disappeared from the governing of Protestant religious culture as the present state of research would have us believe.

I remember how excited I was when I started to read the small volume in Hungarian entitled "Calvin's Letters to the Women." I thought I would discover in it information regarding the female colleagues of the great reformer. The presumption turned out to be incorrect. This work contained letters that Calvin had written to women in captivity or of high social standing who played the role of patron. I do not understand why the Reformation failed to produce even a single great female figure of the church. If I think of the contribution that Saint Teresa of Ávila made to Roman Catholicism in the middle of the sixteenth century, I must conclude that the reformers missed out on a big opportunity.

In fact, Saint Teresa of Ávila is not, perhaps, the best example of women who made significant contributions to the Catholic Church at this time, because she was an exceptional person and not the manifestation of a general phenomenon within the church. In addition to her intensive work in the caring for souls, Teresa of Ávila was an accomplished author who provided world literature with one of its great works—her spiritual autobiography. Nunhood did, however, represent a mass phenomenon within the church, one that offered women a complex array of possible roles. In Hungary, Lea Ráskai, for example, at the beginning of the sixteenth century, worked in a convent. She transcribed the Hungarian-language biographies of saints into the vernacular of her era and complied them into codices to be read by her fellow nuns. One might say that she lived the life of an intellectual as did many other nuns who provided instruction to young novices. Those who lived in the convents could have risen to become abbesses or remained domestic servants, though the latter were not usually members of the order. Cloisters and convents served as places of refuge for the unfortunate or people of extraordinary disposition who wished to live apart from the world. In any case, the church transformed them into unique places of civilization and learning.

I promised at the beginning of this essay that I would not write about personal faith. Here, without reference to a given individual, I would repeat: in the convents women could practice a special form of piety proceeding from their own faith. I do not know if the piety of female religious differed from that of male religious. The opportunity to exercise personal religious devotion certainly existed for both. The Protestantism that emerged from the Reformation did not permit this. It also abolished monasticism for men, though the role of priest remained a possibility for them. I regard the exclusion of women as one of the theologically inexplicable acts of the Reformation.

At the time of the Reformation, Calvin provided women with some duties in the church, placing certain widows in the role of pastoral worker, or, in modern terminology, deaconess. Calvin referred to Paul the Apostle, who believed that certifiable devout women over the age of sixty could serve within the congregation. He designated the difficult tasks of caring for the poor and sick to these women, who occupied the lowest position among the four orders of servants of the church. Ultimately, however, this theologically attractive thought was not put into practice. Philip Benedict showed in his monograph on Calvinism that, in exceptional cases, women served as caretakers for the poor in some cities in France during the sixteenth century despite the general absence of active deaconesses.

Accordingly, after laypeople of both sexes had promoted the acceptance of evangelical ideas through preaching, the ordained clergy consisted of men. They introduced the new doctrines into the church. The canonical visitation registers that I have already utilized to present data regarding tenants, village judges and soldiers represent an excellent source of information regarding the modes of such entry into the church. I refer to them as canonical visitation registers for the sake of simplicity, because this is the established term that is used to refer to them. These registers are actually a thick dossier preserved at the Primatial Archives in the city of Esztergom which, in addition to the visitation protocols, contain a variety of documents produced between 1559 and 1562 during the preparations for a national synod that was never held. Some of them were published in Slovakia.

The most important information I found in these documents was that individuals could maintain a status independent of the church or the congregation. In a record regarding the tiny village of Bálványszakállas (Balvany, Slovakia) in Komárom County, I read a story about the parish priest, Caspar, who was described as a good Catholic of good morals whose parishioners were similarly good Christians. The one exception among the latter was Luka Posar, who was described as the "biggest heretic." What might have Posar said or done to be characterized as such? It is not worthwhile to spend too much time pondering this question, since lack of information makes it impossible to answer. What is important with regard to Posar is that he was either an actual person who acted according to his own reflections in matters of religion or that authorities believed he existed, thus indicating that they were aware of other cases of individual decision-making. In the my train of thought here, Posar does not represent a person who entered the church, but one who withdrew from it.

The most characteristic consequence of entering the church was that the function of the church building itself underwent transformation. I have once claimed that the church was transformed from the church of the priest to the church of the congregation. I maintain this opinion since the difference between Roman Catholic and Protestant churches is truly very big. The most significant characteristic of Roman Catholic churches is that a priest, usually a bishop, consecrates them before they are put into use. In this way, a building constructed via everyday labor becomes sacred. Its interior contains sacraments. Communion wafer and wine, holy water to be used in baptisms and holy oil to be used in anointing the sick must be kept in the church, if possible in an ornamented ciborium illuminated with a sanctuary lamp. I referred to the Catholic churches as the churches of the priest because these originally secular items became carriers of the sacraments via a priest-conducted rite. Moreover, the Roman Catholic Church is that of the priest because the latter can celebrate mass alone, without the participation of the congregation.

Celebrations may have been held to mark the opening of a new Protestant church, though the building did not undergo transmutation. And although the Protestants recognize sacraments, they have no permanent carriers. There are no consecrated objects and items that must be kept in the church. Finally, and most importantly: no rites can be performed in Protestant churches without the participation of the congregation. The pastor can enter the church alone, if he wants, but can only preach if he has an audience and can only administer the Lord's Supper if there are members of the congregation present who wish to take it. No matter how suitable a building is for hosting religious services, it is not a church unless there are believers inside it. This is why I refer to the Protestant Church as the church of the congregation.

The nature of the church thus changed with the introduction of the evangelical teachings. However, the various denominations did not conduct uniform changes to the interiors of their churches. The Lutherans removed only the sacraments; the altar remained. The Reformed removed the sacraments as well as the altars and other ornaments from their previously Roman Catholic churches. The depiction of certain "heretical churches," that is, Lutheran or Reformed churches, as "nicely adorned" and others as "just like a shed" in this excellent source from which I gathered my data is thus understandable.

As long as the Catholic church visitors write about "heretical churches" everything is clear. The faithful unsurprisingly transformed their churches according to the spirit of the new teachings. Descriptions of most Catholic churches, priests and congregations offer no new information either. Most Catholic priests were married or had lovers, though the church visitors did not make a particularly big deal about this. It appears that this did not bother the members of the congregation either. Neither do I concern myself with this issue. I acknowledge that the priests in question from the perspective of the representatives of the official church could be genuine Catholics, despite their wives and lovers.

Two Types of Ritual in the Same Church

Problems emerge when one reads in the record the vivid description of a Catholic priest as one who was not only unsteady in body, but "wavered between two directions" in spirit as well. To put it more clearly: he administered communion to some of the congregation under both kinds, while the other half was taking it under one kind. At first I did not believe my eyes. However, its multiple repetition excludes the possibility of error. The same priest administered communion to some of the faithful under both kinds and to others under one kind in the very same church. This occurred in the village of Récse (Rača) in Pozsony County as well as far from it in the village of Kovarc (Kovarce) in the archdeaconry of Tapolcsány (both in Slovakia). In certain places, the priest claimed that he had been forced to administer communion in two different ways. Among the latter were parish priests Mihály—described as being of "true faith"—and Miklós in the villages of Nagyfalu (Veličná, Slovakia) and Privigye (Prievidza, Slovakia), respectively. Others, such as János, the incumbent of Bazin (Pezinok, Slovakia), said or were said to have offered communion under both kinds to those "who so desired."

Here I must note that taking Holy Communion or the Lord's Supper under one or two kinds became the most ardently debated issue between the various Christian denominations. Present-day historians have differing opinions about it, and I believe that the matter of the Eucharist still represents one of the primary points of controversy in the Vatican-initiated ecumenical negotiations. For laypeople, the subject is difficult to understand, though the origin of the doctrine can be traced back to two actual events. Paul the Apostle learned that the Christians of Corinth were undisciplined in taking their collective meals, neglecting to wait for one another when they began to eat and consuming everything they could find without discrimination. And I add: they behaved as was customary at a Greek feast. However, Paul wanted them to come together as a Christian congregation and to partake of their common meal in remembrance of Christ's crucifixion.

Paul decided to write a letter to them. In it he presented to them the Last Supper that Christ shared with his apostles as a model. According to Paul in his First Epistle to the Corinthians, Christ handed bread to his disciples and said: "This is my body, which is for you; do this in remembrance of me." After eating also "he took the cup" and said: "This cup is the new covenant in my blood; do this, whenever you drink it, in remembrance of me." He then concluded: "For whenever you eat this bread, and drink this cup, you proclaim the Lord's death until he comes."

One can imagine how many explanations these mysterious, originally Greek-language sentences engendered, although the fundamental rite is identical within every Christian church: the ritualistic repetition of the Last Supper belongs to liturgical practice. At the same time, endless debates emerged regarding whether the bread and the wine used in communion became the real body and blood of Christ or whether they contain the body and blood of Christ in the course of the rite or if they simply recall Christ's crucifixion and resurrection. Certain Christian churches essentially distinguish themselves from others on the basis of their conclusions with regard to this matter.

The other subject of contention, using lay terminology, regarded whether the congregation could take communion under both kinds or one kind. Both kinds refers to both bread and wine, while one kind refers to bread only. That is, the debate surrounded the problem of whether both the priest and members of the congregation or only the priest could take communion under both kinds. According to Roman teachings that originated in the Early Middle Ages, only priests received communion in bread, which later was substituted by wafer in order to avoid the crumbling of the body of Christ, and wine, although members of many so-called heretical movements secretly took bread and wine stolen from the church. According to the teaching of universal priesthood, every believer was a priest, thus every member of the congregation received bread and wine. This is characteristic of all Protestant denominations.

Fairly recent research, as well as that of the distinguished twentieth-century Hungarian historian Elemér Mályusz, shows that Latin Christian religious practices began to change in Hungary in the period prior to the Reformation, resulting in the official administration of communion under both kinds in certain places. I cannot make any comment in this regard. However, the canonical visitors whose protocols I am analyzing regarded receiving the sacrament under both kinds as a non-Catholic practice. With regard to regular Catholic communion, these visitors wrote this or something similar: the priest "administers the sacraments according to the rite of the Mother Church of Rome."

The irregularity in this regard was something like this: the priest performs all sacraments according to the rite of the Mother Church, though "it is said that he administers communion under both kinds to those who want it." According to the canonical visitation register, everything was "beautiful" at the Roman Catholic church in Mosóc (Mošovce, Slovakia): in addition to many other devotional objects, the church contained six gilded chalices and four golden crosses; the parishioners all praised the parish priest, who was a native of the village, for his administration of the sacraments according to standard Roman Catholic practice, "although he did offer the Eucharist to certain people under both kinds." At other locations, such as Bazin,

> the people are partially Catholic and partially infected with the Lutheran heresy. Parish priest János ... allegedly administers the Eucharist under both kinds to those who want it.

The priests themselves did not indicate that they had heard about the possibility of communion under both kinds within the Roman Catholic Church, and the textual interconnections of the source make it clear: communion under one kind and communion under both kinds took place within separate rites. The priests concealed this fact from the canonical visitors. If it nevertheless became clear that this was the case, they claimed that some members of the congregation had forced them to offer communion under both kinds or that they did so by obeying the will of their parishioners. Many avoided, or attempted to avoid, detection.

Certain incumbents just happened not to be at home when the canonical visitors arrived. Why, perhaps, did they have to leave when they were surely aware of the arriving guests? The seven high-ranking visitors did not go so far as to take up quarters in the countryside. They commuted continually between the city of Nagyszombat (Trnava, Slovakia) and various communities within the Archdiocese of Esztergom. They escaped the notice of nobody in the district. There had been no canonical visits for decades and convoys of ornate carriages were not an everyday sight on the roads between small villages. This is not even to mention the honor that pious Catholic priests must have felt to meet the confidants of the archbishop. If somebody avoided such a privilege, they must have had good reason to do so. Instead of leaving their homes, some priests attempted to evade detection by returning the wafer, holy water and holy oil that they no longer used on an everyday basis to their accustomed places in the church before the arrival of their distinguished guests. Or else they placed ordinary water and oil in containers designated for holy water and holy oil. However, the canonical visitors seem to have successfully uncovered such deceptions, as they did in villages such as Cseszte (Častá, Slovakia) and Joka (Jelka, Slovakia).

I have no reason to presume that the emissaries of the Archbishop of Esztergom did not write down what they experienced during their visits. I examined the records of these visits at the Primatial Archives. Subsequent ornate copies of these records are preserved at the archives, as are the originals. The attributes of the script in which the latter were written confirm their authenticity. They may be connected not only to preparations for the synod that never took place, but also to the endeavors of Emperor Ferdinand I to obtain authorization from the pope to conduct communion under both kinds on some of the territory over which he ruled. There is ample evidence suggesting that the emperor believed that the desire of the faithful to receive communion under both kinds served as a motor of the spread of the heresy.

If the objective of the canonical visits centered on church politics, the visitors presumably did not find out about the irregularities by accident, but inquired specifically about circumstances surrounding Holy Communion. In this case, those who provided the visitors with information in this regard could not be considered informers, perhaps not even defenders of the faith, but simply opportunists of the type that exist in every culture. These people do not have a place in the present train of thought. They are in no way original.

However, those who requested communion of both kinds and one kind in the same church from the same priest were original. Information regarding such members of the congregation indicate that they practiced their religion based on personal conviction. We do not know precisely why some people continued to take communion according to the Roman Catholic practice and why others requested to receive this sacrament under both kinds.

If I think about the followers of the so-called heretical movements who took communion under both kinds in secret, in the forest, using sacraments stolen from the church, I would say that they were putting the principle of equality before God into practice. One may surmise that, along with the ideas of Martin Luther, the notion of universal priesthood motivated their actions, the same doctrine that the first lay evangelical preachers presumably espoused. However, this again raises the fundamental question: why did the tenets of Christian egalitarianism and universal priesthood fail to attract all believers?

I cannot answer this question. I can only place even greater emphasis on the fact that the practice of receiving communion under both kinds was the product of personal choice. The emphasis is stronger here than it was in the case of lay preachers, because it does not merely involve people constituting an identical society under the broad definition of the term. The people who insisted upon taking communion in two different ways were the inhabitants of small villages. According to a source originating 80 years later, the population of the villages in question ranged from 111 to 1,500. Assuming that children constituted about half of the population at this time, one may presume that between around 50 and 700 people who went to the same church functioning under the direction of the same priest in these villages decided to take communion differently.

This issue should be examined from the perspective of sociology and social psychology. I sought supplementary sources but could find none. It is thus impossible to determine the gender and social composition of the local communities both before and after they split over the practice of taking communion. The most I can do is to register the fact of simultaneous acceptance and rejection.

I must also acknowledge the fact that neither side took exclusive control of the church in a given village. The practice of two different rituals seems to have coexisted peacefully. However, I verified that congregations that received communion in two different ways at the time of the canonical visits later became unified in their evangelical faith and took the communion unanimously under two kinds. Entering the church does not therefore appear to have necessarily implied a sudden change. It could have happened that an increasing part of the congregation embraced the new teachings before finally reaching a majority.

I do not detect the influence of the parish priests in this decision. They do not appear to have taken a leading role. I believe their claim that they administered communion under both kinds according to the wishes of individual members of the congregation more or less in secret. The canonical visitors believed this as well. They were aware that the parish priest was naturally inclined to adapt to the needs of the congregation. With regard to the village of Szmrecsány (Smrečany, Slovakia), they wrote that the priest Ambrus had administered communion under both kinds "in order to please" certain people. Another priest, who was incidentally old and who based on his age could have also disseminated the evangelical faith, claimed that he had denied the request of peasants to administer communion under both kinds.

The social situation of the local incumbent made it impossible for him to take the initiative, to assume the role of the first preacher of the new faith. What did the lay preacher, whether man or woman, and the friar do? If their words fell upon deaf ears, they simply continued on their way, went home or returned to the cloister. The parish priest, however, would have been placing his livelihood at risk. If he failed to convince his parishioners to adopt the new teachings, he had no place to go. He could have hardly expected church superiors to transfer him to a new parish. Might he have counted upon the patrons? They invited whomever they pleased to the churches operating under their authority.

Patrons in a Secondary Role

Due to the secrecy surrounding the practice of heretical communion, one can scarcely conjecture that the patrons served as agents of religious change. Why would the priests have attempted to conceal something to which the patron had assented? I do not know the names of the majority of patrons. The well-known rapid change of land ownership in the sixteenth century deterred me from making an attempt to determine the identity of those whom the source does not name. The canonical visitors certainly do not portray a particularly flattering image of those identified by name.

The patrons play a secondary role, to say the least, in the visitation registers, whereas the broad opinion of historians is that they forced or—to use a more moderate term—induced people to accept the teachings of the Reformation. The prominent historian Gyula Szekfű, for example, wrote with regard to the relationship between aristocratic landowners and religious renewal that one of the lords, Péter Perényi, compelled the entire population of certain villages to consume speck on days of fasting. I do not know how to translate this into the language of facts. Did they herd the inhabitants of several villages into a hall and force them to eat bacon? Who did this? Perényi personally or somebody acting under his orders?

There exists a trustworthy source regarding the religious attitude of Péter Perényi, namely the letter of a Catholic high priest about his short stay at one of Perényi's castles. He went there as an emissary of Ferdinand I. According to his report, Péter Perényi—who had long been considered the most ardent Lutheran—participated in a Lutheran religious service during Christmastime at the castle chapel while in the parish church Catholic holy mass was being celebrated. And somewhat later, officials at the Szepes Chamber recorded complaints from tenants originating from the time of Péter Perényi. Among their many complaints, not one concerned religious matters. Szekfű refers to an eighteenth-century author as his source. I believe that the subchapter regarding the coercive behavior of the patrons represents the nadir of his work in terms of methodology. I do not want to dwell on this matter at length, because Szekfű showed in a thousand other places that he could handle primary sources with great expertise. The Reformation obviously did not inspire within him a great degree of sympathy. Too bad that he exercised an influence over so many historians.

The undoubtedly reliable canonical visitation register, which is of inestimable value amid the scarcity of primary sources in Hungary from this period, does not portray the patrons as being particularly interested in matters of religion. The register's depiction of the poor condition of many churches and parsonages is particularly conspicuous. The canonical visitors even found reason to criticize the state of certain churches that functioned under the personal patronage of the Archbishop of Esztergom despite the fact that they knew the register was prepared for his use. Perhaps they dared to express even such modest criticism because they did not blame the patrons for the "deteriorated" state of the ecclesiastical buildings. I deduce this from the fact that if they found a church or parsonage to be in poor condition, they requested the local congregation or the churchwarden to conduct the necessary repairs. Patrons apparently either did not engage in such work or were not expected by ecclesiastical authorities to do so. This explains why some churches on the estate of a given lord were in magnificent condition, while others were falling into ruin.

The canonical visitors stated, for example, that among the churches on the estate of András Báthori, Dévény (Devín, Slovakia) had been nicely renovated following the depredations of the Ottomans, while those in Taksony (Matúškovo, Slovakia) and Szeli (Saliby, Slovakia) were "unclean and filthy," that in Szerdahely (Dunajská Streda, Slovakia) was "pretty dilapidated" and that in Kürt (Sady, Slovakia) was "rebuilt." According to the visitors, the church under the patronage of the Forgách family in Szentmárton (Svätý Martin, Slovakia) was "neglected," while that in Maróť (Moravce, Slovakia) had been reconstructed after the Turks destroyed it. The visitors recorded that the churches in the Fugger villages were mostly in good condition, though the parsonage was falling apart at one location. The church in Sasvár (Šaštín, Slovakia) under the shared patronage of the Czobor, Révay and Bakich families was in order, though the parsonages in this and several other villages had fallen into disrepair.

The patrons were either concerned about the condition of church buildings or they were not. Similarly, they were either concerned about the religious practices of the faithful or they were not. According to the source in question, they were rather unconcerned. The personality, qualifications and confessional affiliation of the parish incumbents and the religious sympathies of the congregation were of no interest to them. According to the canonical visitors, there lived under the patronage of one of Rome's greatest supporters, the Fugger family, a parish priest named Bertalan, who espoused religious ideas that could be termed Reformed and did not attempt to conceal this fact: "he is propagating cursed heresy among the ignorant and degraded people." When they reprimanded this priest for his actions, he declared that he would rather relinquish his priesthood than celebrate mass.

The situation under so-called co-patronage in which the church belonged to several noble patrons—that is, it did not have one magnate lord patron—was unambiguously bad. These nobles were in continual dispute with one another regarding what needed to be done. Arbitrarily so, because the denominational affiliation of the village had not changed. They removed the altar or other devotional objects from the church, though not even royal dignitaries recoiled from the plundering of churches. To make it absolutely clear: Catholic patrons seized devotional objects and parochial lands from fellow Catholics.

Certain contexts seem to suggest, however, that such noble co-patrons could have played the role of initiators in the acceptance of the new teachings. The visitation record contains two or three instances in which the priest declares that he had administered communion under both kinds in spite of being Roman Catholic, "under the compulsion of the nobles." Since in other cases the "people" or some other term describing the members of the congregation is used to represent the force of compulsion, in this instance responsibility is most probably thrown upon the nobles who collectively exercised the rights stemming from patronage.

Regardless of how it actually was, I must examine the issue of patronage. Many sources and many historians refer to its importance. However, personal curiosity is the primary force that impels me to conduct this analysis. I am curious about the opinion I shall establish regarding the connection between the Reformation and patronage.

6 Patrons in the Reformation

Politics

The theology of the Reformation made the activities of the patrons possible. Secular power received a place in the teachings of both Luther and later reformers. Initially the principle that "all power proceeds from God" prevailed, then Calvin formulated the concept of resistance through elected representatives. However, I do not wish to deal here with theology, but with the fact that the patrons assumed the role of the highest secular head of the Protestant denominations. To my knowledge, representatives of the churches never once protested against it.

The free cities of Switzerland took the lead in this issue. The elected magistrates of these cities, first of all that of Zürich, where Ulrich Zwingli served as pastor, decided already in 1523 to introduce the evangelical teachings. In Zürich, as in Bern and Basel, the city council functioned in the role of patron. The council of Geneva began to consider religious change only in the 1530s, somewhat later than its counterparts in Zürich, Bern, Basel and other free cities of Switzerland. The turning point in Geneva took place in 1541, when John Calvin, who had previously worked for a short period of time in the city, was invited to serve as the town's pastor. In Geneva, the Reformed congregational model—referred to as Calvinist at many places in Europe, including Hungary—evolved during the time Calvin served as pastor, but as a direct result of the intentions of the city council.

Rulers were inclined to choose the Lutheran course. John Frederick, who succeeded Frederick the Wise, who died in 1525, as Elector of Saxony, was almost naturally the first to do so. His proclamation concerning the monopoly of the evangelical teachings in Saxony was the cause of great personal shock to Luther, who was forced into the role of church organizer even though this task contradicted the doctrine of universal priesthood. According to this principle, the congregation had the right to decide who was the true preacher of the Gospel and who was a false teacher. In practice, the theologically warranted doctrine did not prove to be successful, at least in the short period of time that the Saxon congregations had at their disposal. As Luther himself concluded, it resulted in chaos and norms thus had to be established. After visiting some congregations in 1529, Martin Luther reluctantly began to compose the *Large Catechism* and the *Small Catechism.* In these works, Luther regulated the everyday practice of worship among the evangelically minded and he put down the main theses in a dialogical, easy-to-understand form.

I know of no other church organizers who sustained personal shocks of this kind. However, the introduction or rejection of the evangelical teachings caused a greater degree of commotion in certain countries. This led to the burning of both books and people on one side and then the other. The decision of Henry VIII of England in 1532 to assume the role of secular Superior Head of the English church and the consequent events in the country entailed a degree of martyrdom and murder that the rulers of Hungary would not have even dared to imagine. We usually discuss the events in connection to the English king's scandalous marriages and divorces, although they were the product of a very important political intention.

Political ambition represented the motive of all rulers who undertook the role of primary secular superior of the Protestant churches. I naturally do not exclude the possibility that personal faith and intellectual sympathy also motivated these rulers, though the consequence of their actions was in any case political in nature. The espousal of the evangelical faith represented a stand against imperial rule and Rome in Germany, while in other places it was directed specifically against the papacy. Reformation history developed the term "political Reformation" in order to account for this factor. It refers to the process of eradicating—with a greater or lesser degree of force—Roman Catholic doctrine from the church rites conducted in a given country after its king or diet proclaimed the exclusivity of Lutheran teachings. This process could entail the extermination of the Roman Catholic church's representatives, as happened with exceptional cruelty in Denmark.

Such events existed in rudimentary form within Hungary's power structure as well. One only has to think of the struggles that King Matthias Corvinus waged against the Holy Roman Empire or of his attempt to prevent Rome from interfering in the affairs of Hungary. His successors as king of Hungary focused their efforts on reducing the secular authority of the Roman church. With regard to the coexistence of two religions in medieval Hungary, I have already shown that disputes regarding the patronage of landowners ended with the defeat of the church in 1504. There had previously been disagreement concerning the lease of church tithes resulting from the pragmatic decision of certain bishops to lease the right of tithe collecting to landowners. By doing so, they exempted themselves from the tenuous task of collecting produce placed at the perimeter of the peasant plots and transporting it in an often slightly spoiled state to the episcopal storehouses. The landlord paid money instead. But might another landlord have paid more? The practice emerged among bishops of leasing the tithes to those who offered the most rather than to the lord of the relevant estate. A law was passed in 1495 that prohibited prelates from conducting such business with their tithes.

In the end, political reformation did not take place although there was no lack of personal sympathy on the side of the rulers. I think back to Szerémi's assertion that members of the royal court had introduced Lutheran teachings. He was right. Although not explicitly Lutheran, I would certainly not claim that the atmosphere at the court of Buda was strictly loyal to Rome either. George Margrave of Brandenburg, one of Luther's early followers, was among the tutors of King Louis II of Hungary and later became the leading voice of the Protestant prince-electors who opposed the emperor. The intellectually relaxed atmosphere at the court became even more pronounced with the arrival of Queen Mary of Hungary to Buda in 1521. It is telling that her brother, Holy Roman Emperor Charles V, often criticized Mary's statements in support of the new teachings. Following the death of her husband, Louis II, at the Battle of Mohács in 1526, Martin Luther sent the queen dowager the work "The Four Psalms of Comfort" in order to console her.

Supreme secular authority in Hungary came the closest to the Reformation at this time. The juncture at which it occurred explains why the relationship did not expand. The Turk was in the country. The long-time enemy had by this time penetrated the interior of Hungary, destroying the royal army and killing the king in the process. Under these circumstances, it would not have been possible to conduct politics on the basis of intellectual sympathy even if it had been customary to do so.

The Reformation did not represent political power. It could be utilized to strengthen political authority, but was infinitely less effective than that which the pope ensured. The religious reformers exercised an enormous intellectual impact on their believers, though they maintained no additional influence and did not even attempt to acquire such influence. Professors and pastors operated at obscure locations. Neither branch of the Reformation demanded secular power or a church leader. They did not want to put anybody in the place of the pope because every denomination that grew out of the Reformation espoused the principle of equality before God. Later, long after 1526, they chose church superiors for practical reasons. In some countries the latter were called bishops even though they did not possess the rights of Catholic bishops: they owned no land and did not claim tithes on the land of others, nor did they consecrate priests or consecrate churches.

Máté Gönczi became the first elected Lutheran bishop in Hungary in 1550. Who had heard of this village priest? What would secular leaders want from him? Nobody stood behind Gönczi and he possessed no military authority. On the other side, after the fall of Nándorfehérvár the pope sent one high-ranking envoy after another to Hungary. As the embodiment of Christian unity they promised help against the "pagan" Turk. I suspect that Pope Leo X dispatched Cardinal Cajetan, who was well known for his questioning of Luther at the Diet of Augsburg in 1518 and his composition of the papal bull threating him with excommunication in 1520, to hold talks in Hungary in 1524 with the intention of warning to the Buda court.

The year 1526 brought an end to the possible wavering of the Hungarian royals between evangelical and Roman Catholic sympathies. It would have been crazy to turn away from Rome while in the clutches of the Ottomans. Not even King John Szapolyai embraced the evangelical faith, although Pope Clement VII excommunicated him in 1529 as punishment for his Turkish connections. The king waited until the pope took him back into the church a few years later. Incidentally, John—who had powerful relatives in Poland—attempted to oppose the emperor politically. He used a traditional strand of Hungarian politics connected with the region known today as East Central Europe. After 1526, however, this system of connections did not function according to the expectations of John. The other king who was elected in 1526, Ferdinand I, was the brother of Charles V and represented an explicitly Western orientation and connection with the Holy Roman Empire. Later, in 1558, Ferdinand himself became emperor.

I once believed that these events—the struggles between the two kings, the civil war and the opportunity for easy intervention—had lured Suleiman the Magnificent ever closer, and eventually deeper into Hungary. However, the historian of the Ottoman Empire Pál Fodor convinced me that the sultan's ambitions with regard to Hungary did not depend on these factors and that potential conquests—Buda just as Byzantium—gleamed before the Ottomans as a "golden apple" on the horizon. In 1541, the great sultan occupied Buda and held an Islamic religious service in the Matthias Church, thus expressing his decision to rule the city and the region permanently.

Suleiman the Magnificent divided the country into three parts. The son of John Szapolyai, John Sigismund Szapolyai, received the eastern part of the country—that is, John Szapolyai's widow, Queen Isabella, received it in the name of her underage son—while Ferdinand I received the western part of the country and the sultan himself retained possession of the middle part, incorporating it into the Ottoman Empire.

There Are No Patrons in Ottoman Hungary

I will begin my analysis of patrons in Hungary during this period with those in the Ottoman-controlled part of the country. This is an easy topic because, in short, no patrons were active there: neither those who had adopted the evangelical faith, nor those who insisted on their old faith. Instead, they all fled. Some of them settled tenants on their lands located outside the portions of Hungary under Turkish dominion. The large majority of peasants remained in place.

Ottoman authorities displayed an interest in Christian religious affairs for a decade or two. According to traditional historiography, they supported denominations that opposed the Catholicism of the emperor. However, Ferenc Szakály, who has reconsidered the issue, concluded that, although they had made attempts to win the allegiance of the Protestants, the Ottomans had been rejected. More recently, according to Pál Fodor, the Turks built greater rapport with the Eastern Orthodox. This is understandable: they were already familiar with one another. The Byzantine patriarch retained his headquarters in Constantinople, or Istanbul, even after the city fell to the Ottomans in 1453 and became the capital of the Ottoman Empire. The Eastern Orthodox Church was thus able to incorporate itself into the administration of conquered territories during the Empire's expansion into the Balkans. However, this did not occur in Hungary. For a period of time Ottoman authorities in the country simply treated the Orthodox church differently than the rest. Fodor has concluded that following their initial interest in religious affairs in Hungary, which essentially entailed playing the various churches off against one another, the Turkish authorities became completely indifferent to such matters beginning around the year 1570.

It was the simple people who maintained the Christian churches. In addition to their pastors and school rectors, itinerant preachers and Franciscan friars contributed to the intellectual upkeep of them, which in light of what I have stated about the spiritual atmosphere of the country during the Dózsa movement and after will not surprise the reader. A Franciscan friary functioned in the town of Gyöngyös throughout the period of Ottoman rule. Much data exists about this. As for itinerant Catholic priests in Ottoman Hungary during the sixteenth century, there is only speculation. We know for sure only that such priests existed in the seventeenth century, when with great difficulty Roman Catholic authorities provided them with the title of licentiate because their lack of education prevented them from being consecrated as priests. I cannot imagine that such people did not earlier travel through Turkish-controlled territory, obviously without the knowledge of authorities. Why would only itinerant preachers who proclaimed the evangelical faith have appeared?

There were undoubtedly itinerant preachers propagating the Gospel in Ottoman Hungary. We do not know many of them by name during this period, just as we do not know many of them by name from the 1520s. In fact, I do not feel that it is fair to write so cursorily about them because they were very interesting, enterprising people who had a crucial role in the dissemination of the evangelical faith. However, there is no point in trying to imagine who they were. Obviously they were often refugees who found themselves in humiliating situations, much like the Christian inhabitants of Ottoman Hungary in general. Research should be carried out about them. Here I will write only about the prominent itinerant preachers in this part of the divided kingdom since they are the ones with whom we are familiar.

Among the well-known itinerant preachers active in Ottoman Hungary was Mihály Sztárai whom I have already mentioned. He studied at the University of Padua. He claimed to have organized 120 evangelical congregations on the banks of the Drava River between 1544 and 1551. Sztárai does not indicate whom he left to serve as pastors and teachers at these congregations after he moved on to the next place. I have no doubt that he himself found a solution or helped simple people to find one. He was familiar with the ability of the community to organize itself. After leaving this part of the country much later, Sztárai began to write satirical dramas in which he consistently portrayed the town or village judge as uneducated, though wise. Sztárai was a resourceful, multifaceted personality. Not one of his contemporaries appears in various records and narratives as often as he does. Both his friends and enemies continually dealt with him. They regarded him as both a learned theologian and a wizard scholar, known in Hungarian as *garabonciás.*

István Szegedi Kis was perhaps not explicitly an itinerant preacher, but simply appeared at many places in Ottoman Hungary. After studying in Wittenberg, he spent his entire life working there. He was active in populous places like Gyula, Cegléd, Makó, Tolna and Temesvár (Timişoara, Romania) for relatively long periods of time. He maintained very good relations with simple people: when he fell into Turkish captivity in the village of Csehi in 1561, Ferenc Mező and his wife organized a country-wide, ultimately successful campaign for his freedom. Ferenc Szakály uncovered the social roots of the immense interest that surrounded Szegedi Kis. In addition to his personal relations, I am astounded at the scholarly work of this eternally roaming man. Among the evangelical preachers in Hungary, only Szegedi Kis produced theological works that have received recognition within international scholarship. After his death, Szegedi Kis's son took these works abroad and they were published in Switzerland and England. I simply do not understand how Szegedi Kis proved capable of such an achievement.

I also marvel at the simple people who lived in Ottoman Hungary. Because Szegedi Kis produced something exceptional, whereas the learned people who were active in schools and congregations there were not working in an exceptional fashion. The simple people turned to them with great interest. Pál Thuri Farkas, the rector of the school in Tolna at which several teachers taught and provided secondary-level training, wrote that they would soon run out of things to teach students because they already knew so much. There was also a school of high caliber in Ráckeve. Its most famous student was István Budai Parmenius, who established the foundations for his later widely respected erudition at this school. Budai Parmenius lived in Oxford for a long period of time before dying during an expedition to the New World in 1581.

Public religious discussions between Catholic priests and evangelical preachers attracted the greatest degree of attention. The Ottoman officials who were frequently called upon to serve as arbiters in these debates sometimes backed one side and sometimes the other. In an abstract sense, this represented playing one religion off against the other; though in practical terms it represented the interest of the simple people, who flocked to certain theological disputations as if going to the theater. And such public discussions did contain elements of the dramatic arts. The priests and preachers who participated in them stepped onto the stage with the intention of winning the sympathies of the audience.

With regard to the patrons, the important aspect of all this is that the events did not unfold under their direction. The patrons withdrew and the community assumed their rights and duties. The elected judge and council conducted all affairs of the congregation, both secular and religious, with Ottoman authorities. Everything from renovation of the church steeple to burning witches required permission from the state officials or the persons who presented themselves as such. One had to be able to identify the unavoidable officials within the complex hierarchy of Ottoman administration. Klára Hegyi's description reveals the skills that representatives of the Christian population attained in their negotiating with the offices of the Turks.

If theological considerations served as their primary motive, one might say that they were following the teachings of Calvin, who assigned the duty to lead the congregation to elected bodies called presbyteries. The latter term is derived from the Greek form of *presbiter* meaning "elder." However, the actions of town judges and other elected communal representatives exercising the obligations of the patron were not driven by theological aspects, but by the running of everyday business. All confessions came into contact with Ottoman authorities in this way.

All in all, official pressure did not play a role in the turn of events that made the majority of the inhabitants of Ottoman Hungary evangelical minded by the 1570s. The patrons certainly had no role in it.

The Unique Attitude of Patrons in Transylvania

The eastern part of Hungary that the sultan granted to the successors of King John Szapolyai was composed of a few counties beyond the Tisza River and the region of Transylvania that had been governed by an appointed voivode since the Early Middle Ages. The state that encompassed these territories, the Principality of Transylvania, came into being after Voivode of Transylvania Stephen Báthory became the king of Poland in December 1575. We refer to the eastern part of Hungary as Transylvania as a kind of collective name based on previous habit.

The patrons began to behave in a unique manner at the initiative of the widow of John Szapolyai, the queen consort of Hungary Isabella Jagiellon. Isabella was not by nature a conventional person. Had she been conventional, she would have long before withdrawn from the chaotic circumstances that surrounded her in Hungary. Isabella became widowed just ten days after giving birth to John Sigismund when her husband, King John, was killed in battle during the suppression of a rebellion in Transylvania. She could have thereafter calmly gone back to her homeland of Poland. Her return to Poland would have found some support in Hungary, since the birth of her son had disrupted numerous political plans in the country. However, the widow continued to act as queen in Hungary. For many years Isabella attempted to maintain a balance between her supporters and enemies. The decision of the sultan again produced a situation in which a commonplace young widow, even if a queen, would have sought refuge elsewhere. Isabella, however, decided instead to travel by oxcart in the absence of a better mode of transport to the location where the rebellion against her late husband had recently taken place.

The queen took her first action regarding religion in 1543, when she made the astounding decision—one that prompted vehement opposition from her ecclesiastical supporters—to approve the evangelical-minded Confession of the Transylvanian Saxons. Her deeds in matters of religion are fascinating. I have written about them several times. One of the studies closely connected with the phenomenon of Isabella and the churches is the *Hungarian Schooling* piece in this volume. The queen breathed, so to say, tolerance in spite of the fact that she felt no personal sympathy for the new teachings. She was not simply Catholic, but had received a very strict Catholic education. With the acceptance of the Confession of the Transylvanian Saxons, she nevertheless assumed the role of the supreme secular patron of the new church. In 1557, Queen Isabella publicly revealed the principle that had guided her actions, supporting in her name and the name of her son the decision of the Diet that "everybody should follow the faith of their choice," and addressing the Estates she declared "We are bound to defend every church according to our royal office and dignity."

Only one other Roman Catholic sovereign made a similar statement, albeit in far less formal circumstances. This ruler was Sigismund I of Poland, whom his subjects referred to as "Sigismund the Old" in expression of the sympathy they felt toward him. Sigismund told a papal nuncio sent to him to convey the pope's dissatisfaction with the unimpeded spread of the new teachings in Poland: "Permit me to rule over the goats as well as the sheep." He was referring to words attributed to Christ. In the Gospel According to Matthew it is written that Christ said that at the time of the Last Judgement the saved shall be separated from the damned as a shepherd separates the sheep from the goats. Even if Sigismund did not really say that, the contemporary anecdote itself demonstrates his reputation as an originally-minded ruler.

This Old Sigismund was the father of Queen Isabella. He had died by the time a group of Transylvanian politicians sent her back to Poland. These politicians believed that without the troublesome presence of Queen Isabella and John Sigismund, they could bring Transylvania under the authority of Ferdinand I. This plan, in fact, worked, though amid the prevailing political power relations it proved to be short-lived and Isabella and the teenaged John Sigismund were called upon to return to Transylvania. While in Poland, Isabella had the opportunity to see the fruits of her father's peerless religious policy, which strengthened the relations between the king and his subjects, thereby serving to enhance royal authority.

We do not know if Isabella received counsel from her father regarding the handling of religious affairs before that, when she had to assume the rule in Transylvania, or if their similarity of personal nature impelled them to react in the same way to the appearance of evangelical teachings. In any case, on her return, Queen Isabella resumed the royal policies that were practiced nowhere else but in Transylvania and Poland. I feel unconfortable as I am writing this. Is it normal to mention sixteenth-century Poland and Transylvania in one breath? Old Sigismund reigned over a territory stretching from the Baltics to the Black Sea. And his tolerant religious policies played a significant role in the foundation in 1569 of the Polish-Lithuanian Commonwealth, the largest country in Europe and also one of the most powerful.

The kings of Poland and, subsequently, the common monarchs of the Polish-Lithuanian Commonwealth could afford to be tolerant. And it was with this tolerance that they undermined the unity of the enormous territory that had come under their control; not only the unity of the Roman Catholic, but that of the Eastern Orthodox Church as well. The rulers of Transylvania, to the contrary, could not afford not to be tolerant. They had gained their authority not as a result of their own political actions, but at the volition of the sultan. And not throughout an immense territory, but over a mere corner of the medieval Kingdom of Hungary. By the time they began to rule, most of their subjects had turned away from the Roman church. Amid such circumstances they could have engaged in much unrestrained action. However, they did not do so, perhaps following the example of Isabella.

Tolerance produced the same result in Transylvania as it had in Poland in spite of the great differences between the two countries. The rupture of religious unity weakened the estates that represented the counterbalance to royal authority. For those living in our present-day culture, tolerance is certainly more appealing than the exercise of religious force, though in the hands of the monarchs they served an identical purpose—to strengthen and preserve authority. Through their religious tolerance, the rulers of sixteenth-century Transylvania relinquished control over religious affairs to the estates, in practice to the Transylvanian Diet. They allowed the lords and the envoys to debate about this issue among themselves. That was the policy also of John Sigismund, who was christened Roman Catholic, then became Evangelical, at the age of 22 converted to the Reformed faith, and subsequently became a Unitarian. Although there are other opinions as well, I believe that he followed his subjects from one denomination to the other. The highest degree of tolerance is not merely accepting another religion, but joining it.

The estates of Transylvania fell into the trap. They accepted the Catholic Queen Isabella and John Sigismund both as a Catholic and as a Protestant, and after them accepted all sixteenth-century Catholic rulers in their role as the supreme secular head of the Protestants. What else could they have done? They demanded that Isabella establish and maintain at state expense Protestant schools at the vacated Dominican cloister in Kolozsvár (Cluj-Napoca, Romania) and the Franciscan houses in Marosvásárhely (Târgu Mureş, Romania) and Várad (Oradea, Romania). There was some contention regarding the funding of these schools. It was not customary among sixteenth-century sovereigns to utilize their own revenue to maintain schools. However, the fact that the instruction at these schools would take place according to teachings that were contrary to the religious beliefs of the queen was not even mentioned. Under the prevailing circumstances, it was natural for the estates to demand the establishment of schools teaching the precepts of their own religion and it was natural for the queen to establish them. In the end, the obligation of the state to maintain such schools was enacted into law.

The Catholic rulers of sixteenth-century Transylvania thus financed the operations of Protestant schools. This situation was unparalleled throughout

Europe. Though I must qualify this assertion: I have not checked to see whether state-run Protestant schools operated under the Catholic kings of Poland. It is, however, certain that religious conditions were similar in Poland and Transylvania during the sixteenth century. All existing Christian confessions appeared in both countries. Anti-Trinitarians, who later came to be known as Unitarians, were able to establish churches in Poland and Transylvania at a time when they were persecuted throughout the rest of Europe. The strictly Roman Catholic Stephen Báthory confirmed the appointment of the first Unitarian Bishop of Transylvania. Báthory attained the greatest degree of power as the supreme patron of the Protestants: in 1572 he received the right of excommunication from the Transylvanian Diet.

To my knowledge, Stephen Báthory never exercised this right. Supreme secular authority exposed its subjects to no religious violence in sixteenth-century Transylvania. It may seem that royal tyranny motivated the unsuccessful intellectual humiliation and actual physical humiliation of Ferenc Dávid. The Unitarian bishop had transcended the doctrinal boundaries that the Diet had established at his initiative for Unitarianism, one of the four recognized denominations in Transylvania, and he was therefore pressured to retract his newest teachings. Ferenc Dávid had moved throughout his life from stronger churches to weaker ones. He began his life as a Roman Catholic before converting to Lutheranism, then to Calvinism and, finally, to Unitarianism. He was elected to serve as bishop at all phases of this spiritual odyssey. In 1578, after ensuring the existence of Unitarianism in his capacity of bishop, Dávid resumed his religious journey in the direction of Sabbatarianism and the rejection of Christ's quality as Redeemer. Secular authorities convicted him. During his final hearing, the physically crippled old man was so weak that his son-in-law had to repeat his whispered words. However, Dávid had remained sound in spirit: he upheld all of his new religious assertions. He died in his state of terminal weakness as a prisoner in the fortress of Déva (Deva, Romania).

I believe that secular authority determined the fate of Ferenc Dávid in formal terms only and that, in truth, his very own Unitarian Church sacrificed him. After receiving confirmation from the Transylvanian Diet, this church became institutionalized and refused to engage in further religious conflict and risk possible persecution. To be sure, I do not know what kind of persecution the deniers of the Holy Trinity feared. Nobody was executed as a result of their religious beliefs in sixteenth-century Transylvania. In my opinion, Báthory exercised an extreme form of tolerance with regard to Ferenc Dávid. He tolerated Unitarian intolerance.

Meanwhile, tolerance quietly began to erode the patronage rights of the landowners. The sovereign reached above the heads of the lords to the community. In sixteenth-century Transylvania, "everybody" freely followed their chosen religion. This did not happen without problems; there was undoubtedly much contention regarding the practical exercise of this right. The Diet adopted laws concerning the freedom of religion with conspicuous frequency. If a law works, it does not have to be repeatedly enacted. The freedom of congregations to choose their own priest nevertheless represented the essence of religious practice in sixteenth-century Transylvania.

The right to freely elect the priest was not unknown in medieval Hungary. The kings donated it—infrequently—as a privilege to some communities. The free election of the priest in sixteenth-century Transylvania was another matter. There it was not a privilege but part of the system, the basic element in the functioning of the church organizations. The system was shaped most probably by the wars after 1526 between the two kings when John and Ferdinand donated estates prodigally, and the grantee was either installed into the donation or was not. Many communities could not have even known who the local landowner was when they invited one preacher to replace another or when the congregation became dissatisfied with somebody's service. To whom should they have turned to discuss the matter of the local pastor? And even if they found the pertinent lord, did it matter to him who was preaching in a godforsaken village when he could not have even been sure who his king was?

We do know that some lords were, in fact, very interested in who was preaching in such villages. Great patrons of the evangelical teachings lived in the eastern part of the country. Among them, for example, was Péter Petrovics, one of the guardians of John Sigismund. Under pressure from Petrovics, local pastors elected Márton Kálmáncsehi Sánta, who professed Helvetian ideas alien to their taste as their bishop in 1556. He worked in Debrecen until his death the next year, establishing the foundations for the city's legendary affiliation with the Reformed church during this period.

The town of Debrecen took advantage of opportunities stemming from the political upheavals. The region lying at the juncture of the three parts of Hungary suffered greatly from this turmoil, though also derived great benefit from it. The municipal council began to behave as if it represented a city that was not dependent on the power of the landowners, moving with agility among the various authorities and, by the end of the sixteenth century, gaining the status of free royal city. Debrecen thus became the only Reformed city among the free royal cities of Hungary. The Great Church of Debrecen, the most renowned space of Reformed worship in Hungary, was built only in the nineteenth century. There had previously been no such magnificent church in Debrecen as in other cities. However, the elected representatives of the community had acted with the consciousness of free citizens.

At other locations, the elected council made decisions in the name of "everyone." In Transylvania the congregation exercised the freedom of religion as a body. For quite a long period of time, the lords restricted the rights of Roman Catholics by banishing the Catholic priests from Transylvania. This was a severe blow for those affected but did not extirpate the basic freedom to elect the pastor. In declaring the right to elect Catholic priests, the Transylvanian Diet stipulated that if a city or village asks for "teachers of Roman religion" their request will be fulfilled by the prince. That is, the supreme patron, not the landowner—who was obviously not supposed to take part in the maneuver—took care of the community's collective religious affairs.

The religious tolerance of the rulers, which I must again emphasize was driven by political considerations, had a paradoxical impact on the Eastern Orthodox church. This began with the Transylvanian Saxons, who in the Middle Ages had gained collective prerogatives. All Saxons of Transylvania exercised religious freedom as a body. There were no problems with this. However, the otherness of the Romanians who lived in their vicinity, often on their own lands, did disturb the Saxons. The latter complained particularly about Romanian customs regarding marriage and divorce, which they considered to be excessively lax and therefore of questionable morality. They started to proselytize the Romanians.

The Saxons took action through the council of Szeben (Sibiu, Romania). We know for certain that this city installed Cyrillic letters on its printing press and published a Lutheran catechism in the Romanian language at its own expense in 1544. Books published at this press represented, including those published in the Romanian voievodats, the first ever printed in the Romanian language. However, we do not know whether the Romanian Protestant congregations were formed out of their own initiative or under pressure from the wealthy Saxons.

The influence of the Reformation on the Orthodox Romanians of Transylvania was, again, a unique phenomenon in Europe. The assertion that the Eastern Orthodox religion did not cross paths with evangelical teachings is a historical platitude. The two certainly did cross paths in Transylvania. And the princes took advantage of this new opportunity to practice tolerance. First, John Sigismund in 1566 assented to the appointment of György Szentgyörgyi—who despite being known to history by this Hungarian name undoubtedly spoke Romanian as his native language and was originally a member of the Orthodox church—to be elected as a Romanian Reformed bishop. Then attention shifted toward Romanians who had remained Eastern Orthodox. Until that time, they had not maintained an official church organization: then, in 1574, Stephen Báthory persuaded the Transylvanian Diet to recognize the right of the Orthodox to elect their bishops. Gyulafehérvár (Alba Iulia, Romania) became the headquarters of the first Eastern Orthodox diocese. A Romanian priest named Ghenadie became the first head of it. Another Orthodox diocese was subsequently established in northern Transylvania with its capital in Rév (Vadu Crişului, Romania). And again tolerance: they provided the Transylvanian Romanian Orthodox bishops with the right to travel abroad following their appointment to have themselves ordained.

In Transylvania, the community practiced freedom of religion corporately and independently from the landowner. This right worked in accordance with its use and possible obstruction.

The Patrons of Habsburg Hungary Are Indifferent

The right of patronage of the landowners was preserved in the third part of the divided country, the Habsburg-ruled Kingdom of Hungary. In Latin, these rights were called *ius patronatus*, the content of which Reformation historiography usually interprets in this way: *cuius regio, eius religio*, that is, "whose realm, his religion." However, I will remind the reader here at the beginning of this subchapter of the interpretation previously exemplified in the charter of Đurađ Branković. According to this document, the principle of *cuius regio, eius patronatus* prevailed during the Middle Ages, that is, "whose realm, his patronage." This means that the landowner was the patron of the churches on his or her estate regardless of his or her religious affiliation.

Patrons did come under attack from the Roman church regarding the free exercise of their patronage. I do not know exactly when the conflict began to take place. However, I have already described how this ended with the victory of the secular forces in 1504. The Diet punished a high-handed bishop by confiscating the revenue he derived from the relevant church. I have also described why there could not have been any dispute regarding the placement of Orthodox priests in a given parish: because the representatives of this church did not gain seats in the Diet and its priests lived on tenant holdings.

The status of churches that formed as a result of the Reformation was very similar to that of the Orthodox church. They were of low social standing. No Protestant clergyman ever participated in the activity of the Diet in any capacity, while the Catholic clergy always retained its position in the legislature. The prelates were sitting alongside the secular magnates, while the representatives of church institutions had common consultations with the envoys of counties and absent magnates. This traditional regulation continued to exist even at a time when the large majority of the secular members of the Diet were Protestant.

None of the Protestant denominations had a church superior who exercised authority over the entire country, whereas the Archbishop of Esztergom was the head of the entire Catholic Church in Hungary. Bishops consecrated the

Catholic priests, the king appointed the prelates and the pope approved the appointment by the rulers. On the other hand, because the priesthood did not represent a sacrament according to the evangelical tenets, nobody consecrated Protestant clergymen. After their bishops or their church superiors termed otherwise were elected, they ordained the pastors with the "laying on of hands"—an act in which no other internal or external church organization had the right to interfere. Some speculate that initially, when no superiors yet functioned, the laying on of hands was done at the University of Wittenberg. I feel it impossible to imagine every pastor who espoused the evangelical faith travelling so far for that reason.

The Protestant pastor, who was most often married and sometimes had a large family, took up residence at the parsonage belonging to a given congregation. The curate and—if there was one—the bachelor teachers lived usually together with the pastor and his family. The most distinguished curates and teachers were usually unmarried because they regarded their position as preparation for their further studies. They saved up money or sought benefactors for foreign academic peregrination.

I do not want to thereby suggest that the majority of the Protestant intellectuals attended university in the sixteenth century. I mention this because I have the impression that our understanding of the ecclesiastical intellectuals contains the cause of the misconception that in Hungary the congregation was obliged to follow the religion of the landowner.

We know something about the intellectuals that attended foreign universities for at least some period of time. This is essentially a consequence of the miserable source conditions in Hungary. It is easier to find somebody in the *matricula* of students at universities than it is to find them in the available data regarding Hungarian schools. It is characteristic of the lack of sources regarding Hungary that not one list of students at school in the country exists from the sixteenth century, with the exception of a post-1580 registry of the Debrecen Reformed College.

The other reason for which we are familiar exclusively with the sixteenth-century ecclesiastical intellectuals who attended university is that they became the ministers of larger congregations. This was natural. It is hard to overestimate the difficulty that people from places such as Szikszó, for instance, an isolated village located in northeastern Hungary and the birthplace of the outstanding Reformed pastor, Bálint Szikszai Hellopoeus, encountered on their way to universities. I find it natural that somebody who managed to reach there in the sixteenth century did not want to return to a small hinterland village in Hungary. This was a rational attitude among the intellectuals. The highly qualified people about whom I have written as working in small villages located in Ottoman Hungary I regard as exceptions. They must have been driven by missionary zeal to choose that hard life. Extraordinary people were ready to follow such a calling, but one could not expect anybody to do so.

Some sixteenth-century sources may have survived from larger settlements, which were often market towns. These settlements either had better opportunities for preserving documents or else documents originating from these towns were later considered more important and more likely placed in archives than those from villages. With luck, one may uncover surviving information regarding intellectuals who lived and worked in these larger places at the local archives. As for villages, I searched through all the possible locations of village sources at the National Archives of Hungary but not one of them contained anything from the sixteenth century, with the exception of tax registers, which, of course, exist in large numbers. I enjoy reading them, and on occasion they refer to the village priest or teacher, mostly by their first name. Thus one can embark on the research of village ministers' education on the basis of some first names. It proves to be successful in very few cases.

We are also familiar with sixteenth-century intellectuals who attended university because these people wrote works that were published in print. And if there is a book, scholarship casts itself upon the person of the author. The first Hungarian grammar book written in the Hungarian language and the author of this work provide a very informative manifestation of this fact. This book was published anonymously in 1549. Ferenc Kazinczy, the most eminent philologist at the turn of the nineteenth century, already dealt with it but the invaluable RMNY reveals that it took the efforts of several scholars to identify its author, Mátyás Dévai Bíró. It is hardly necessary to specify that Dévai Bíró attended several universities.

Finally, we know something about sixteenth-century intellectuals who studied at universities because they came into contact with the powerful lords, the patrons. This, again, is the result of the way intellectuals naturally behave. There is an extensive body of literature regarding the methods with which the intellectuals of the period sought and found their protectors. Intellectuals ranging from Erasmus, who is regarded as the prototype of the scholar who withdraws from the world, to Péter Bornemisza, one of the greatest Lutheran pastors of sixteenth-century Hungary, utilized complicated methods. Erasmus did not fail to appear at the royal court during his stay in England and wrote a book to be used for the instruction of the future Emperor Charles V in exchange for no little material compensation. Bornemisza gained access to the most powerful aristocratic circles in Hungary, those of the Salm, Országh, Enyingi Török and Balassa families, among others. I must note that such behavior can be found also among intellectuals who were active during much later periods, notably Descartes. The latter, who was accustomed to the pleasant French climate, succumbed to the hard Swedish winter as a member of the court of Queen Christina in 1650.

The powerful patron provided both material and social support. Historiography is fortunate to have access to a large amount of sources that were produced almost incidentally regarding relations between patrons and intellectuals. Letters preserved at the archives of noble families provide information regarding ministers and teachers who were active in the milieu of powerful patrons. We thus know that the son of János Sylvester, the translator of the first printed Hungarian-language translation of the New Testament, was named Tódor. We know this because Sylvester wrote to his patron, Tamás Nádasdy, about Tódor's sickness and the Nádasdy family has preserved this letter in its archives which are kept in an exemplary fashion.

All in all, what is important about this is that we are familiar with sixteenth-century Protestant intellectuals who worked in larger towns and cities, castles and lordly residences. It was easy to gain the impression that the fate of the teachings that these intellectuals represented depended on the patrons. In his 1957 book *A reformáció jegyében* (In the Spirit of the Reformation), János Horváth wrote the history of the Reformation in Hungary focusing on individual patrons and estates. He was very influential as a historian; nevertheless, it was not he who devised the notion that the community was obliged to follow the religion of the landowner. I could not determine precisely who first propounded the idea.

Translated into the language of facts, it means, for example, that when the magnate Elek Thurzó became Lutheran in the 1530s, he issued a decree—or conveyed his wish in some other manner—that Roman Catholic priests leave the churches located on his estates throughout northern Hungary. If Thurzó did so, where did he find Lutheran pastors to replace the priests? The first two Hungarian students left, though not from Thurzó's estates, to study at the University of Wittenberg in 1522. There was no Lutheran bishop at this time, thus pastors could not have been ordained by imposition of hands. What conclusion might be drawn from this other than that Elek Thurzó ordered bishop-consecrated Catholic priests to cease regarding the bread and wine given in the Eucharist as the true body and blood of Christ, but as containing their presence merely in the course of the rite? Is it possible to command this?

If this had been the case, there would have been innumerable instances in which the lord would have demanded that the communities living on his estates follow his religion. There were hundreds of churches located on the lands of a given landowner. On the immense estates in southwestern Hungary belonging to the Zrínyi family, notably those of the three sons of the hero of Szigetvár who had become Lutheran—János, György and Kristóf—such a measure would have affected thousands of churches. Increasing power entailed patronage over a greater number of churches. Although lords were able to achieve many things they wanted, especially when they acted collectively, not even they could conjure out of nothing such a massive number of pastors propagating the evangelical faith.

As Catholics, the patrons had not concerned themselves much with the religious practices of village priests and congregations. As the 1515 decree of the Synod of Veszprém demonstrates, many churches had no priest: the synod prohibited priests from bringing the faithful of other parishes under their authority. Obviously these priests could have committed such a transgression only if no priest was located in the relevant parish. The canonical visitation register I have used so intensively states the same: many village parochial churches had no incumbents. In some instances, priests travelled to some of these villages from other locations to conduct religious services, while in other instances those living in places without a priest went elsewhere to receive communion or have their children baptized. Canonical visitors sometimes failed to specify the way in which the problem of religious practice in vacant parishes was resolved.

One might believe that the patrons, in the zeal of changing religions, took steps to address this situation. In fact, they did not. Sixteenth-century Protestant church regulations indicate that there was a shortage of pastors in the same way as the 1515 Synod of Veszprém decree did. The Protestants also prohibited individual pastors from serving more than one congregation. Since all churches stood on somebody's land, it would logically have been the duty of the patron to assign clergymen to them. This, however, did not happen.

The lords did, undoubtedly, take an interest in the highly educated intellectuals. They also lavishly supported the foreign studies of low-status youth. That appears to have been part of aristocratic self-fashioning. But what about the village priests? According to the Veszprém decree, they should be educated: though the precise degree of education was not specified, they should be familiar with certain liturgical texts, possess the necessary liturgical books and should receive the holy orders. The sixteenth-century Protestant regulations stipulated similar obligations, naturally not including receipt of the holy orders. Church superiors examined evangelical—in other words, Lutheran and Calvinist—ministers at the time of their ordination, though the regulations do not reveal the contents of the examinations they had to pass in order to be ordained.

Let us face the facts: the majority of village clergy within both the Roman Catholic and Protestant churches was poorly educated. The level of learning among school rectors could not have been much higher. István György Tóth made several definitely disparaging statements about this. In my opinion, it would be surprising if sixteenth-century Hungary would have been capable of producing a large number of highly educated intellectuals. And I regard the fact that so many people—though still far too few to meet the needs of the laity—strove to attain the office of village priest or schoolmaster to be a manifestation of intellectual interest. By modern standards, they were not educated. Their knowledge, which they shared with the parishioners in the church and in the spaces of their everyday interactions, was based on experience and listening.

I have thus returned to the community, because simple people required and supported the multitude of teachers and low clergy. Outstanding intellectuals were supported by the lords, who provided them with homes located near the castle and availed themselves of their pastoral care. Following the change of religion, these evangelical intellectuals did not receive wealth comparable to that of the Catholic high clergy's large estates. They were provided with a vineyard or two, a pig and various other trivial things. During the chaos of the civil war, the lords themselves took possession of Catholic church-owned estates. Never—not even during the time in which almost the entire aristocracy had become Protestant—was the idea of transferring to the Protestant churches the lands of the Roman Catholic Church that had been left without parishioners ever proposed.

However, the pose of the preacher castigating the princes is not appropriate for the historian. I should have described the conditions of religious practice and clergy in villages dispassionately. I now emphasize without emotion: there were not enough priests active in sixteenth-century Hungary to make it possible for patrons to force communities to emulate their change of religion. There are, moreover, many facts suggesting that they did not even want to interfere with local parish religion. Partially because they had little concern for the affairs of the simple people and partially because they had no reason to want to use force against them. Their seigneurial rights were not affected by the religious affiliation of the people living on their estates. They followed the principle *cuius regio, eius patronatus*—"whose realm, his patronage." They did so rightfully. This was the norm that the sovereigns of Royal Hungary never called into question.

The issue of communal religious practice thus also became a domain of seigneurial non-interference, just as the freedom of the tenants to take surnames, marry and govern their children.

The lords began to propound the notion *cuius regio, eius religio*—"whose realm, his religion" —when movements acting under the rallying cry of freedom of Protestant religious practice began to oppose the Catholic king. Indirectly it was the co-patrons who turned religion into a political issue. They did not have their own churches but had to share the dignity and the honor of patronage with others. In addition there were the landless nobles who lived on the estates of others and whose numbers grew high as a result of aristocratic avarice. Under everyday circumstances they had no voice whatsoever in religious affairs. The attention of princes of Transylvania Gábor Bethlen and György Rákóczi II turned toward these elements. They constituted the multitudes. Bethlen and Rákóczi began to discuss the freedom of religion *una cum templis*—together with the churches. The principle *cuius regio, eius religio* adapted from the rich storehouse of ideas that emerged during the German Reformation took hold in Hungary from the 1620s on. By then, matters of religion became closely tied not to the relationship between the landlord and the tenant, but to that between the estates and the crown.

Fig. 5. Vita Stephani Szegedini, in: *Theologiae sincerae loci communes*. Basilieae, 1585. Front Page

7 Conclusion: What Did the Reformation Mean for the Communities?

Simple Answers

As I have perhaps managed to make clear in the text, I define the Reformation as the teachings of Luther and those reformers who arose in his footsteps, primarily Zwingli and Calvin, as well as the establishment of church organizations that espoused these teachings. Temporally, I confine the validity of the term to the sixteenth century, although new religious denominations that regard and call themselves evangelical and espouse teachings which they deduce from Biblical books are emerging in both North America and Europe to this day. However, these denominations do not refer to Luther and his contemporaries, but to later church founders. I think that placing such congregations in the framework of some kind of unending Reformation would give rise to the unfortunate analogy of permanent revolution.

Thus the Reformation about which I have written provided members of the community above all with the possibility to doubt. The Reformation called into question knowledge that had become part of their essential beings. This applies to everybody—both to those who accepted the teachings of the Reformation and to those who rejected them. By reception of these teachings, I mean familiarity with them. Information from Hungary reveals that the community was broadly familiar with the tenets of the Reformation and that simple people took a vivid interest in them. Other data suggest that the roots of this interest were not new. The Reformation thus encountered existing knowledge.

During the disputes regarding the new teachings, some people chose to retain the old knowledge, the language that they already spoke well, while others chose to accept the new teachings and to learn the new church language. This change was perhaps less traumatic in this religiously mixed kingdom than it was in places where people had previously known the teachings of only one church.

I see the simple people in the role of initiator. Thus I do not wish to assert that the community established the new teachings. Emphasis on the influence of the reformers in the Reformation does not permit such an assumption. However, I do maintain that to a greater or lesser degree the abilities and awareness of simple people spurred the reception in Hungary of Reformation teachings, with which somebody had somewhere become acquainted and which anonymous people propagated in the country.

In the process of reception, authorities applied no coercion on a normative level. By European comparison, the decision regarding whether to accept or reject evangelical teachings resulted in very few victims among the simple people of Hungary. This was the case both before the Battle of Mohács and subsequently in all three parts of the divided country. Over time, the followers of the Reformation came to constitute the majority of the population living under both Christian and Muslim authority. Whether patrons played a role in this process or not was, however, an open question.

With regard to Transylvania, I would highlight two important circumstances: first, the use of religious tolerance as a means of exercising power; and second, the Orthodox Church's encounter with the Reformation—a meeting that was unparalleled in the history of Christian churches. I did not write about this with regard to the Kingdom of Hungary, because there it was a more limited phenomenon.

I must respond to the research question asking whether the Reformation transformed the landowner-tenant relationship with a resolute "no." The Reformation did not disrupt the flow of authority. The Protestant lord moved no closer to the Protestant subjects than he did to his Roman Catholic peers. I do, however, consider the uniqueness of Hungary's social order that emerged from the lessons of the Dózsa rebellion to be of outstanding significance. The lord did not take advantage of his theoretically unlimited prerogatives, because experience had shown that it was inadvisable to interfere in certain affairs of the peasants. With the Reformation, religious practice became one such affair.

The foundation of new church organizations affected the majority of the community. It was a question of faith, thus I did not examine the degree of the certainty of salvation that the Catholic and Protestant churches proclaimed.

More Complex Answers

The fact that Hungary experienced a golden age in terms of education and learning during the period of Protestant predominance from the 1570s to approximately the end of the century constitutes part of Reformation history in a complex way. Tibor Klaniczay examined the manifestations of this intellectual vitality. There is much evidence supporting the notion of such an intellectual climax in Hungary even if the scarcity of sources from this period renders this hard to demonstrate. I am working here with a quantifiable phenomenon:

namely, that printed books were published in every native tongue used in Hungary during this thirty-year period. A similar situation emerged during the period of the Enlightenment 150 years later. Monarchs initiated this during the Enlightenment, while individual and collective patrons and more often simple intellectuals stood behind it during the Reformation. In the latter period, the majority of printers, those who ordered books and the authors of the works were Protestants—and in the case of those who wrote books in the vernacular, 80 percent belonged to Protestant denominations.

As I wrote at the beginning of my analysis, the subject of native languages in Hungary in the period prior to the Reformation was not particularly contentious. After 1526, however, the issue of mother tongue assumed some political resonance as a result of the fact that one of the elected kings, Ferdinand I, did not learn Hungarian. It is true that the king, as other members of the Habsburg dynasty, did not learn the languages of other countries ruled by them either. It cannot be coincidental that the first member of the dynasty to learn Hungarian did so at the time of the seventeenth-century wars of independence. Although the historian can treat Ferdinand's inability to speak Hungarian as a mere fact, those who lived in Hungary during his reign regarded it with great antipathy. Ferdinand became a "foreign" king and the Hungarian estates treated his Habsburg successors as foreigners for a long time.

The inhabitants of Hungary nevertheless continued to handle the issue of native language among them in the same way. Therefore, with regard to the golden age, I emphasize the content of books rather than the language in which they were printed. Figures on the printed material can be seen in the *Golden Age and Decay* piece of this volume. They show that literary fiction constituted 30.7 percent of all published printed matter, which amounted to 37 percent of all works published in the vernacular, and 54 percent of all printed matter published in popular form. All literary fiction published in popular form was written in the vernaculars. In terms of content, ecclesiastical and theological works as well as the edition of texts from classical antiquity comprised the majority of the printed output in all languages and forms before 1570. A considerable part of all published prints in Hungary between 1526 and 1570 belonged to the latter category.

The proportionally large number of works published in the vernacular demonstrate that demand for secular themes grew sharply around 1570. In my opinion, the origin of this demand went far beyond intellectual circles, because the intellectuals were able to read in foreign languages. If I add that around half of all printed matter was published in popular form, then I can say that I have detected demand from people of everyday education. I believe that people of the latter type usually attended a local or nearby school for a certain period of time and retained some of the knowledge acquired there. In my attempt to find a suitable modern analogy, the tax form came to mind. Ordinary people are familiar with the tax form, though many cannot complete one even though doing so represents an elementary task, at least in principle. I, as someone with the highest degree of education attainable in Hungary, know what data to include in the form, though I still have not ever managed to fill one out properly. As a result of my negative experiences, I consign this task to an intellectual expert, an accountant. That is, the people of everyday education know something, but are not specialists with regard to knowledge of any sort. Such people began to take particular interest in the printed word around the decade of the 1570s.

Far from all of my colleagues agree with this opinion. The longstanding notion first emerges among them that the simple people of the sixteenth century were largely illiterate. Thus, this argument goes, the books published for them were useless. The claim may be also put forward to counter my opinion that popular printed matter did not exist at that time.

In response to the first assertion, I respond that those who wrote the works in question were well acquainted with their potential readers. They worked not in the centres of scholarship, but in peasant-inhabited communities. They were pastors or schoolmasters by primary occupation, and the community provided their everyday social environment. When, for example, István Bencédi Székely, the preacher of Gönc, stated that he wrote his Hungarian world chronicle published in 1559 for those who could read Hungarian, this meant that a community of such readers existed. Beginning in 1538, the university-trained Bencédi Székely served as a schoolmaster and, subsequently, minister in the districts of Szikszó, Szántó, Liszka and Gönc in northeastern Hungary. If anybody would have known what could be sold as reading material, such an intellectual surely would.

The second claim—that popular printed matter did not exist in the sixteenth century—presents a technical problem. The type of popular book that was quite common in France distinguished by the color of its cover did not, in fact, appear in Hungary. However, books were published in Hungary that were manifestly intended for those who read with some difficulty and did not want to spend too much money on reading material. Under the conditions that prevailed in Hungary at the time, these can be characterized as popular books. However, since the term "popular book" is too serious, they should instead be called pulp literature. Written culture of this type appeared in the stands of market vendors after 1570.

In sixteenth-century Hungary, in my definition, popular printed matter, or pulp literature, was composed of publications that were a maximum of 30 pages in length, used large fonts and appeared in octavo, with large margins. The content of such popular printed matter was remarkably diverse. This included biblical stories rendered into verses. The tale of Wife Judit became particularly popular. Many authors wrote adaptations of the story about the woman, who saved the people of Israel from King Ahasuerus of Persia. It was presented in popular form as well. How breathtaking it must have been to read about Judith's undressing. Will she really get into bed with Ahasuerus? Then the terrible turn of events: the tyrant writhing in blood between the white sheets. Popular literature also included accounts of travels to exotic places such as "The Land of the Moors," that is, Africa. Stories were also published regarding Hungarian history, classical antiquity or contemporary events that took place far away from Hungary. The translation of a Renaissance novella also appeared in popular form.

The impact of these publications and pulp literature manifested itself in folk tales. Readers found many elements of this literature to be so enthralling that they subsequently transmitted them verbally. The figure of King Matthias the Just or *Szép Ilonka* ("Beautiful Ilonka"), who was originally Helen of Troy, entered Hungarian folk tales via pulp literature.

That there was not a single Roman Catholic among the authors of secular literature published in the vernacular is the result of a complex phenomenon. This is the reason for which I gave this subchapter the title "More Complex Answers." Theological factors do not explain this circumstance. The Roman Catholic religion did not prohibit the writing of travelogues or glorifications of ancient heroes, who were, incidentally, by definition Catholic. And if the theme of heroes was foreign to Roman Catholic authors, why did they not write the legends of the saints in Hungarian? Why did they not write about the royal saints? Why did Archbishop Oláh's work on Attila in Latin remain in the drawer all his life, while rural Protestant clergymen and schoolmasters published stories in Hungarian amid much more modest material conditions?

I almost wrote that vernacular literature came to be Protestant-written because the Protestant intellectuals came from the communities. There was not a single aristocratic Protestant pastor or schoolmaster in the sixteenth century. Subsequently there was only one—Tamás Esterházy, the brother of the later palatine of Hungary, Miklós Esterházy, at the very beginning of the seventeenth century. However, I cannot write this, because the Roman Catholic clergy was not composed only of lords. I would refute my earlier assertions if I were to forget here about the friars who moved among the simple people or about other simple Catholic priests.

I have no explanation. There is, however, an answer to the question of what the community received from the Reformation. Because vernacular literature, whether sold in the form of pulp or thick books, worked with themes that were denominationally unbiased. The community, whether it had supported the Reformation or remained Catholic, could read this literature. The importance of this fact is equal to that which we attach to the impact of books and the printed word.

Here I recapitulate the simple answers which I have just outlined. They say basically the same as the complex one: the Reformation was a huge intellectual experience for all simple people. It must have been, first of all, a spiritual shock to listen to the negation of nearly everything they were brought up with. Everybody came across the new language of Christianity, be it under a tree, in the pub or in the church, and could decide whether to learn it or to resist the persuasion of the new ministers. In addition, people were offered the opportunity to learn about the world from the printed book without religious biases.

Bibliography

The following is a list of works cited or consulted and suggestions for further reading.

Almási, Gábor. "Az Oláh Miklós elleni gyűlöletről: szélsőséges nemzeti-társadalmi előítéletek humanista körökben" [Radical social-national prejudices among humanists: on the hatred against Nicolaus Olaus]. In *Mindennapi választások. Tanulmányok Péter Katalin 70. születésnapjára* [Everyday Decisions. Studies in Honor of the 70th Birthday of Katalin Péter, edited by Gabriella Erdélyi and Péter Tusor, 585–616. Budapest, 2007. http://mek.oszk.hu/09300/09378/09378.pdf

András Vári. "Wirrwarr der Herrschaftstypen?: Herrschaftselemente und regionale Typologien von Herrschaft über Bauern." In *Historie und Eigen-Sinn: Festschrift für Jan Peters zum 65. Geburtstag*, edited by Axel Lubinski, Thomas Rudert, and Martina Schattkowsky, 115–27. Weimar, 1997.

Bak, János M. "Delinquent Lords and Forsaken Serfs." In *Society in Change*, edited by S.B. Vardy and H.A. Vardy, 291–304. Boulder, Col., 1983.

Bak, János, et al. *The Laws of the Medieval Kingdom of Hungary. Decreta Regni Maedievalis Hungariae, 1000–1490*, 3 vol. Bakersfield, 1989–1997.

Balázs, Mihály. *Teológia és irodalom. Az Erdélyen kívüli antitrinitarizmus kezdetei* [Theology and Literature. The Beginnings of Antitrinitarism outside of Transylvania]. Budapest, 1998.

Barta, Gábor and Antal Fekete-Nagy. *Parasztháború 1514-ben* [Peasant War in 1514]. Budapest, 1973.

Bárth, Dániel. *Esküvő, keresztelő, avatás. Egyház és népi kultúra a kora újkori Magyarországon* [Marriage Ceremony, Baptism, Ordination. Church and Popular Culture in Early Modern Hungary]. Budapest, 2005.

Benedict, Philip. *Christ's Churches Purely Reformed: A Social History of Calvinism*. New Haven, 2002.

Berkner, Lutz K. "Inheritance, land tenure and peasant family structure – a German regional comparison." In *Family and Inheritance: Rural Society in Western Europe 1200–1800*, edited by Jack Goody, Joan Thirsk and E.P. Thompson. Cambridge, 1979.

Blickle, Peter. *Der Bauernkrieg: Die Revolution des Gemeinen Mannes*. Munich, 1998.

Bucko, V., ed. *Reformné hnutie v arcibiskupstve ostrihomskom do r. 1564* [Reformatio in archidioecesi Strigoniensi ad a. 1564]. Bratislava, 1939.

Bunyitay, V., R. Rapaics, J. Karácsonyi, F. Kollányi, and J. Lukcsics, eds. *Egyháztörténelmi Emlékek a Magyarországi Hitújítás korából* [Sources on Church History at the Time of the Reformation], 5 vol., Budapest, 1902–12.

C. Tóth, Norbert and Tibor Neumann. *Keresztesekből lázadók: Tanulmányok 1514 Magyarországáról* [Crusaders turned into Rebels. Studies on Hungary in 1514]. Budapest, 2015.

Caspers, Charles, Gerard Lukken, and Gerard Rouwhorst, eds. *Bread of Heaven: Customs and Practices surrounding Holy Communion: Essays in the History of Liturgy and Culture.* Kampen, 1995.

Chirot, Daniel, ed. *The Origins of Backwardness in Eastern Europe: Economics and Politics from the Middle Ages Until the Early Twentieth Century.* Berkeley, Los Angeles and Oxford, 1989.

Craciun, Maria and Fulton Elaine, eds. *Communities of Devotion: Religion and society in East Central Europe.* Farnham, 2011.

Craciun, Maria, Ovidiu Ghitta, and Graeme Murdock, eds. *Confessional Identity in East Central Europe.* Aldershot, 2001.

Csepregi, Zoltán. "Konfessionsbildung und Einheitsbestrebungen im Königreich Ungarn zur Regierungszeit Ferdinands I." *Archiv für Reformationsgeschichte*, 94 (2003): 243 –75.

Csepregi, Zoltán. *A reformáció nyelve: A magyarországi reformáció első negyedszázadának vizsgálata alapján* [The Language of the Reformation: An Analysis of the first 25 years of the Reformation in Hungary]. Budapest, 2013.

Csukovits, Enikő. *Középkori magyar zarándokok* [Medieval Hungarian Pilgrims]. Budapest, 2003.

Dávid, Ferenc. *De falsa et vera unius Dei Patris, Filii et Spiritus Sanctus cognitione libri duo.* Albae Juliae, 1568. Introd. Pirnát, Antal. Budapest, 1988.

Davies, Norman. *God's Playground: A History of Poland.* Vol 1: The Origins to 1795. New York, 1984. many editions

Delumeau, Jean. *Catholicism between Luther and Voltaire.* London, 1977.

Demény, Ludovic. "Untersuchung der bedeutendsten Urkunden über den Aufstand von Bobîlna." *Nouvelles Études d'Histoire.* Bucuresti, 1960.

Dykema, Peter A. and Heiko A. Oberman, eds. *Anticlericalism in Late Medieval and Early Modern Europe.* Leiden, 1993.

Eddie, S. A. *Freedom's Price: Serfdom, Subjection and Reform in Prussia, 1648–1848.* Oxford, 2013.

Eisenstein, Elizabeth. *The Printing Revolution in Early Modern Europe.* Cambridge, 1983.

Engel, Pál. *The Realm of St Stephen: A History of Medieval Hungary, 895–1526.* London and New York, 2001.

Engels, Friedrich. *The Peasant War in Germany.* www.marxists.org./archive/marx/works/1850/peasant-war-Germany (accessed: 28 November, 2016)

Erasmus, Desiderius. *Paraclesis.* In English translation: *Christian Humanism and the Reformation: Selected Writings of Erasmus*, edited by John C. Olin. New York, 1987.

Erdélyi, Gabriella. *A Cloister on Trial: Religious Culture and Everyday Life in Late Medieval Hungary.* Farnham, 2015.

Erdélyi, Gabriella. "Lay agency in religious change: the role of communities and landlords in Reform and Reformation." *Hungarian Historical Journal* 2 (2013): 35–67.

Erdélyi, Gabriella. "The consumption of the sacred. Popular piety in a late Medieval town in Hungary." *The Journal of Ecclesiastical History* 63 (2012): 31–60.

Erdélyi, Gabriella, ed. *Armed Memory: Agency and Peasant Revolts in Central and Southern Europe (1450–1700).* Göttingen, 2016.

Erdő, Péter. *Kirchenrecht im mittelalterlichem Ungarn.* Berlin, 2005.

Erikson, Erik H. *Identity, Youth and Crisis.* New York, 1994.

Fekete Nagy, A., V. Kenéz, L. Solymosi and G. Érszegi, eds. *Monumenta rusticorum in Hungaria rebellium anno MDXIV.* Publicationes Archivi Nationalis II, Fontes 12. Budapest, 1979.

Galeski, Boguslaw, *Basic Concepts of Rural Sociology*, edited by Theodor Shanin and Peter Worsley with the assistance of Ann Allen. Manchester, 1972.

Gawthrop, Richard and Gerald Strauss. "Protestantism and Literacy in Early Modern Germany." *Past and Present* 104 (1984): 31–56.

Gurevich, Aaron. *The Origins of European Individualism*, The Making of Europe Series, edited by Jacques Le Goff. Oxford and Cambridge, Mass., 1995.

Hammann, Gottfried. *Die Geschichte der christlichen Diakonie. Praktizierte Nächstenliebe von der Antike zur Reformationszeit.* Göttingen, 2003.

Hegyi, Klára. *Török berendezkedés Magyarországon* [Ottoman administration in Hungary]. Budapest, 1995.

Hermann, Arthur und Wilhelm Kahle, eds. *Die reformatorischen Kirchen Litauens.* Erlangen, 1998.

Herma van Voss, Lex, Els Hiemstra-Kuperus, and Elise van Nederveen Meerkerk, eds. *The Ashgate Companion to the History of Textile Workers 1650–2000.* Farnham, 2010.

Hill, Christopher. *Reformation to Industrial Revolution: A Social and Economic History of Britain, 1530–1780.* London, 1967.

Himl, Pavel. *Die „armben Leüte" und die Macht.* Stuttgart, 2003.

History of Labor Relations 1650–2000 [Project] Internationaal Instituut voor Sociale Geschiedenis (accessed: November 5, 2016).

Hroch, Miroslav and Luďa Klusáková, eds. *Criteria and Indicators of Backwardness: Essays on Uneven Development in European History.* Prague, 1996.

H. Hubert Gabriella. *A régi magyar gyülekezeti ének* [The old Hungarian church song]. Budapest, 2004.

Hussey, J. M. *The Orthodox Church in the Byzantine Empire.* Oxford, 2010.

Josepho Alberigo, Josepho A. Dosetti Perikle, P. Joannou Claudio Leonardi and Paolo Prodi, eds. *Conciliorum Oecumenicorum Decreta.* Bologna, 1973.

Kaak, Heinrich and Martina Schattkowsky, eds. *Herrschaft: Machtentfaltung über adligen und fürstlichen Grundbesitz in der Frühen Neuzeit.* Köln, 2003.

Karant-Nunn, Susan C. "Changing One's Mind: Transformations of Reformation History from a Germanist's Perspective." *Renaissance Quarterly* 58 (2005): 1101–27.

Klaniczay, Tibor. "A magyar reformáció irodalma" [The Literature of the Hungarian Reformation]. *Irodalomtörténeti Közlemények* 61 (1957): 12–47.

Klaniczay, Tibor. "Die Benennungen „Hungaria" und „Pannonia" als Mittel der Identitätssuche der Ungarn." In *Antike Rezeption und nationale Identität in der Renaissance insbesondere in Deutschland und in Ungarn,*" edited by Tibor Klaniczay, Katalin S. Németh and Paul Gerhart Schmidt. Budapest, 1993: 83–100.

Klußmann, Jan, ed. *Leibeigenschaft. Bäuerliche Unfreiheit in der frühen Neuzeit.* Köln und Weimar, Wien, 2003.
Koselleck, Reinhart. *Zeitschichten. Studien zur Historik.* Frankfurt am Main, 2000.
Kovács, Ábrahám and Baráth, Béla Levente. *Calvinism on the Peripheries: Religion and Civil Society in Europe.* Budapest, 2009.
Kristó, Gyula. *Nem magyar népek a középkori Magyarországon* [Non-Hungarian People in Medieval Hungary]. Budapest, 2003.
Kubinyi, András. "Nemesi szabadság - jobbágyi szabadság - falusi önkormányzat a késő középkorban" [Noble Freedom - Serf Freedom - Village Municipal Government in the Late Middle Ages]. In *A középkor szeretete. Történeti tanulmányok Sz. Jónás Ilona tiszteletére* [The Love of the Middle Ages. Studies in Honor of Ilona Sz. Jónás], edited by Gábor Klaniczay and Balázs Nagy, 245–56. Budapest, 1999.
Lázs, Sándor. *Apácaműveltség Magyarországon a 15–16. század fordulóján* [The Erudition of Nuns in Hungary at the Turn of the Fifteenth and Sixteenth Centuries]. Budapest, 2015.
Leopold Ranke. *History of the Reformation in Germany.* London, 1905; 1st edition in German in 1881–82.
Leppin, Volker. *Martin Luther.* Darmstadt, 2006.
Levin, Eve. *Sex and Society in the World of the Orthodox Slavs 900–1700.* Ithaca, New York, 1995.
Lortz, Joseph. *Die Reformation in Deutschland.* 2 vol. Freiburg im Breisgau, 1939–40. Translated by Ronald Walls as *The Reformation in Germany*, 2 vol. New York and London, 1968.
Louthan, Howard and Graeme Murdock, eds. *A Companion to the Reformation in Central Europe.* Leiden and London, 2015.
Madas, Edit. *Középkori prédikációirodalmunk* [Our medieval sermon literature in Hungary]. Debrecen, 2002.
Makkai, László. *A magyar puritánusok harca a feudalizmus ellen* [The Hungarian Puritans Fighting Feudalism]. Budapest, 1952.
Maksay, Ferenc, ed. *Urbáriumok XVI–XVII. század* [Manorial Surveys, XVI–XVII Centuries]. Budapest, 1959.
Maksay, Ferenc, ed. *Urbáriumok XVI–XVII. század* [Manorial Surveys, XVI–XVII Centuries]. Budapest, 1959.
Mályusz, Elemér. *Egyházi társadalom a középkori Magyarországon* [Ecclesiastical Society in Medieval Hungary]. Budapest, 1971.
Mályusz, Elemér. *Kaiser Sigismund in Ungarn, 1387–1437.* Budapest, 1990.
Márkus, Dezső, ed. *Corpus Juris Hungarici. Magyar Törvénytár, vol. 4., 1526—1608 évi törvényczikkek.* Budapest, 1899.
Marsina, Richard, and Michal Kušík, eds. *Urbáre feudálnych panstiev na Slovensku* [Manorial Surveys of Feudal Estates in Slovakia]. 2 vols. Bratislava, 1959.
Mead, Margaret. *Male and Female: A Study of the Sexes in a Changing World.* New York, 1949.
Medick, Hans and David Warren Sabean, eds. *Interest and Emotion: Essays on the Study of Family and Kinship.* Cambridge, 1984.
Melius Juhász, Péter. *A Christus közbe iarasarol valo predicacioc…* Debrecen, 1561. Modern edition by Gábor Incze, Budapest, 1948.

Mitterauer, Michael and Sieder, Reinhard. *The European Family: Patriarchy to Partnership.* Oxford, 1982. Chicago, 1984.

Molnár, Antal. *Mezőváros és katolicizmus: katolikus egyház az egri püspökség hódoltsági területein a 17. században* [Market town and Catholicism: the Catholic Church in the diocese of Eger under Ottoman rule]. Budapest, 2005.

Ogilvie, Sheilagh. "Communities and the second serfdom in early modern Bohemia." *Past and Present* 187 (2005): 69–75.

Olesen, Jens E. "Dänemark, Norwegen und Island." In *Dänemark, Norwegen und Sweden im Zeitalter der Reformation und Konfessionalisierung: Nordische Königreiche und Konfession 1500–1660,* edited by Matthias Asche und Anton Schindling, 27–106. Münster, 2003.

Orosz, István. "A hegyaljai mezővárosok társadalma a XVII. században" [The Society of the Hegyalja market towns in the seventeenth century]. In *Agrártörténeti tanulmányok,* edited by István Szabó, 3–70. Budapest, 1960.

Pásztor, Lajos. *A magyarság vallásos élete a Jagellók korában* [The Religious Life of the Hungarians in the Age of the Jagiellos]. Budapest, 1940.

Pesti, Gábor. *Novum Testamentum seu quattuor Evangeliorum volumina lingua Hungarica donate.* Vienna, 1536.

Peter, Blickle. *From the Communal Reformation to the Revolution of the Common Man.* Leiden, 1998.

Péter, Katalin. "A jobbágy házasodási szabadsága az örökös jobbágyság korában." [The Freedom of Serfs to Marry in the Time of Perpetual Serfdom]. In *Tanulmányok Szakály Ferenc emlékére* [Studies in Memory of Ferenc Szakály], edited by Pál Fodor, Géza Páffy and István György Tóth. Budapest, 2002: 333–52.

Péter, Katalin. "Női családfők Sárospatakon a 16. és 17. században" [Female heads of household in Sárospatak in the sixteenth and seventeenth centuries]. *Századok* 123 (1989) 5–6: 563–605.

Péter, Katalin. "The way from the church of the priest to the church of the congregation." In *Frontiers of Faith: Religious Exchange and the Constitution of Religious Identities 1400–1750,* edited by Eszter Andor and István György Tóth. Budapest, 2001: 9–20.

Péter, Katalin. "Vázlat a jobbágyok nevéről és névhasználatáról az örökös jobbágyság korában" [An Outline of the Name and Usage of Names of Peasants in the Time of Perpetual Serfdom]. In *Historia manet: volum omagial - Demény Lajos Emlékkönyv 75* [Historia manet: Studies in Honor of Lajos Demény 75], edited by S. Tüdős Kinga and Violeta Barbu, 85–118. Bucharest and Kolozsvár, 2001.

Peters, Christine. *Patterns of Piety:* Women, Gender and Religion in Late Medieval and Reformation England. Cambridge, 2003.

Pettegree, Andrew. *Reformation and the Culture of Persuasion.* Cambridge, 2005.

Prodan, David. *Urbariile țării Făgărasului* [Urbars of the Land Fogaras] 1. Bucuresti, 1970.

Pruzsinszky Pál ed. et transl. *Kálvin levelei a nőkhöz* [Calvin's letters to women]. Budapest, 1909.

Redfield, Robert. *Peasant Society and Culture: An Anthropological Approach to Civilization.* Chicago, 1956.

Révész, Imre. *A magyarországi protestantizmus történelme* [The History of Hungarian Protestantism]. Budapest, 1925.

Romsics, Ignác. *Clio bűvöletében. Magyar történetírás a 19–20. században* [Enchanted by Clio. Hungarian Historical Scholarship in the Nineteenth and Twentieth Centuries]. Budapest, 2011.

Scott, J. C. *Weapons of the Weak: Everyday Forms of Peasant Resistance.* New Haven, 1985.

Scribner, R. W. *For the Sake of Simple Folk: Popular Propaganda for the German Reformation.* Cambridge, 1981.

Shanin, Teodor, ed. *Peasants and Peasant Societies.* London, 1989.

Shilling, Heinz. "Confessionalization in the Empire. Religious and Societal Change in Germany between 1555 and 1620." In *Religion, Political Culture and the Emergence of Early Modern Society: Essays in German and Dutch History*, edited by Heinz Schilling, 205–45. Leiden, New York, and Cologne, 1992.

Skarica, Máté. "Stephani Szegedini Vita." In Skarica, *Theologiae sincerae loci communes.* Basileae, 1599. Online: Beinecke Rare Book and Manuscript Library.

Solymosi, László, ed. *A veszprémi egyház 1515. évi zsinati határozatai* [The Synodal Decretals of the Diocese of Veszprém in 1515]. Budapest, 1997.

Spufford, Margaret. *Small Books and Pleasant Histories: Popular Fiction and its Readership in Seventeenth-Century England.* Cambridge, 1981.

Szabó, István. *A jobbágy birtoklása az örökös jobbágyság korában, Értekezések a TörténetiTudományok Köréből XXXV új sorozat* [The Holdings of Serfs in the Era of Hereditary Serfdom. Papers from the Historical Sciences XXXV New Series]. Budapest, 1947.

Szekfű Gyula, *Magyar Történet.* A *tizenhatodik század* [Hungarian History: The Sixteenth Century], vol. 4. Budapest, 1935–36.

Szent Biblia [Holy Bible] … .[Translated by Gáspár Károlyi et alii]. Vizsoly, 1590.

Szerémi, György. *Emlékirata Magyarország romlásáról* [Letter Concerning the Decay of Hungary, text in Latin], edited by Gusztáv Wenzel. Pest, 1857. archive.org/details/emlkiratamagya00szer (accessed: 29 November, 2016)

Szilády, Áron, ed. *16. századbeli magyar költők művei* [The Works of Sixteenth-Century Hungarian Poets], Régi Magyar Költők Tára, 2. Budapest, 1880.

Szűcs, Jenő. "A ferences obszervancia és az 1514. évi parasztháború. Egy kódex tanúsága" [The Franciscan Observants and the Peasant War of 1514]. *Levéltári Közlemények* 43 (1972): 213–63.

Szűcs, Jenő. "Die Ideologie des Bauernkrieges." In *Aus der Geschichte der Ostmitteleuropäischen Bauernbewegungen im 16.–17. Jahrhundert*, edited by Gusztáv Heckenast, 157–88. Budapest, 1977.

Szűcs, Jenő. "Ferences ellenzéki áramlat a magyar parasztháború és reformáció hátterében" [Franciscan Oppositional Currents in the Background of the Hungarian Peasant War and the Reformation]. *Irodalomtörténeti Közlemények* 78 (1974): 409–35.

Szűcs, Jenő. "Megosztott parasztság-egységesülő jobbágyság. A paraszti társadalom átalakulása a 13. században" [A Divided Peasantry – Unifying Serfdom. The Transformation of Peasant Society in the Thirteenth Century]. *Századok* 115 (1981) 1: 3–65, 2: 263–319.

Teleki, József. *A Hunyadiak kora Magyarországon* [The Age of the Hunyadis in Hungary]. 1. Pest, 1852. online: library.hungaricana.hu

Teresa of Ávila. *Life by Herself.* Penguin Classics, 1988.

Tóth, István György. *Literacy and Written Culture in Early Modern Central Europe*. Budapest, 2000.

Tradigo, Alfredo. *Icons and Saints of the Eastern Orthodox Church*. Los Angeles, 2006.

Tygieski, Wojciech. *Politics of Patronage in Renaissance Poland*. Warsaw, 1990.

Veress, Éva. "Háztartás, telek és termelés hegyaljai és bodrogközi jobbágyfalvakban a XVI. század derekán" [Household, Plot of Land and Production in the Serf Villages of Hegyalja and Bodrogköz in the Middle of the Sixteenth Century]. In *Jobbágytelek és parasztgazdaság* [Serf Plots of Land and Peasant Economy], edited by László Makkai, 285–426. Budapest, 1966.

Weber, Max. *The Protestant Ethic and the Spirit of Capitalism*. London, 1930; 1st edition in German in 1904–05.

Wohlfeil, Reiner. "Reform, Reformation." In *Geschichtliche Grundbegriffe*, vol. 5, edited by Otto Brunner. Stuttgart, 1984, 313–35.

Zamoyski, Adam. *Poland: A History*. London, 2009.

Závodszky, Levente. *A Szent István, Szent László és Kálmán korabeli törvények és zsinati határozatok forrásai* [Sources of the Laws and Synodal Decretals Issued during the Time of Kings Saint Stephen, Saint Ladislaus and Coloman]. Budapest, 1904.

Zoványi, Jenő. *A reformáczió Magyarországon 1565-ig* [The Reformation in Hungary until 1565]. Budapest, 1922.

Part II
Confessional Cultures and Beyond

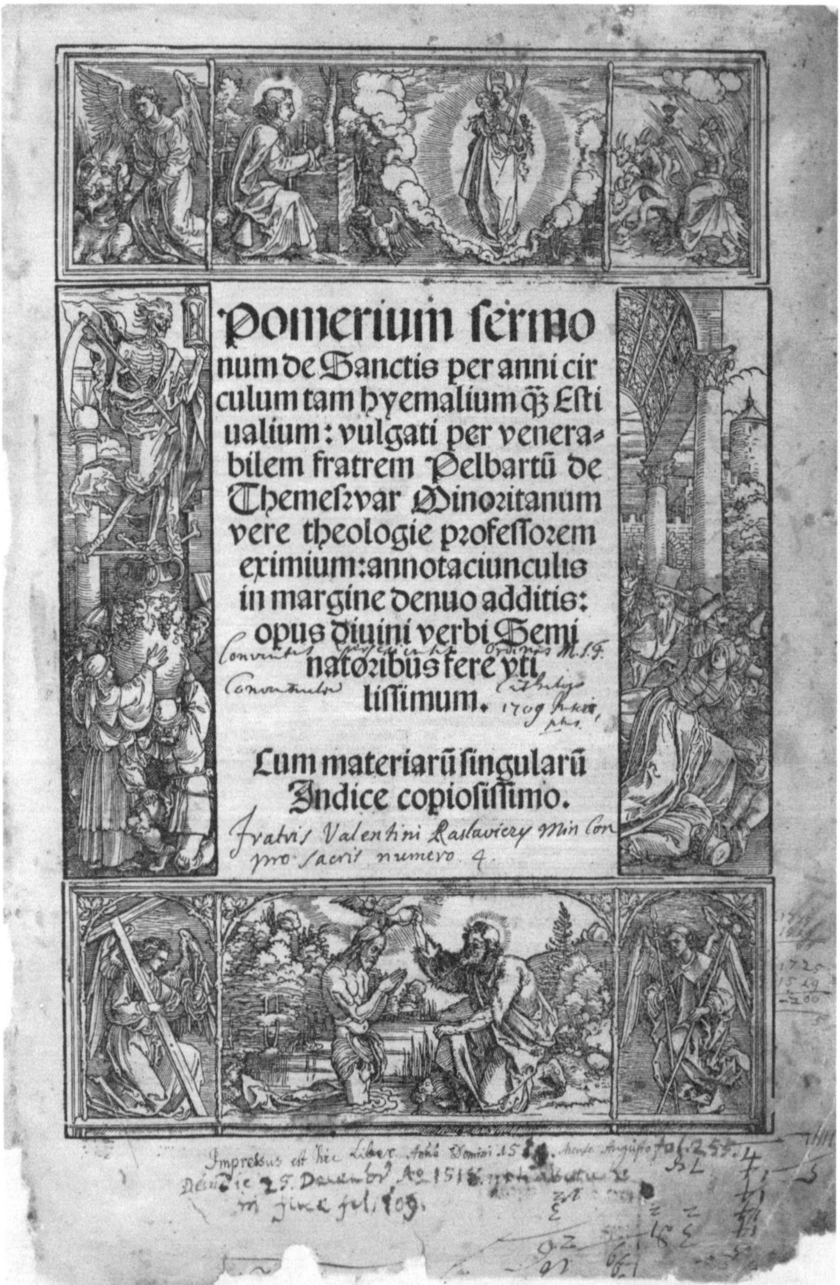

Fig. 6. Pelbartus de Themeswar, *Pomerium sermonum de sanctis*. Front Page

1 The Apocalyptic Mood in Sixteenth-Century Hungary

Sixteenth-century people thought that they were living in the end times just before the second coming of Christ.[1] They learned to believe this from secular texts as well as sermons from the pulpit. While exploring the making of this belief, I used, with the exception of the Carthusian Anonymous who was a very well-informed man,[2] contemporary or near-contemporary published texts. I did not deal with works that the author or the author's circle left in the drawer. One could call this procedure into question. I argue that it is justified because in the era of book printing, publication indicates at least two things: the intention of the author to have an impact on his or her audience; and the contention of the publisher that the book will have a market. Since sixteenth-century authors and publishers in Hungary were familiar with the demand for printed matter among readers, I presume that the contents of published works indeed reached their audiences. There is not much other data available that indicates whether sixteenth-century texts reached readers or not. However, it is true that we are no longer seeking readers in the traditional sense of the word. Seen from this perspective, István György Tóth's change of interests is very revealing. He, who after Kálmán Benda was the second most prominent figure associated with statistical literacy research in Hungary, more than ten years ago accepted the concept of the cultural uses of writing and of printed material like other scholars interested in the matter. That turn can be ascribed to the influence of Roger Chartier's interpretation of popular culture. According to this interpretation, popular culture can best be approached by exploring the popular uses of the instruments of culture.[3]

1 This chapter was first published in Hungarian: "Az utolsó idők hangulata a 16. századi Magyarországon," *Történelmi Szemle* 47 (2005) 3–4: 277–86.

2 His name has not been preserved. In Hungarian we call him Kartauzi Névtelen. He was, in the first half of the sixteenth century, the caretaker of a rich charterhouse.

3 See the volume "Pratiques d'écriture" of *Annales. Histoire, Sciences Sociales* 56 (2001) 4. Studies in it concerning Hungary include István György Tóth, "Une société aux lisières de l'alphabet," 863–80; Gábor Klaniczay and Ildikó Kristóf, "Écritures saintes et pactes diaboliques. Les usages religieux de l'écrit (Moyen Âge et Temps modernes)," 947–80.

In this essay, I expand Chartier's understanding of the uses of writing, incorporating into it the notion of learning, which includes reading, reading out loud as well as the listening to sermons or lectures.

The End Times Today

The connection of the human present with the imminence of the Final Judgement was neither unique to the sixteenth century nor to Hungary. Within the Christian cultural sphere, this Bible-based notion of the present exists today just as it did at the time of church organization. The concept of the Final Judgement has been taught ever since the beginning of theological education. Today this concept is the subject of instruction at prominent arts and sciences universities in Germany and England, for example. In countries such as France and Hungary, the Final Judgement is regularly taught at separate theological universities. And children throughout the world learn about it during Christian religious instruction. The members of large religious communities, most often located in North America, presumably await the second coming of Christ on a specific date based on what they learned regarding the Final Judgement. The Christian historical outlook founded upon the connection between the present and the coming Final Judgement does not serve as a basis for periodization that can be used in historiography.

Biblical Time

Biblical historical philosophy worked with the idea of endless time. However, all Christian-based historical concepts, including that in Hungary, have identified the beginning of earthly time with Creation and its future ending with the second coming of Christ and the Final Judgement.[4] The beginning and its unique aspects have conspicuously failed to engage the interest of historians. The only fact upon which they have come to mutual agreement is that human history has lasted 6,000 years. As the eminent sixteenth-century Hungarian author István Bencédi Székely wrote, "the old rabbis" introduced this concept.[5] Bencédi Székely's assertion was correct: the 6,000-year concept drew on an old, uncertain Jewish tradition that did not appear in the books of the Bible.[6]

4 I am using the term "time" according to the interpretation of the theoretical physicist Stephen Hawking in the book *A Brief History of Time* (New York, 1988).

5 István Bencédi Székely, *Krónika ez világnak jeles dolgairól* [Chronicle of the Illustrious Things of the World] (Krakow, 1559).

6 For the best surveys of the calculation of time published until now, see Ernst Bernheim, *Mittelalterliche Zeitanschauungen in ihrem Einfluss auf Politik und Geschichtsschreibung. I.*

The temporal disparities in the beginning of human history were insignificant. This circumstance is reflected clearly in the odd discrepancy in the chronologies of István Bencédi Székely and János Apáczai Csere, both of whom were very familiar with European scholarship and espoused up-to-date viewpoints: based on the 6,000-year concept, Bencédi Székely concluded that Christ had been born in 3962, while Apáczai Csere concluded that he had been born in 3947.[7] I find the strange aspect of this to be that the year of the end of the world did not move closer during the hundred years that separated the work of Bencédi Székely and Apáczai Csere, but, in fact, moved fifteen years farther into the future. However, the authors in question measured time in thousands of years and were probably little interested in such a small disparity which arose from the fact that historians dated the story of Noah slightly differently. Although Creation signified the beginning of time, all historians with a biblical vision started their narrative of events with Noah. This is logical: according to the writings included in the Bible, through the divine grace to Noah were a few members of the human race saved from the flood that inundated the sinful world. History is thus continuous from the time of Noah.

However, the ending point—the Final Judgement—was more important than the beginning. The conviction that Christ would one day return and pronounce eternal judgement represented one of the fundamental teachings of Christianity from the very beginning. Only the Crucifixion and Resurrection of Jesus representing the essence of Christianity are more important. Interestingly, no firm period boundaries emerged regarding the events that had transformed the destiny of all humanity. The authors of the great histories did not use the Resurrection of Christ as the starting point for their narratives. As the annual cycle of feast days developed within the Western Christian Church during the fourth century, the event of the resurrection became the movable feast of Easter calculated by the movement of the moon.

Preparation for the Final Judgement, a living custom within Christianity since the beginning, was not, however, connected to the celebration of Easter. From the layman's secular perspective, it seems logical to presume that, since without ascension there can be no second coming, Easter and the Final Judgement must be somehow connected. But they are not. Since the Christian annual cycle of feasts took shape, the

---

Antichrist und Friedenfürst (Tübingen, 1918) and James Westfall Thompson, *A History of Historical Writing: From the Earliest Times to the End of the Seventeenth Century*, 2 vol. (New York, 1954).

7 See Székely, *Krónika*, 79v; and János Apáczai Csere, *Magyar Encyclopaedia, avagy minden eddig feltalált, igaz és hasznos bölcsességnek szép rendbe foglalása és magyar nyelven világra bocsátása* [Hungarian Encyclopedia, or Placement of Every True and Useful Wisdom Yet Invented into Nice Order and Release to the World in the Hungarian Language] (Utrecht, 1653). Text edition: Apáczai Csere János, *Magyar Encyclopaedia* [Hungarian Encyclopaedia], ed. Imre Bán (Budapest, 1959), 317.

Final Judgement has become the topic of sermons preached on the four Sundays before Christmas.

Advent Sermons

The connection between the topic of the second coming of Christ and Sunday sermons during Advent has been so solid within Christianity that not even the Reformation or the subsequent organization of churches could change it. Both Protestants and Catholics preach about the return of Christ and the Final Judgement during Advent. In the sixteenth century, great Hungarian theologians, including—in chronological order—the Calvinist Péter Melius Juhász, the Lutherans Péter Bornemisza, György Kulcsár and István Bejthe and the Catholic Miklós Telegdi, compiled model sermon books containing mandatory or recommended sermons for every Sunday of the year. All of these books begin the year with sermons for the Advent season.[8] Therefore, it is not surprising either that the small book that the Pietist Moravian Church funded in the eighteenth century designating biblical text for each day of the year—a booklet that has been translated into 50 languages—used the same scriptural passages for Advent Sundays in 2005 as the Franciscan friar Pelbárt Temesvári did in Hungary during the second half of the fifteenth century.[9]

Periodization might be derived from the way in which scholars or preachers characterized the present in which they lived. However, the biblical historical outlook did not provide much room for variation, because the Bible and the Church Fathers whose beliefs were founded upon the Bible identified the phenomena that would characterize the times before the Final Judgement. These produced extremely complex theological and dogmatic systems, or else the sciences retroactively reconstructed complex systems pertaining to notions regarding the characteristics of the Final Judgement. According to a rather marked scientific theory, the estimation of the period before the return of Christ depended upon the role in which the theologians of various ages viewed the Antichrist.[10] The distinguished author Albert Schweitzer developed another theory, which is also comprehensible for lay readers, focusing on the changing essence of mysticism.[11] The difference between these two

8 Data regarding all the relevant authors and texts can be found in RMNY 1 194, 333, 334, 374, 552. There was also a Lutheran layman named Kristóf Sóvári Soós: see RMNY 2, 828.

9 *Die täglichen Losungen und Lehrtexte der Brüdergemeine für das Jahr 2005. Ausgabe für die Schweiz* (Basel, 2004), 128–36.

10 See the summary: Robert E. Lerner, "The Black Death and Western European Eschatological Mentalities," *The American Historical Review* 86 (1981): 533–52.

11 Albert Schweitzer, *The Mysticism of Paul the Apostle* (Baltimore-London, 1998, first edition in 1931).

theories is embodied in the fact that Schweitzer does not even mention the protagonist of the other theory—the Antichrist.

Both theories—as well as the many others of which I am not aware—would provide an excellent foundation for theological and dogmatic historical periodization. With regard to secular history, they only help insofar as they question the frequently articulated notion that the Bible trammeled thought. Here I would not go back as far as the difference of opinion between the Doctors of the Church, for instance Augustine and Thomas Aquinas, though I would mention that the concept of the Antichrist became the subject of popular culture—that is, it entered the pages of folk tales.[12] Obviously, the figure of the Antichrist would have not captured the imaginations of simple people if it had always been discussed using the same type of ritualized language. I will cite other instances from Hungary to exemplify the divergent modes of discussing the same, tightly determined theme of the Final Judgement.

Cheerful and Gloomy Sermons on the Final Judgement

Many people talked about the Final Judgement since four Sundays a year provided ample opportunity for preaching about it. The texts of these sermons give the reader the feeling that everybody constructed their concrete messages based on personal considerations. "Everybody" naturally represented the few people who were capable of doing this. Examined objectively, the texts regarding the Final Judgement differ from one another according to the specific thread that their authors selected from the multilayered fabric of the biblical prophesies. They could choose the mostly cheerful words of Christ contained in the gospels, thus suggesting that people would generally find salvation at the time of the Final Judgement. However, the Old Testament prophets or John the Apostle in the Book of Revelation offered frightening texts. In profane terms: it was possible to select among the sources describing the Final Judgement.[13]

The possibility of selecting was related to the subjective aspect of the topic. The authors could select the mood to project in their works according to their personal beliefs and attitudes toward faith or theological teachings. I attempted to find out

12 Wilhelm Bousset, *The Antichrist Legend: A Chapter in Christian and Jewish Folklore* (Kessinger, 2003; first edition in German in 1896).

13 Researchers generally focus on the authors who worked with the horrifying sources. See the summary of the results of such research: Pál Ács, "'Apocalypsis cum figuris'. A régi magyar irodalom történelemképe" ["Apocalypsis cum figuris": The Image of History of Old Hungarian Literature] in id., *"Az idő ósága". Történetiség és történetszemlélet a régi magyar irodalomban* ["The Ancientness of Time": Historicity and Historical Vision in Old Hungarian Literature] (Budapest, 2001), 149–64.

whether any authors wrote both cheerful and gloomy works about Christ's expected return and the Final Judgement. I found no evidence of authors who did so: the preachers or historical philosophers I examined wrote about these events according to either one mood or the other. And although by no means all works have survived, the results of my investigation seem to be plausible. If in no other way, authors are generally consistent with regard to the tone of their works.[14]

In Hungary, Pelbárt Temesvári represents the example of the cheerful narrator of the Final Judgement. His sermons are usually regarded as the most beautiful and as standing the closest in spirit to the faithful. Many of this author's Latin texts and model sermons, which are easily translated into the vernacular, have survived in several different editions. Temesvári's magnificent volume *Sermones Pomerii [. . .] de tempore* contains 16 Advent sermons regarding the return of Christ. A total of 127 other sermons are about other biblical themes and the saints.[15] Temesvári proposed four sermons for each Sunday during Advent because he believed that the people would "hate" to listen to the same thing every time: "That is pleasant which is rare," he wrote in the introduction of *Sermones Pomerii [. . .] de tempore.*[16]

We are unaware of the homiletic considerations of other preachers in Hungary during this period. We do not know the degree to which they regarded entertainment of the faithful to be one of their tasks. However, it is certain that they held sermons regarding the second coming of Christ during the Advent season. The author of the Döbrentei Codex did so with a clumsy train of thought and the Carthusian Anonymous with radiant self-confidence. And they described how one should imagine the return of Christ. Pelbárt Temesvári, who based his Advent sermons on the words of Christ from the gospels of the apostles, portrayed the Final Judgement as an almost joyful event. According to Temesvári, the flowering of the trees would portend the arrival of the Final Judgement in which the faithful would likely not perish for eternity. He even concluded his sermon bearing the alarming title "With Regard to

14 This is the everyday experience of readers. We recognize the new texts of familiar writers after reading just a few lines. And this is what the present theory is about. Barthes wrote about the automatism of the author's art, claiming that individual differences emerge "from the individual and secret mythology of the author." See Roland Barthes, *Le plaisir du texte* (Paris, 1973).

15 *Sermones Pomerii fratris Pelbarti de Temeswar divi ordinis sancti Francisci de tempore*, 1498. There were many more editions that are bibliographically difficult to identify. I used the edition at the National Széchényi Library in Budapest. See Károly Szabó and Árpád Hellebrant, *Régi magyar könyvtár. III. Magyar szerzőktől külföldön 1480-tól 1711-ig megjelent nem magyar nyelvű nyomtatványoknak könyvészeti kézikönyve* [Old Hungarian Library. III. Bibliographical Handbook of Non-Hungarian Language Works from Hungarian Authors Published Abroad from 1480 to 1711]. vol.1, (1480–1670) (Budapest, 1896), 95. Table of Contents: 2–15v.

16 See prologue of *Sermones Pomerii fratris Pelbarti de Temeswar divi ordinis sancti Francisci de tempore*, unnumbered page.

the Dreadful Omens" with the reassuring words that "we shall be saved through the grace of Christ; he does not desire the eternal death of anybody."[17]

The Carthusian Anonymous, in contrast to Temesvári, describes the Final Judgement in very somber terms. Even today, his text provides very dismal reading. One must bear in mind, however, that the text of the unidentified Carthusian author must be seen within the context of his battle against the "haughty, pestilent Lutheran heresy that has corrupted almost all of Europe" and had begun to spread even among "the chosen Hungarian people."[18] He based his sermons on the words of the Old Testament prophets rather than on the books of the New Testament. And at the end of his sermon on the third Sunday of Advent, he declared that, contrary to hearsay indicating otherwise, the "doctors interpreting Holy Scripture" state that all sin and all sinners will be condemned to eternal hellfire at the time of the Final Judgement. According to the Carthusian author, this would make the world as smooth as a "scrubbed board."[19]

For the Carthusian Anonymous, the notion that not all sinners would perish and be subjected to eternal damnation at the time of the Final Judgement represented "midwife talk."[20] The author presumably used this expressive term as an allusion to the teachings of Luther. The reference to a typically female occupation also reflects a circumstance that has been perceived by historical scholarship, though is hard to prove with sources—namely, that women were particularly receptive to the new teachings. A religious would unlikely refer to that which another religious, Pelbárt Temesvári, depicted as salvation derived from the grace of Christ as "midwife talk."[21] If he was really thinking of the Lutheran teachings, then the Carthusian author was well-informed. Around 1527, when he put together his Hungarian-language codex for the simple folk, young people, and monks with a lower competence in Latin, no evangelical work had yet been published in Hungary.[22] At this time, one could only hear about the new teachings.

17 Ibid., 16–18.

18 *Régi Magyar Codexek: Érdy Codex*, 2 vol. [Old Hungarian Codices: Érdy Codex], ed. György Volf (Budapest, 1876), XXIX.

19 Ibid., vol. 1, 27.

20 Ibid.

21 The possible antagonism between Pelbárt Temesvári and the Carthusian Anonymous is conspicuous because Áron Szilády once told György Volf, the publisher of the Érdy Codex, that while reading the Carthusian he is continually reminded of Temesvári. See György Volf's foreword in *Régi Magyar Codexek*, vol. 1, VI–VII. Since Volf's comment the Carthusian is considered to be the remaker or reviser of Temesvári.

22 The codex was prepared because its anonymous author in this way wanted to compensate for the lack of a vernacular Bible. According to the author, "all peoples have the Holy Scripture in their own language, only the Hungarian does not." See *Régi Magyar Codexek*, vol. 1, XIII. The text gives the reader the impression that the Carthusian was familiar with the Erasmian idea that all peoples should have their own vernacular Bible, though had misunderstood it, since the Bible had not been translated into all of the vernacular languages spoken in and around

Cheerful and Gloomy Historical Philosophy

A Protestant historical philosophy (this genre produced no Catholic authors in this period) appeared only much later. Because this genre focused on interpretation of the present as the end times, it inevitably dealt with the notions of the second coming of Christ and the Final Judgement. There is a very clear difference between sermons regarding the return of Christ and works of historical philosophy, since the former addressed many other themes besides the Final Judgement. Preachers held sermons about the birth of Christ at Christmastime, about the resurrection of Christ on Easter, about the descent of the Holy Spirit upon the Apostles on Pentecost and about saints and selected biblical events on other occasions. The Final Judgement was the theme of around eleven percent of all those presented in the Pelbárt Temesvári volume.[23] This presumably represents the general proportions.

The historical philosophies hardly dealt with anything else. And they used extremely complex periodization. The 6,000 years were divided into three periods of 2,000 years. This was furthermore connected to one of Daniel's prophesies about the fall and rise of empires.[24] András Batizi's 1544 tract written in verse represents the earliest and clearest known text that appeared in Hungary regarding this complex historical perspective. The title of this tract was "Meglött és megleendő dolgoknak, teremtéstül fogva mind az ítéletig való história" [History of Past and Future Things, from Creation until the Final Judgement], though it is also known from its opening line as "Az én beszédemet ti meghallgassátok" [Listen to My Speech].[25] We know that Batizi spent around one year in Wittenberg and that he remained in contact with Philip Melanchthon, to whom he once sent a letter from the town of Eperjes (Prešov, Slovakia). Batizi enjoyed great prestige among his Protestant contemporaries in Hungary. He was a prolific writer. In addition to a catechism, András Batizi wrote several tracts in verse and con-

---

Hungary. I disagree with the frequently cited opinion of Rabán Gerézdi that the anonymous Carthusian lacked a vernacular program. See Rabán Gerézdi, "Az első magyar világkrónika 1559" [The First Hungarian World Chronicle], in idem, *Janus Pannoniustól Balassi Bálintig. Tanulmányok* [From Janus Pannonius to Bálint Balassi. Studies] (Budapest, 1968), 374.

23 Out of a total of 143 sermons, 16 were about the second coming of Christ and the Final Judgement. Ibid., 2–15v: table of contents.

24 Daniel 2: 1–47.

25 Batizi had many editions in and around the period in question. This is why I refer to the first text edition: András Batizi, "Meglött és megleendő dolgoknak, teremtéstül fogva mind az ítéletig való história," in *XVI. századbeli magyar költők művei*, vol. 1, 1527–1546 [Works of Sixteenth-Century Hungarian Poets, vol. 1, 1527–1546], ed. Áron Szilády (Budapest, 1880), 95–113, 423–25.

gregational songs that have survived to the present day. All of these were published multiple times.[26]

"Listen to My Speech" describes the course of the millennia since the Creation as interpreted by the prophets as well as the rise and fall of empires until the expected impending return of Christ. It claims that the appearance of the Antichrist will signal the approach of the end times. The tract identified "Turkish arms, the country of Mohamed" and "the bogus science, the deceit of the pope" as the Antichrist that would assail Christ in the end times.[27]

This historical philosophy corresponds to certain biblical texts and is found in medieval chronicles as well. Here it can be nothing else than Protestant in spirit. It was not a case of a Catholic author characterizing the pope as the Antichrist. Identifying the person of the pope with the concept of the Antichrist is in its own simple way a great idea. Using the words of Géza Kathona, Hungarian scholarship calls it "the Wittenberg history vision."[28] Melanchthon was likely its fabricator. The German scholar and reformer built an entire historical concept upon the common knowledge about the Final Judgement and used the anti-papal teachings in order to identify the originally vaguely defined and impersonal Antichrist with the Bishop of Rome. In Protestant Reformation pamphleteering, the Antichrist was sometimes the pope, sometimes Charles V and sometimes the Ottoman sultan.

András Batizi went even farther. Using his scholarly ingenuity and his capacity for abstract thinking, he transformed the Antichrist into a dual figure. For Batizi, the Antichrist could simultaneously be "Turkish arms" and the "deceit of the pope." He presented his teaching about the probable end of the world in a joyful text. The words he used to describe the historical turning point of the birth of Christ were befitting of a goliard poet. In this text, Batizi wrote that "our lord . . . was born into the world from a beautiful virgin girl." The phrase "beautiful virgin girl" is only slightly different than the appellations "the virgin" or "virgin mother" that others used to describe Mary. It lends a buoyancy typical of the genre to the pathetic tract on historical theory. This is a happy and joyful end. Despite the fact that many negative phenomena portended the return of Christ, Batizi recommended that everybody "wait cheerfully for the lord Jesus Christ."

Others were more obscure and often much bleaker. András Szkhárosi Horvát, for example, wrote an extremely dismal treatise under the revealing title "Az

26 RMNY 1, 769.

27 Batizi, "Meglött és megleendő dolgoknak," 103.

28 Géza Kathona, *Károlyi Gáspár történeti világképe. Tanulmány a XVI. századi apokaliptika történetéből* [The Historical World View of Gáspár Károlyi. Essay on the History of Sixteenth-Century Apocalyptic Thinking] (Debrecen, 1943).

átokról" [On the Curse].[29] This work is based on the chapter 28 of the Book of Deuteronomy which, at its beginning, describes in detail the blessings that those who live according to the commandments of the Lord shall receive. Szkhárosi Horvát, however, chose to ignore this pleasant passage. He very likely made a conscious decision to frighten his audience, electing instead to focus on the second part of this chapter of the Old Testament depicting the terrible suffering that those who failed to follow the will of God on earth would undergo before the Final Judgement.

Gáspár Károlyi, who later produced the first integral translation of the Bible in Hungarian, adopted a much more nuanced approach than Szkhárosi. In 1563, Károlyi published a treatise entitled "Két könyv minden országoknak és királyoknak jó és gonosz szerencséjeknek okairul" [Two Books about the Causes of the Good and Evil Fortune of All Countries and Kings] regarding the imminent end of the world.[30] The first book portrayed the changing fate of the empires, alluding in thinly disguised fashion to the expected downfall of the still-powerful Habsburg dynasty. The second book described nine signs indicating that the end of the world was approaching. Some of these signs were horrifying, such as the changed climate: it would no longer be possible to distinguish between winter and summer. However, Károlyi on the whole portrayed the events in a positive light from an intellectual standpoint:

> The wisdom of literacy and understanding of the Greek language, the Jewish language as well as the Latin language was never so abundant as it is these days. Take a look at wisdom in other things and you will see that wisdom in external things has never been so copious as it is now and there have never been so many new inventions.[31]

Károlyi, one of the greatest Hungarian scholars, assumed a unique role with the publication of this treatise, becoming the first advocate in Hungary of a distant-reaching representation of history that developed in the course of the seventeenth century and which was based on the concept of the "fullness of time" meaning that the return of Christ and the end of the world would occur after "the unity of the faith and of the knowledge," that is, the rule of pansophia had been achieved.[32] This concept represented the delicate interweaving of religious faith with the unqualified belief in the power of knowledge. Various political presumptions, most often regarding the collapse of some empire formulated ac-

29 András Szkhárosi Horvát, "Az átokról," in *XVI. századbeli magyar költők művei*, 207–14, 458–60.

30 Gáspár Károlyi, "Két könyv minden országoknak és királyoknak jó és gonosz szerencséjeknek okairul" (Debrecen: 1563). See RMNY 1, 192. (Text edition: Gáspár Károlyi, "Két könyv" [Two Books], ed. András Harsányi (Budapest, 1940).

31 Ibid., 104–05.

32 Based mainly on Paul the Apostle's letter to the Ephesians.

cording to the worldly convictions of the author, were connected to this concept as well.

If the simple people of the sixteenth century actually used the knowledge and ideas that the intellectuals taught them, they then had the option of choosing. Whether they, just as the authors of the various texts, were optimistic or pessimistic about the present likely depended on their personal characteristics and inclinations, their mood and their social and political circumstances.

Fig. 7. *Fortuna*, Kolozsvár, 1599–1610. Front Page

2 Confessionally Undivided Hungary After the Reformation

The title of this chapter is intended to encapsulate the following contention: in the immediate wake of the Reformation, the population of Hungary was very diverse and divided from the perspective of denominational belonging, but Hungarian society's natural network of relationships nonetheless continued to function for a long time, confessional diversity notwithstanding.[33] Using more scholarly terminology, one could say that confessionalization took place later and, indeed, in some spheres of life, did not take place at all.

Fatherhood Beyond Denominational Belonging

It is a bit surprising that, based on the parent-child relationship, it is impossible to determine the denomination to which a given family belonged in the period after the Reformation had begun (and in some cases well after it had begun), even though the Reformation brought with it many teachings concerning the role of the father as the head of the family and the father's responsibility for his family members.[34] The example of three fathers and grandfathers in Hungary clearly demonstrates the fundamental similarities between the attitudes concerning fatherhood characteristic of families here. Chronologically, the first was György Thurzó, a man who had many important positions, including serving as palatine as of 1609. He spent a great deal of time with his children, in part because his wife, Erzsébet Czobor, liked to travel and often entrusted them to him, whether they were ill or in good health. When Erzsébet was away, he would send her attentively descriptive letters. "Our daughters are also better and feeling well... The little one is

33 This chapter was published in Hungarian as "A felekezetek felett álló Magyarország a reformáció után", in *Felekezetek és identitás Közép-Európában az újkorban* [Confessions and Identity in Central Europe in the Early Modern Period], ed. Illés Pál Attila (Piliscsaba, 1999), 9–25.

34 Steven Ozment offers a succinct summary of the established view concerning the general affects of the new religious teachings: *When Fathers Ruled: Family Life in Reformation Europe* (Cambridge, Mass.–London, 1983).

very well, I played with her a great deal today." Or, to cite another one of his typical letters, "I kissed Borissenka for your sake."[35] The other example is Miklós Esterházy, who was also a politician and for a long time served as palatine. He showed his love and concern for his children by caring attentively for their mother during her pregnancies. As a grandfather, he was always anxious, at times almost hysterically so, for the safety of his grandchildren. On one occasion, when he was staying in the city of Pozsony (Bratislava, Slovakia) on state business, he learned that one of his grandchildren had an outbreak of pimples. He immediately gave instructions: "with regards to my little grandchild, I understand that there are little red bumps under his chin. It would not hurt, I think, to inform the doctor of this."[36] The third example is Miklós Bethlen, a leading Transylvanian politician and for a time the chancellor. He spent all of his free time with his family, sometimes even neglecting affairs of state because of them. In one of the most difficult moments of his life, he was imprisoned by the emperor, but he nonetheless always remained concerned about his children. He exchanged letters not only with his adult children, but also with his grandchildren. His grandson Miklós was just beginning to learn to read. From prison, Bethlen wrote to his daughter, explaining to her how to teach the boy to read:

> it must not be forced at all, but rather be done as a game. The letters of the alphabet should be stuck to marbles and little pieces of paper, and you should play with him like that.[37]

Thurzó, Esterházy, and Bethlen belonged to the Lutheran, Roman Catholic, and Reformed churches, respectively. All three were knowledgeable on questions of theology, and they were leading secular representatives of their churches. It seems quite unimaginable, however, that they were guided in their roles as attentive fathers by theological teachings. It seems similarly unimaginable that Péter Perényi, who according to his contemporaries was an outrageously bad father, turned his son over to the Ottoman Sultan as a hostage instead of going himself simply out of ignorance of theological matters.[38]

Considering society from the polar opposite perspective, i.e. the perspective of the peasantry, it seems even less likely that the peasants were guided in their

35 Letter of György Thurzó to Erzsébet Czobor, January 4 1596: *Bethlenfalvi gróf Thurzó György levelei nejéhez* [The Letters of Count György Bethlenfalvi Thurzó to his Wife], ed. Edmund Zichy, 2 vol. (Budapest, 1876), vol. 1, 162–63.

36 Lajos Merényi (ed.), Letter of Miklós Esterházy to Erzsébet Thurzó, September 7 1641. Esterházy Miklós családi levelezése [Miklós Esterházy's Family Correspondence], *Történelmi Tár* 4 (1907) 8: 317.

37 Letter of Miklós Bethlen to Júlia Bethlen, Wife of Sándor Teleki, July 28 1709. *Bethlen Miklós levelei* [Letters of Miklós Bethlen], 2 vol., ed. József Jankovics (Budapest, 1987), vol. 2, 1019.

38 For a description of the case, together with a collection of the relevant documents, see Mihály Sztárai, *História Perényi Ferenc kiszabadulásáról* [The History of the Liberation of Ferenc Perényi], ed. Imre Téglásy (Budapest, 1985).

everyday family lives by religious teachings. We can characterize an individual as the head of the family on the basis of his relationship to his children, but the available data do not reveal anything about denominational belonging. For instance, at the beginning of the seventeenth century, a tenant peasant lived on the estate in Szalónak whose son, Péter, went abroad to study. The father ceased to concern himself with his son, as evidenced by the fact that by the time Péter had returned, the father had moved to an unknown location and had done nothing to ensure that his son would get the share of the tenant plot of land he was due.[39] However, we know of another peasant, Vida Tot, who also lived at the beginning of the seventeenth century, whose daughter moved out of his home after getting married. Tot did not break off ties with his daughter. Sources indicate that he paid his daughter a visit when she was pregnant.[40]

We do not know whether the father who was indifferent to his son's fate was of the same denomination as the father who visited his pregnant daughter. We also do not know which denomination György Dienes or János Takácz belonged to. Both men tensely waited for their wives to go into labor, Takácz in a village near Pozsony at the beginning of the seventeenth century, Dienes at the end of the century in northeastern Hungary, in Szabolcs County. Dienes fell into a state of despair when, at the end of the eighth month of the pregnancy, the quadruplets died, in his view because of a blunder made by the midwife.[41] Takácz, in contrast, looked on with joy as the midwife washed his wife in their "conjugal bed" after an easy birth.[42] Perhaps there were bad husbands and fathers who were less enthusiastic about the births of their children.

Fundamentally, it seems most likely that individual habits and characteristics made a man a good father or a bad one, an attentive head of household or an indifferent one. Other factors, such as family traditions, customs, and social norms, played secondary roles, and this probably included the teachings of the various confessions as well.

39 On the trial concerning the plot of land see: *Úriszék. XVI–XVII. századi perszövegek* [Manorial Court. The Texts of Sixteenth-Century and Seventeenth-Century Trials], ed. Endre Varga (Budapest, 1958), 128–29.

40 "Vida Tot… came here once… to see his daughter, since she was pregnant, and he spent one night at his daughter's house." *Magyarországi boszorkány perek 1529–1768* [Hungarian Witch Trials, 1529–1768] 2 vol., ed. Ferenc Schram (Budapest, 1970), 237.

41 "… when his wife would have had to carry them for only one more month, [the midwife] killed the four children by trying to deliver them before their time." Ibid. vol. 2, 50.

42 ".. she then washed the woman of the home in their conjugal bed." Ibid. vol. 3, 232.

Holy Communion, with No Difference According to Confession

One would also presume to find evidence of clear differences in the practice of administering the Lord's Supper or the Eucharist on the basis of confession, since the divergent understandings of the priestly order gave rise to a visible difference. The situation does not demand a particularly detailed explanation. According to the Roman church, only members of the priestly order were to take communion "under both kinds," meaning churchgoers were not offered the chalice containing wine. By contrast, Luther and, in his wake, other leaders of the Reformation rejected the priestly order and consequently allowed every member of the congregation to take communion under both kinds. Visibility, in this context, is not to be understood in any theological sense. Rather, it simply means that everyone could see whether or not the faithful were being given bread and wine, or if only the priest was sipping from the chalice.

One cannot presume that there were, during the time of the early Reformation or the evangelical movement, radically divergent practices among evangelicals or those loyal to the Roman church when it came to communion, since in all likelihood there was considerable confusion and debate on this question, as there was on most church rituals and teachings. We know, for instance, that in the case of investigations of the so-called "Lutheran plague" in Hungary in the 1520s the church authorities themselves were often not certain which teachings or forms of conduct should be considered at odds with the Roman church.[43] This was the case all over Europe.

In order to get a sense of the uncertainty that quite naturally arose everywhere it perhaps suffices simply to recall Luther's experiences in the course of his first church visitation. When Melanchthon managed—almost with the use of force—to persuade him to examine the prevailing circumstances in individual congregations for himself, he was shocked. As he wrote to one of his friends,

> the state of the churches is deplorable everywhere. The peasants learn nothing, except how to abuse their freedom, and they make no confession of their faith, they do not live according to the sacraments, as if religion had freed them from everything.[44]

In 1529, he began the *Small Catechism* with the following words: "The deplorable, miserable conditions which I recently observed when visiting the parishes have

43 Jenő Zoványi: *A reformáció Magyarországon 1565-ig* [The Reformation in Hungary until 1565] (Budapest, 1922), 65–67.

44 Luther to George Spalatin, February (?) 1529: WA Briefe [Wette], 5, 424. https://ia802606.us.archive.org/13/items/lettersmartinlu00luthgoog/lettersmartinlu00luthgoog.pdf (accessed October 12 2016). I could find no English translation published.

constrained and pressed me to put this catechism of Christian doctrine into this brief, plain, and simple form."[45]

The confusion and ambiguity naturally also affected those who did not want to break from the Roman church. Earlier, the situation had been unambiguous: anyone who went to church or held sermons in a church was regarded (and could regard him or herself) as a member of the church. Only after the spread of evangelical teachings did it become unavoidable to explain Roman teachings in a manner that would be broadly comprehensible. The fact that, in the wake of the spread of neologist ideas, the Roman Catholic Church also began to summarize its basic teachings and the rituals and acts of religious practice in easily understandable, question-answer catechisms (much as the reformers were doing) reveals a great deal about the circumstances among Roman Catholics. The Catholic catechism that was the most widely familiar and the most in use, Petrus Canisius' *Small Catechism* (the title of which is a clear reference to Luther), began to be used in Hungary sometime around the late 1570s and early 1580s.[46]

By then, however, the teachings of the various confessions had already become sharply divided in Hungary as they had across Europe, and these divergent teachings had reached catechisms intended for the simple, uneducated people. In 1538, István Bencédi Székely composed and published the first Lutheran catechism in Hungarian.[47] Not long before February 1551, the first Roman Catholic catechism was published in Hungarian,[48] and the first Calvinist catechism in Hungarian was published in 1562.[49] By then, it had become very clear what expectations were placed on the faithful and the clergymen by each individual confession.

However, the practice of administering the Eucharist under both kinds was not regarded as a clear criterion on the basis of which one could distinguish the various confessions. One finds clear evidence of this in the records of the visitors who submitted reports on the circumstances and affairs of the church and the parishes in the Archdiocese of Esztergom in the territory of Northwestern Hungary.[50] The visitors, who had been entrusted by Miklós Oláh, Archbishop of Esztergom, with the task of doing preparatory work for a national Catholic Synod, were essentially

45 Martin Luther's The Small Catechism http://www.cph.org/images/topics/pdf/smallcatechism/preface.pdf (accessed: October 12, 2016).

46 Petrus Canisius. Parvus Catechismus. Tyrnaviae, [between 1578 and 1583]. RMNY 1, 471.

47 István Székely, *Keresztyénségnek fundamentumáról való tanúság* [In Witness of the Foundation of Christianity]. (Krakow, 1538), RMNy 1, 27.

48 Péter Literatus, *Hungarische Pente-Tafel.* Vienna, [between 1549 and 1551, in Hungarian]. RMNY 1, 81.

49 Péter Melius Juhász, *Catekismus… Calvinus János írása szerint* [Catechism… According to the Writing of John Calvin] (Debrecen, 1562), RMNy 1, 182.

50 It is the same source that I used in the first part of this volume so intensively. The scarcity of material in Hungary of this period makes it most valuable.

reviving the institution of diocesan visitation to parishes, a practice that had long fallen into neglect in Hungary.

Essentially, they were charged with the task of determining whether the parish priests were guiding parish religion "in accordance with the customs of the Roman Church" or whether they should be regarded as "heretics." With regard to heretics they were remarkably well informed. They drew distinctions among the individual Protestant confessions and theological tendencies.[51] In some places, a priest or an entire congregation was pronounced "heretical" without any clear explanation, while in other places subtle distinctions were drawn. They made note of "Lutheran" priests and congregations, but also wrote of "sacramentarians," by which they essentially meant the later Calvinists. They even knew of groups within the Swiss confession, the members of which they regarded as followers of Ulrich Zwingli or Thomas Grynaeus. One of the visitors suspected that followers of Zwingli were living in the village of Galánta (Galanta, Slovakia), a settlement in which there had not been a priest for ten years.[52] A patron in the village of Szentmária (Liptovská Mara, Slovakia) who was domineering in his dealings with his co-patrons was characterized as a student of Grynaeus.[53]

The visitors easily identified people who were non-Catholic. Usually, the condition of the church itself was enough to betray such a congregation. According to some of the visitors, the churches resembled stables and pigsties, while others noted only that the usual adornments and accoutrements were missing. The churches did not have decorations, devotional objects, or holy water. In other words, they were clearly used by the congregations for rituals that were based on the new teachings.[54]

It is striking, however, that, whether openly or in secret, many priests who considered themselves Roman Catholic and who were not stamped as heretics by the visitors administered the Eucharist under both kinds. The appearance of the churches in which they served clearly indicated that they belonged to the Roman Catholic Church. They did not remove any of the furnishings or devotional objects from their churches that were part of the Roman Catholic services. They considered themselves (and indeed were considered by the visitors) members of the Catholic Church because, with the exception of Holy Communion, they performed all other rights in accordance with Catholic practices.

---

51 A copy of the visitation record survives in the Prímási Levéltár [Primatial Archive, Esztergom] Archivum Ecclesiasticum Vetus, with no reference number. Detailed edition: Vojtech Bucko, ed., *Reformné hnutie v arcibiskupstve ostrihomskom do r. 1564 (Reformatio in archidioecesi Strigoniensi ad a. 1564)* (Bratislava, 1939), 124–233.

52 "Populus inobediens, nescitur Lutheranam an Cynglyanam amplectatur heresym. … A decennio fere nullum habuere parochum." Ibid. 146.

53 Rakoczky "Grynei eruditionem, eloquentiam, copiam, ardorem animi, presertim in tali causa habeat…" Ibid. 167.

54 Ibid., passim.

Thus, for instance, in 1562, the church, the altarpieces, and the devotional objects (in other words, all of the things necessary for the church rituals) in Dévény (Devín, Slovakia) were in splendid condition. The priest had been ordained by a bishop, and at least to the extent that the visitor was able to determine on the basis of what he was told by the members of the congregation, the priest "performed every sacrament according to the rites of the Roman Church." Nonetheless, it was said of him that, "along with others, he receives Holy Communion under both kinds." He himself denied this, and the church visitor did not regard him as a "heretic." He concluded his report with the contention that the priest performed every ritual and held every service in accordance with Catholic practices. Obviously, he placed no emphasis on the fact that the priest was married.[55] The church in the village of Récse (Rača, Slovakia) was in similarly good condition, and the devotional objects were also clearly well cared for. According to the visitor, the parish priest, a man named Sebestyén, seemed to be a good Catholic, and "he celebrates all services according to the customs of the Catholic mother Church." However, it was said of him that he administered Holy Communion under both kinds for anyone who asked.[56]

Many similar contentions were made on the basis of oral evidence, but in several cases it is not clear how the visitors knew that communion was being given under both kinds, though they wrote about this practice as if it were a fact. For instance, according to one of the visitors, the village priest of Szmrecsány (Smrečany, Slovakia), Ambrus, administered communion in accordance with the requests made by the parishioners, but "in other matters, he acted according to the rituals of the Roman church."[57] In Trsztena (Trstená, Slovakia), a young priest kept the village church in good condition and respectfully decorated. He administered communion under both kinds, but in everything else he followed the old customs.[58] In Dubova (Dubová, Slovakia), an old, simple priest maintained the church and the sacraments and performed mass according to Catholic customs. There was,

55 "Ecclesia huius oppidi quamvis per Turcas fuerit compusta, iam tamen est restaurata et decenter servatur… Parochus huius loci Bartholomeus Justipolitanus, ordinatus Parencii per Reverendum Petrum Grythy episcopum… Sacramentum Eucaristiae, Crisma, oleum Sanctam, fons Baptismatis, aqua Benedicta ornamenta altarium et indumenta sacerdotalia honorifice, locoque mundissimo servantur, et omnia Sacramenta iuxta ritum Sanctae Romanae Ecclesie perspective parochum administrantur, quod eciam parochiani sui fatentur, a quibusdam tamen exteris dicebatur eundem parochum cum nonnullis sub utraque specie communicari. Ipse tamen fortiter id negabat, horas canonicas orat, missas latine celebrat cum indumentis et apparatibus solitis, concionatur ex postillis catholicorum scriptorium, mulierem habet…." Ibid. 141.

56 "Sebastianus plebanus homo, ut apparet, Catholicus, sacramenta omnia iuxta ritum Sancte Matris Ecclesie administrat, fama tame n est de illo, quod sacramentum Eucharistiae sub utraque specie volentibus distribueret." Ibid. 143.

57 "Eucharistiam pro accipiencium affectu distribuit, in aliis suis condicionibus iuxta ritum Sanctae Romanae Ecclesiae procedit." Ibid. 169.

58 "Ecclesiam bona tenet condicione omni decore ornatam. Sub utraque specie tamen communicat, alia omnia iuxta veterem consuetudinem observat." Ibid. 174.

however, one exception. He administered communion under both kinds.[59] A young priest in Szentmihály (Liptovský Michal, Slovakia), who was an educated and pleasant man, kept his church in good condition and beautifully decorated. Nonetheless, he offered communion to the parishioners under both kinds.[60] In general, the record books make little mention of details.

It is rather striking, in contrast with all this, that the visitors made no record of a priest who was, in their assessment, a "heretic," but who administered communion in one kind. In other words, non-Catholics took communion under both kinds, but the converse did not happen. Taking communion under both kinds was not a sign of "heresy" in the middle of the sixteenth century in Hungary.

This complex situation, rich with contradiction, cannot be explained simply as the consequence of ignorance or unfamiliarity with matters of theology. While it is clearly likely that there were village priests who were not fully armed, as it were, with complete knowledge of church teachings—and it is reasonable to presume that they were not entirely aware of the implications of all of their actions—the assessments of the priests that were recorded in the record books were made by archdeacons who had been prepared to serve as visitors. They perhaps knew perfectly well that at the Council of Trent there had been heated debates concerning the participation of the laity in Holy Communion under both kinds, in large part at the urgings of Hungarian prelates. In the end, the decision was made to allow members of the laity to drink from the chalice in places where the church risked losing followers if it were to ban communion under both kinds, for instance in parishes under the authority of the Archbishop of Esztergom.[61]

This decision illustrates very clearly that the desire to partake in communion under both kinds was a matter more profound than mere teachings or dogmas. Theologically, the origins of the practice can be traced back to the early Christian church and the Church Fathers.[62] In practice, in the Middle Ages it was an issue that was always emphasized by the movements that were challenging the authority of the Roman church. People who had only an approximate understanding of church teachings insisted on it. Before the Reformation, "heretical" peasants would take communion under both kinds in deep forests, using wine taken from the church, and one of the factions of the Hussites was given the name Utraquist because of its insistence on partaking in communion under both kinds ("sub utraque specie").

59 "Ecclesiam, sacramenta, ceremonias more tenet Romano, dempto, quod sub utraque specie communicat." Ibid. 174

60 "Non indoctus, neque inhumanus, bonis preditus moribus, ecclesiam bona tenet conditione cum decente decore et ceremoniis, communicat nihilominus sub utraque specie." Ibid. 177.

61 The editor of the visitation records, Vojtech Bucko, has collected the relevant documents and details: ibid. 234–55.

62 The Second Vatican Council addressed the question with this in mind and decided to permit the administration of Holy Communion under both kinds.

According to Luther, who in one of his early works insisted that "all Christians are truly of the spiritual estate, and there is no difference among them, ... we are all consecrated as priests by baptism,"[63] the administration of communion under both kinds is an expression of equality before God. In all likelihood, simple people shared this view, but we have no sources concerning their opinions. We do not know why some of them were so insistent on the importance of partaking in communion under both kinds or why others simply took notice of the fact that the priests were of a different standing from them.

By the time the church structures had grown rigid, this was no longer an issue. From then on, people were born into a given confession. The possibility of choosing from among the different confessions had passed, or at least, as a form of conversion, it had become very complicated. The data in the visitation records compiled at the behest of Miklós Oláh are particularly important in part for this reason. They show very clearly that in the decades during the spread of evangelical ideas people sympathizing with different confessions could still take part in the same manner in the only common Christian sacrament apart from baptism: communion.

Church Songs without Confessional Difference

A particular kind of source, namely the church songs or rather the songbooks taken as a whole, suggests that the words that were spoken in the various churches of the various confessions were not necessarily divergent. It is worth considering this source in part simply because we have very little information concerning the religious convictions of the simple people of sixteenth-century Hungary, but everyone heard and sang these songs, since everyone was a churchgoer at the time. Naturally, people remembered and in all likelihood accepted on some level the ideas in the songs that were most frequently sung.

200 church songs in 15 songbooks have survived from the period between 1538 and 1582, i. e. the decades during the spread of Reformation ideas.[64] 24 of them can be considered popular songs because they were published several times. Of these 24, 5 were published in 10 songbooks and 19 were included in 9 songbooks. Thus, they were among the songs that were sung and heard the most often, primarily in the course of religious services, but sources also indicate that church songs were sung at social occasions outside the church and when people were working.

63 Martin Luther, *To the Christian Nobility of the German Nation.* 1520. WA 6, 407. English translation: http://www.iclnct.org/pub/resources/text/wittenberg/luther/web/nblty-03.html (accessed October 12 2016).

64 The data can be found in RMNY 1. I collected the texts on the basis of the index of incipits in RMNy 1.

The largest group of the most popular songs consisted of translations of eleven psalms. It is rather striking that, while in the Book of Psalms there are many songs that are characterized as "for giving thanks," not one of them is among the psalms that were published the most frequently in Hungarian. This is characteristic of the entire body of church songs in Hungarian; they concern not eternal triumph, but present misery. The majority of the most popular songs, 19 in all, begin with emphasis on our current, miserable, fallen state. In two of the songs, the cause of human misery was the work of the devil, while in the others it was God's wrath, provoked by the sins of the Hungarians. According to 20 of the songs concerning our fallen state, our sufferings are God's punishment for our sins. In each song, the punishment is delivered by the enemy, but only two songs give explicit mention of this enemy: "the pagans." The other striking feature of the songs is that while most of them concerned war and the blows delivered by the enemy, they made almost no mention of physical suffering. Only two of the 24 most popular songs deal with physical suffering. Finally, the songs share one common feature, namely faith in the future. The songs, which speak of our fallen state, our sins, and our spiritual sufferings, all conclude with the reassurance that God will surely rescue us.

The texts of the songs are beautiful and often moving and disturbing. The fact that most of them can be found in songbooks that are still in use today gives a clear indication of their powerful expressiveness. Their most striking feature, however, is not their beauty, but rather the fact that they are confessionally neutral. To put this more precisely, they are very clearly Christian, but they cannot be tied to any particular denomination. None of them deal with theological teachings, and they do not touch on the passionately debated questions of faith.

The most popular songs do not concern religious teachings, although songs about such teachings were written in the sixteenth century. Among the 200 surviving church songs, there are some that touch on church teachings, but they are not among the 24 most popular. In several cases, the texts of these songs are every bit as moving as the texts of the most popular songs. Five of the 24 songs that were published most frequently do not deal with the misery of the present, but they are also not didactic. Instead, they speak of the tranquil wonder of having found the true faith, and they asked for faith.

The evidence suggests that the people who compiled the songbooks felt that it would not be easy to popularize didactic songs concerning baptism, Holy Communion, or prayer. They did not expect churchgoers to have a firm grasp of the subtleties of theological debates or to appreciate the sometimes hidden divergences in the dogmas of the various confessions.

This hypothesis finds support in the general content of the songbooks. Scholars have identified the denominations to which individual publications belonged on the basis of the person who compiled them or, in some cases, on the basis of the denomination of the printer or the layout of the book. The layout of the songbooks was different for each denomination. However, the authors of the songs could have belonged to any denomination.

Perhaps the most illustrative example of a songbook lacking all confessional bias is the collection by Lutheran Bishop Péter Bornemisza entitled "Énekek három rendbe," or "Songs in Three Orders."[65] It was published in 1582. The first section contains the church songs, 193 in total. Clearly, Bornemisza collected the most frequently used songs. 91 of the songs are found in six other songbooks, and the book includes all of the 24 most popular songs. In some cases Bornemisza's collection includes the name of the author of the particular text. On the basis of this, we know that almost half of the texts in the songbook compiled by the Lutheran bishop were written by authors who were not Lutherans.

This is true, essentially, of the other major collections of songs as well. For instance, in 1556, a collection of songs was published entitled "A keresztyéni gyülekezetben való isteni dicséretek," or "Divine Hymns for the Christian Congregation," a collection which is known in the literature as the songbook of Várad.[66] At the time, the sharp and often vehement debates among representatives of the various Protestant denominations either had already taken place or were underway. However, one finds, in this songbook, texts by both Lutheran and Calvinist authors. Provost of Esztergom Miklós Telegdi, who later became bishop, included church songs in his book of sermons, which was published in 1577.[67] Of the six songs, four had already been published in the Protestant songbooks.

Thus, both the songs and the songbooks that were published and used in the decades of the early Reformation reflect an attitude that transcended confessional differences and rivalries. Even at a time of vehement debates concerning questions of faith, church songs did not become a means of expressing confessional conflicts.

However, this should not be misunderstood to suggest that the songs washed over the fundamental confessional divisions entirely. They did not. For instance, in descriptions of the sufferings of the present, one of the recurring motifs is the mention of having to live alongside "idolaters," in other words, people who belonged to different denominations. However, this was not a particularly prominent characteristic of the songs: for the texts in question, or rather their authors and presumably also the churchgoers who sang them, in a manner that was unusual and even surprising did not shy away from accepting responsibility. "Idolatry," when according to the texts it was the cause of suffering, is described in the songs as "our sin." Similarly, if we hope to win God's mercy and grace, the precondition for this is not that "they" convert, but rather that "we" find the real faith.

65 RMNY 1, 513.
66 RMNY 1, 222.
67 RMNY 1, 374.

Confessional Coexistence

Put simply, these songs essentially summarize everything on the basis of which one can contend that in the period beginning in the middle and ending roughly at the close of the sixteenth century there was not necessarily conflict among people belonging to different denominations in Hungary. As long as neither individuals nor authorities from outside the communities stirred up trouble, the people in these communities lived peacefully with one another.

With regards to this, the portrait given by Bishop of Vác György Draskovich of the city of Pozsony, in which three denominations lived side by side, is typical. Draskovich wrote in his visitation record that in earlier times Protestants had also partaken in Holy Communion at the altars of the guilds, but by the time he traveled to the city to examine conditions in the churches, they had abandoned this practice completely. Similarly, very few Protestants took part in the Corpus Christi procession. He questioned the city alderman about this, who replied that he cannot compel anyone to participate. "This is true," the bishop wrote in parentheses.[68]

This took place in 1634. In other words, before 1634, Protestant craftsmen had taken part in Catholic ceremonies. Draskovich's text suggests that they did so voluntarily, since both in his view and in the view of the city alderman one could not have compelled them to participate. The source does not indicate precisely which Protestant denomination the people who had earlier taken part in the Catholic ceremonies had belonged to. The bishop refers to them simply as "acatholici." However, he gives a few glimpses into the relationships among the Protestant denominations. For instance, he notes that in the outer city there had at one point been a Hungarian preacher and a Slavic preacher, but now there was only one. This preacher preached "to the Slavs in Slavic, according to their Lutheran religion, and to the Hungarians in Hungarian, in the Calvinist manner."[69]

Draskovich compiled his visitation records for internal use by the Catholic Church. There is, therefore, no reason to suspect that he distorted the facts. Indeed, he seems to have been more objective than prejudiced in favor of the Catholic Church. For instance, he did not fail to include information that suggested that the Protestant churchgoers made considerably larger donations to their congregations than the Catholics. The Catholic priests and teachers received most of their incomes from the city, while the Protestant preachers, teachers, and the organist were paid not out of the city coffers, but rather with monies gathered during collection, which everyone gave voluntarily. Teachers, furthermore, were paid using the tuitions paid

68 "Neminem se (quasi vero) cogere posse respondit." *Pázmány Péter egyházlátogatási jegyzőkönyvei 1616–1637* [The visitation records of Péter Pázmány. ed. Margit Beke (Budapest, 1994), 179.

69 "Dicitur iste Sclavis Sclavonice, Lutherano dogmate, Ungarice Ungaricis, Calviniano concionari." Ibid.

by the girls and boys they taught. The bishop also noted that there were more pupils in the "famous" school of the Lutherans then there were in that of the Jesuits.[70]

Thus, in all likelihood the account offered by Draskovich of his experiences in Pozsony offers a relatively accurate portrait of the circumstances in the city. We must nonetheless raise the question of credibility simply because the body of data he provides is remarkably valuable. It is valuable in part simply because we know very little about everyday social conduct in times of peace in this early period. The available sources frequently provide information concerning groups that were active, but few records were made concerning customary events of everyday life. Furthermore, the visitation record is valuable because it contains data concerning people who belonged to the same community, but different denominations. We have very few such sources, perhaps simply because there were very few places where the members of a given community belonged to different denominations. It is also possible, however, that historians simply have failed to give the question of the coexistence of denominations the attention it deserves and therefore have not sought the relevant sources.

Among the data on violence against members of a specific denomination, perhaps the most familiar is the infamous "lutherani comburantur" law, which was issued by the Diet in 1523 and later revised. The law entitled anyone to apprehend and burn Lutherans anywhere in the land.[71] The most familiar event took place in 1675, when many Protestant preachers and teachers were sentenced to galley labor.[72] Works on the history of this period make less frequent mention of the violence against the Sabbatarians, which came to its culmination in a trial in 1638 under the rule of the Prince of Transylvania, György Rákóczi I.[73] Whether these are familiar facts or details that are less frequently discussed, it is quite clear that the tools of aggression were in the hands of the prevailing secular authorities. It is also quite clear that the acts of violence that were committed by the secular authorities or by the church authorities who enjoyed their support could be listed almost ad infinitum, but in Hungary no one suffered a fate comparable to that of Thomas More, nor was there any slaughter comparable to the bloodshed of the Saint Bartholomew's Day massacre.[74] For

70 Ibid. 176–79.

71 1523/54th. article. 1525/4th article. *The Laws of the Medieval Kingdom of Hungary*, vol. 4. ed. Péter Banyó and Martyn Rady (Idyllwild and Budapest, 2012).

72 For a major publication of sources on these events, see László Makkai, ed., *A magyarországi gályarab prédikátorok emlékezete* [Remembrance of the Hungarian Galley-Slave Preachers] (Budapest, 1976).

73 Róbert Dán, *Az erdélyi szombatosok és Péchi Simon* [The Sabbatarians of Transylvania and Simon Péchi] (Budapest, 1987), 289–314.

74 Kálmán Benda has called attention to the relativeness of religious violence: "Habsburg politika és rendi ellenállás a 17. század elején" [Habsburg Policies and the Estates' Opposition at the Beginning of the Seventeenth Century] *Történelmi Szemle* 13 (1970): 404–27.

complex and interrelated reasons, the authorities in Hungary seem in all likelihood to have been compelled to practice a certain degree of tolerance.

Similarly, many sources survive concerning violence and aggression in issues of religion committed by the simple people. They share two features. The first is that popular violence was created in times of war or in times of tension that had been fostered by some external factor. The second is that, strikingly, they were not directed against secular or church authorities.

The movements that were launched under the banner of Protestant religious freedom gave rise to wars. In the course of these wars, acts of horrific violence were committed, and many of the people who in recent times were beatified died as martyrs during the conflicts.[75] The acts of church patrons served as external factors that gave rise to acts of violence committed by simple people. In many places, churches were vandalized and preachers were tortured when the local landowners, abusing their rights or power, changed the denominational belonging of the church on their estates. One does not need to present a long list of the many instances of such violence. The fact that these events were often discussed at the Diet gives a clear indication of their significance. For instance, in 1662 the members of the Diet, the majority of which was Catholic, discussed at length the offenses committed against Protestant congregations. Palatine Ferenc Wesselényi, who himself was Catholic, protested officially and in firm language against the acts of landowners who had taken possession of churches.[76]

In Pozsony, conflict also broke out because of the construction of the Lutheran church in the outer city. More precisely, conflict broke out because the Royal Chamber did not grant permission for construction of the church. Draskovich made note of the first signs of the events that led to this: by 1634, Protestant guild members who earlier had attended Catholic ceremonies no longer did so. The connection between the refusal of the Chamber to grant permission for the construction of the church and a change of mood among members of the Protestant community may have been clear at the time, because collections were taken for the construction of the church, although usually the holder of the right of patronage had a church built. Draskovich also learned of the plans of the "heretics" in the outer city to build a small church on the site where they were holding services, for which they had already obtained several thousand forints in cash and in pledges.[77] In 1635, the patron, i. e. the Chamber, refused to give permission for construction. This gave rise to hostility and

75 Pope John Paul II beatified some of these saints when he traveled to Slovakia.

76 For the records of the 1662 national diet see András Fabó, *Az 1662-diki országgyűlés* [The National Diet of 1662] (Budapest, 1874), 102–5.

77 "Fama fert velle eos eo loco ubi nunc conciones ascultant insigne templum extruere in quem finem habent in paratis pauca aliquot millia florenorum, in promissis et quidem certis plurima millia." *Pázmány Péter egyházlátogatási jegyzőkönyvei*, 179.

conflict among the people of various denominations in the city, which lasted for decades and was continuously inflamed by measures taken by the authorities.

Similar events took place later and in other locations. Far from Pozsony, in Sárospatak, where the majority of the population had long been Calvinist, the appearance of Jesuits in 1663 did not bring about any upheavals. The Catholic landowner, Zsófia Báthory, gave them a few houses and a considerable sum of money for the construction of a church. The nobility of Zemplén County protested, but the people of Sárospatak observed the religious customs of the Jesuits, which were strange to them, with more curiosity than hostility: for instance, the processions in the streets, the morality plays, and the other practices that the Jesuits brought with them. Initially, the relationship between the Jesuits and the inhabitants of the town was good, as evidenced by the fact that the city alderman and even the preachers paid visits to the Jesuits in their house. Anger only broke out against the Jesuits when Zsófia Báthory gave them the famous college and the church, which had been a Protestant church for roughly 150 years.[78]

Then began the wars. The town and the church buildings were taken over several times by rivalling political camps, anti-Habsburg and pro-Habsburg forces. When control of the town changed hands, the clergymen always left their buildings, and the denizens of the town would remove all of the devotional objects of the other denomination from the churches. Relationships among the people of Sárospatak who belonged to different denominations grew so embittered that in 1690 the locals helped the soldiers drive the preacher from the town and occupy the barn that had been used by Calvinists to hold religious services.[79] The Jesuits and the pastors seem to have considered the whole thing tragicomic by the end. Once, as a preacher named Pál Debreceni Ember was moving out of the vicarage near the church, Father Palicz, the Jesuit prior, yelled, "Israel also suffered during the flight from Egypt!" Pál Ember replied, "the pharaoh paid the price for Israel's flight from Egypt."[80]

The hostilities, of course, brought only grief, and confessionalization was inevitable. Understandably, the individual denominations created their own borders. The lives of the simple faithful, however, perhaps had been easier before almost insurmountable walls were erected between the different denominations.

78 Katalin Péter, "A jezsuiták működésének első szakasza Sárospatakon" [The First Phase of the Activity of the Jesuits in Sárospatak], in *Az értelmiség a 17. századi Magyarországon* [Intellectuals in Seventeenth-Century Hungary], ed. István Zombori (Szeged, 1988), 103–116.

79 It was called "horreum ligneum": Pro annius residentiae Societatis Jesu 106. Egyetemi Könyvtár Kézirattára [The Manuscript Collection of the Library of the Eötvös Loránd University], AB 95.

80 Prothocollum venerabilis tractus Zemplen. A Sárospataki Református Kollégium Levéltára 3. 68. [Archive of the Sárospatak Reformed College]. Sárospatak.

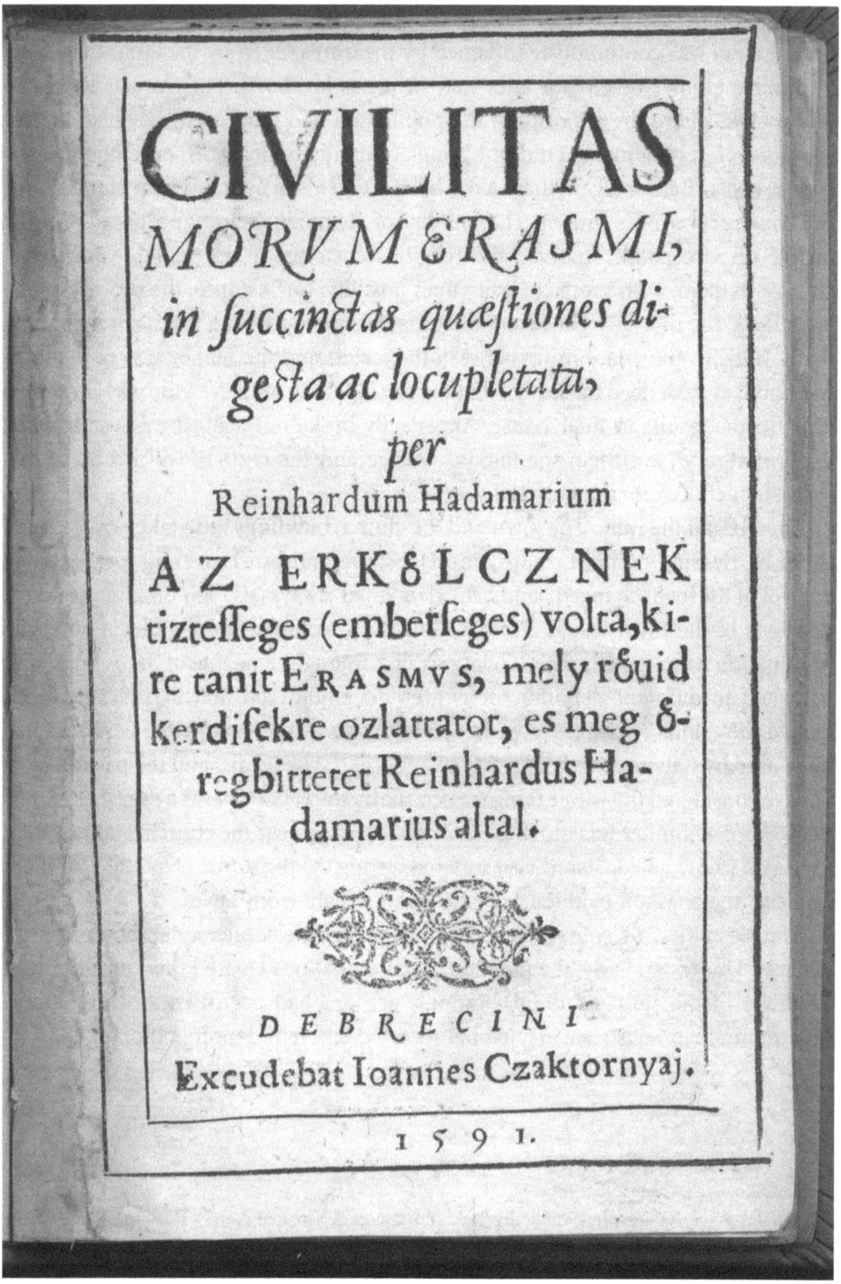
CIVILITAS
MORVM ERASMI,
in ſuccinctas quæſtiones di-
geſta ac locupletata,
per
Reinhardum Hadamarium
AZ ERKÖLCZNEK
tizteſſeges (emberſeges) volta, ki-
re tanit ERASMVS, mely röuid
kerdiſekre ozlattatot, es meg ö-
regbittetet Reinhardus Ha-
damarius altal.
DEBRECINI
Excudebat Ioannes Czaktornyaj.
1591.

Fig. 8. *Desiderii Erasmi Roterodami Colloquia familiaria, et Encomium moriae.* Front Page

3 Golden Age and Decay in Intellectual Culture at the Turn of the Seventeenth Century

The Problem[81]

In 1563, Gáspár Károlyi identified "the wisdom of the understanding of writing," "the wisdom of external things" and the "abundance" of "new inventions" as the defining characteristics of his age.[82] In 1656, János Apáczai Csere stated that Hungarian children "are from the cradle immersed in the bottomless depths of ignorance and as adults never see the light of day and the benefit of the homeland."[83]

These two outstanding intellectuals, both of whom had acquired immense prestige among their contemporaries and were familiar with domestic and international conditions, had thus arrived to opposite conclusions regarding the intellectual climate in Hungary. Although the assertions of both Károlyi and Apáczai Csere were likely exaggerated, they were nevertheless generally characteristic of the era.

Intellectuals who lived in Hungary amid the physical destruction of the sixteenth century usually expressed satisfaction with their circumstances, while those who lived in the country amid the relative tranquility of the seventeenth century almost all complained about the bleakness and obtuseness of the prevailing environment. This change in mood is reflected clearly in the easygoing attitude of the first Bible translators into Hungarian as opposed to the obvious self-consciousness of seventeenth-century linguistic authors. János Sylvester wrote with natural pride in reference to his translation of the New Testament that "The Word of God can now be read in Hungarian as well."[84] István Geleji Katona and Pál Medgyesi en-

81 This chapter was first published in Hungarian: "Aranykor és romlás és szellemi műveltség állapotában a 17. század fordulóján," *Történelmi Szemle* 27 (1984) 1–2 [For the 65th birthday of Zsigmond Pál Pach]: 80–102.

82 Gáspár Károlyi, *Két könyv*, 159.

83 János Apáczai Csere, *Az iskolák fölöttébb szükséges voltáról* [The Exceedingly Necessary Nature of Schools], ed. Gábor Szigethy (Budapest, 1981), 3.

84 *Uj testamentum magyar nyelven* [New Testament in the Hungarian Language], trans. János

gaged in an intense dispute over the regulations governing the translation of religious texts. This controversy lasted for a longer time than it took for Gáspár Károlyi and his associates to translate the entire Bible. Hungarians living in the sixteenth century were proud of their mother tongue because it could be used to express all their thoughts. Later they regarded the Hungarian language to be lacking in flexibility. It was as if they were pioneers who had to make the language suitable for general use on their own.

The mood of the intellectuals can usually be regarded as a reliable measure of the state of learning and culture. The opinions of Károlyi and Apáczai Csere deserve special attention among such appraisals. They merit close examination not primarily because of their intellectual authority, but because their claims serve to reinforce a latent suspicion.

Economic history raised this suspicion regarding statements concerning the so-called "divergence." If culture and education indeed develop according to economic possibilities, then the intellectual conditions that took shape in seventeenth-century Hungary in conjunction with the latter could not have represented a simple continuation of those which had existed previously. According to economic history, the level of economic development in Hungary was roughly compatible with that of countries in Western Europe until the early seventeenth century. The disparity in economic development between Hungary and Western Europe was already present in embryonic form during the final third of the sixteenth century, though only in the early 1600s did it become apparent: Hungary had become part of the group of agrarian countries that had assumed a disadvantageous position in the international division of labor.[85]

If this is true, then some kind of change very likely took place in the cultural conditions at this time as well. The difference of opinion between Károlyi and Apáczai Csere could reflect a difference in two separate periods of cultural history.

The cultural consequences of the emergence of the great European division of labor have received recognition in Hungary only within literary history. This discipline constructed a Marxist idea of the Baroque as a distinct period in the history of culture throughout Europe, based on analysis of the repercussions of economic change.[86] Literary historians also conducted a consistent analysis of the unique characteristics of Baroque literature in Hungary.[87] However, no detailed explora-

Sylvester (Újsziget, 1541), A IV. 2. Facsimile edition with an introduction by Béla Varjas (Budapest, 1960).

85 The leading Hungarian scholar in this field was Zsigmond Pál Pach. His studies appeared in English: Zsigmond Pál Pach, *Hungary and the European Economy in Early Modern Time (Collected Studies)*, (Abingdon, 1994).

86 Tibor Klaniczay's introduction to the chapter on Baroque literature in *A Magyar irodalom története*, 2 vol. [The History of Hungarian Literature] (Budapest, 1964), 113–21.

87 Ibid., 123–617.

tion of cultural history encompassing the broad spectrum of culture has yet been made—neither with regard to this period nor with regard to the previous era. Naturally no attempt to make comparisons between them has yet been made either. Therefore, the problems contained in the conclusions of economic history —notably that cultural conditions in Hungary underwent a negative transformation of some sort parallel to the detrimental change in economic circumstances in the country—have not been examined.

Attempt at Comparison

It is likely impossible to conduct a comprehensive analysis of cultural conditions. Most cultural phenomena cannot be evaluated numerically and are not therefore suitable for objective comparison. Of those cultural factors that can be quantified, only one appears to provide the opportunity for such comparison: printed matter as reflected in the two volumes of *Régi Magyarországi Nyomtatványok* (Early Hungarian Printings), which contains both the number and themes of published works.[88]

In my analysis of it, I have chosen to disregard data regarding Hungarian-language prints published outside Hungary. The reason for this is that there is no information available regarding the number of works that non-Hungarian inhabitants of Hungary published abroad in their mother tongues.[89] In light of the fact that as of the early sixteenth century an ever greater proportion of Hungary's population was non-Hungarian, to examine only Hungarian-language works published abroad would lead to distorted conclusions. Therefore, for lack of a better solution, I have chosen to omit all data regarding mother-tongue works from Hungary published abroad.

The designation "vernacular" refers collectively to all those spoken in Hungary. I only specify the precise language in certain instances. This also applies, *mutatis mutandis*, to church languages as well: I have taken into account not only Latin, but also Old Church Slavonic, classifying both of them under the category "dead languages." And finally: the heading "theological and ecclesiastical works" includes Catholic, Protestant as well as Eastern Orthodox printed matter.

I am naturally aware that data regarding works printed in Hungary do not provide a complete image of the state of culture in the country. Information

88 RMNY 1–2. I do not cite this work in all instances, because all of my assertions pertaining to this book can be easily verified in its excellent index.

89 Compared to its predecessor, Károly Szabó's *Régi magyar könyvtár*, 2 vol. [Old Hungarian Library], (Budapest, 1879–1885), RMNY indicates so many changes that it is simply impossible to derive conclusions based on the antecedents.

regarding printed matter refers only to certain aspects of intellectual culture, while the number of published works reveals nothing in terms of material culture.

However, the very existence of books in Hungary clearly demonstrates that the great technical revolution of the age—modern book printing—took place in the war-ravaged country as well. The first sixteenth-century book was published in Hungary just three years after the Battle of Mohács in 1526, which led to the Ottoman occupation of a great part of the country and initiated a period in which the number of various types of printed matter grew continually. The data showing the average number of works published per year does not describe technical standards, since it is simply impossible to establish an average in this domain. It is, however, clear that there was an enormous disparity in the technical quality of works published at various workshops.

The beauty of the typeface and technical perfection of the illustrations in printed matter published at the printing workshop that Johannes Honter launched in the city of Brassó (Braşov, Romania) in 1539 were unrivalled throughout Europe. Every work published at Honter's workshop was a masterpiece. At the same time, a printing press operated in Sárvár that produced works of stunningly superficial technical quality.[90]

General technical conditions in Hungary were similar to those in the rest of Europe at the beginning of the period of industrial development: the quality of products depended on the degree of individual skill and access to suitable technical and material prerequisites. Printing houses had only one thing in common at this time: by modern standards, they worked extremely fast. For example, Gáspár Károlyi dated the dedication of his work *Két könyv* (Two books) on December 25, 1563 and this book was published, albeit in rather miserable technical form, by the end of the year. The content, text and illustrations of some printed works offer further information concerning material culture. Again, Johannes Honter must be mentioned first in this regard. Honter's work *Rudimenta Cosmographica* has been republished in original or revised form more than 40 times in countries throughout Europe, thus making him the most popular Hungarian-born author of all time. In addition to many maps, this book shows how to use cartographical instruments, thus making it the first technical documentation to be published in Hungary. Marcello Squarcialupi, the famous Italian physician of the Prince of Transylvania, Kristóf Báthori, subsequently published a book in Kolozsvár on spring water. This book can be classified among the best works on hydrology published anywhere in the world during the period. Numerous other works printed in Hungary during this period, particularly calendars, contain images that are very useful from the standpoint of cultural history.

90 See Béla Varjas's study in the facsimile edition of the New Testament (Budapest, 1960).

However, printed works from this period, no matter how valuable they are in themselves, obviously provide no basis for conducting any type of systematic examination of material culture.

Moreover, one could make a lengthy list of the topics that are not reflected in the data regarding printed matter published in Hungary. This body of printed matter nevertheless undoubtedly represents the instruments of intellectual culture that were the easiest to acquire in Hungary at the time.

These published works most certainly display the lowest level of intellectual culture among those who were consumers of the written word and very likely reflect the demands of average readers as well. However, they do not reveal very much regarding their authors and the intellectual élite in general. Existing library catalogues indicate that those with a high degree of intellectual demand bought books abroad as well, and that a great deal of literature and perhaps scientific works remained in manuscript form. Printed literature, on the other hand, certainly reached its audience. This is the nature of books and their market: if they are published, people purchase them and read them. There is no reason to believe that things were any different in the sixteenth and seventeenth centuries.

The numbers therefore suggest that two groups of phenomena can be studied: the structure of culture that demonstrably reached the reading public; and the identity of the reading public, which remains a faceless mass using this approach, though its broad composition can nevertheless very likely be determined.

The tables showing data regarding all types of printed matter at the end of this chapter thus provide information regarding the intellectual demand of the average consumer and of that segment of the reading public that did not belong to the intellectual élite.

Data regarding all printed matter does not, however, accurately represent the lowest level of intellectual culture of book readers. Seen from the perspective of traditional cultural history, calendars and literary fiction could represent the lower boundary of intellectual culture simply because we usually regard them to be of a lower order than scientific works. One must be aware, however, that during the sixteenth century calendars were not a genre necessarily intended for the broad public and that there was no tripe among literary fiction.

Thus I defined the lower boundary of intellectual culture according to the form of printed matter. *Octavos* of fewer than 30 pages and even smaller printed matter in *sextodecimo* format appear in separate tables at the end of this chapter. I regard these as the vehicles for transmitting the lowest grade of intellectual culture. Or perhaps: one might presume that works printed in these formats were destined for the broadest audiences.

Three Periods

I divided my examination into three periods lasting from 1529 to 1635. The beginning year presents itself naturally: the first sixteenth-century book was published in Hungary in 1529. The ending year is, on the one hand, practical and random: I chose it simply because the first two volumes of *Régi Magyarországi Nyomtatványok* describe printed matter until 1635.[91] On the other hand, several historical factors serve to define period boundaries around this year. Literary history identifies the year 1640 as the ending phase of the crisis of the Renaissance and the beginning phase of the Baroque period, while economic history asserts that Hungary's disadvantageous economic classification became obvious during the middle of the seventeenth century.[92]

Thus the period between 1529 and 1635—since the evangelical movement first took root in the cities during the 1520s—roughly represents the phase of the Renaissance that began with the Reformation and the subsequent transitional period. The Baroque had, in any case, not yet became dominant during this time. Placing this in direct parallel to economic history, this period includes the decades in which Hungary followed a Western-type path as well as the critical turn of the century, and provides certain cultural-historical facts essentially until the time when the new situation became evident. In short, it provides an ideal basis for comparison.

The interval between 1571 and 1601 signifies an internal division within this lengthy period. These three decades signify longstanding period boundaries within both literary and economic history. In Hungary, the beneficial impact of the great agricultural upturn lasted from the 1570s to around the turn of the century, while the golden era of Renaissance literature took place approximately during the final three decades of the sixteenth century.

According to literary and economic history, the turning points are reflected accurately in the two designated years, 1571 and 1601—there is no need here to justify them. The only conspicuous phenomenon that deserves mention is that book publication follows this division precisely. While studying the material depicted in *Régi Magyarországi Nyomtatványok*, one cannot fail to notice the importance of 1571 and 1601. One would place the temporal boundaries at these points even if he or she had never heard of such a thing, because the depicted printed material makes them perceptible.

91 Since the first publication of this analysis, two further volumes of RMNY have been published covering the period until 1670.

92 My periodization in this text is based on Pál Zsigmond Pách's previously cited studies as well as Tibor Klaniczay's introduction in *The History of Hungarian Literature.*

The importance of the year 1571 is also highlighted in the fact that five works of literary fiction were published in this year. This many books of entertaining literature of this type had never previously been published in a single year and were rarely published in any subsequent year in the sixteenth century. And it is also worth noting: among the authors whose works were published in 1571 was one of the most-read Hungarian-language belletrists of all time, Péter Ilosvai Selymes, and one of the most popular protagonists, King Matthias. As far as the reading experience of the historian is concerned, 1571 brought a great degree of relief.

Descriptions of printed matter from old Hungary are interesting to read only at the beginning, while later they become plain and simply depressing. At the beginning one discovers an enchanting array of themes, unexpected authors and enticing titles. After a while everything quickly becomes monotonous. Theological themes follow one upon another; the names Péter Melius Juhász and Ferenc Dávid emerge time and time again; titles grow ever longer and are difficult to understand even in Hungarian. The low point may have occurred in the year 1568, when 18 theological treatises were published.

And when one begins to feel incapable of reading even one more description of a work in divinity, the following amiably awkward title emerges in 1571: *Szép jeles históriás ének a felséges Mátyás királynak jeles viselt dolgairól, életéről, vitézségéről, mind Bécs megvételéiglen* (Beautiful, Excellent Rhymed Chronicle Regarding the Illustrious Acts, Life and Valor of King Matthias until the Capture of Vienna). Beginning with this year, *RMNY* again provides a long period of enjoyable reading: every third description is interesting, because it describes literary fiction.

The situation was just the opposite in 1601, as if readability was no longer a consideration from this year. In 1599 there were still an instructive-amusing song and a song mocking female vanity among the theological works published during the year. The output in 1600 was conspicuously meager, though included a nice little book serving the individual meditation of the reader. The amount of printed matter that appeared in 1601 was very large, though very dull: four calendars, three collections of mourning poetry, three theological works, three text editions and a Latin grammar. Gáspár Ráskai's *Vitéz Franciskó* (Valliant Francisco), already known from the previous period, was hardly noticeable among all these serious publications. *Vitéz Franciskó* subsequently assumes the quality of a nice memory: it is nearly unparalleled during this period in which there was conspicuously little literary fiction published.

After 1601, the feeling of monotony again overcomes the reader of *RMNY:* Calendar follows upon calendar; the texts of laws appear continually; and there is an extreme abundance of mourning poetry and other occasional poetry. In comparison with the works of the previous period, those published in the post-1601 decades seems to belong to a different culture. Only the frequent appearance of pre-1601 authors create the impression of continuity. Aside from a few theologians, hardly any authors had works published between 1601 and 1635 who had not already gained recognition in the sixteenth century.

The numbers serve to confirm the perhaps excessively subjective-seeming conclusion derived from the experience of reading the headings of *RMNY*, namely that the years between 1529 and 1635 can be divided into three distinct periods: a dynamic beginning period in which works of theology still dominated; an intermediate period showing diverse intellectual vitality; and an ending period in which there was no innovation of any kind.

The Run-Up Period: 1529–1570

The data regarding the first period (Tables 1/1 and 2/1) reveals that works published at this time were intended primarily for intellectuals: three-quarters of them could not be read without the knowledge of dead languages. The topics of printed works refer more directly to a scholarly audience: a full 93 percent of the works were associated with some branch of learning and science. A total of 60 percent of all printed matter published during the period dealt with theology or ecclesiastical subjects. Text editions and works regarding linguistics were in demand, constituting 24 percent of all printed matter published during the period. Only 8 percent of printed matter concerned other sciences.

I did not classify theological works according to denomination, because the various religious orientations could not easily be distinguished from one another during the initial phase of the Reformation. Authors and entrepreneurs who had joined the Reformation undoubtedly continued to publish works from the Church Fathers. The fact that the first translators of the Bible, whom we regard as humanists, cannot be associated with a certain denomination serves to increase the difficulty of such classification. If we take strict consideration of denominational factors, János Sylvester was a Catholic; nevertheless, his New Testament published in the form of a popular book ornamented with nice little illustrations can nevertheless be regarded as one of the first products of the Reformation in Hungary.

Thus only affiliation with the Eastern Orthodox Church was unambiguous during this period: between 1529 and 1570, eleven works associated with this church were published in Hungary—six in Old Church Slavonic, four in Romanian and one bilingual work. The division between Catholic and Protestant works is expedient only from the end of the 1540s. Since, however, no Catholic work was published after that date, the immense majority of theological and ecclesiastical works published between 1540 and 1571 were affiliated with Protestantism. Here I include works associated with denominations that regarded themselves as part of the Reformation, thus the single Anabaptist work published in Hungary as well as those of the anti-Trinitarians.

Although only a small part of the works published during this period dealt with topics other than theology and the sciences or were not text editions, the fact that any such works appeared at all is significant. It shows that at least a small number of those who read printed matter were not intellectuals. The existence of vernacular works in every category, naturally with the exception of text editions, also serves to demonstrate this. Obviously those who had learned Latin in school, though as adults were no longer masters of the language, also read works regarding the sciences.

The data does not reflect the composition of non-intellectual readers, though the dedications of certain works refer to them, either by name or according to their social standing. Dedications such as that of author Mihály Sztárai in 1566—"to all pious readers" —were not uncommon.

Dedications naturally most often cited patrons, though those addressed generally to "all readers" and "the pious Christian" call attention to possible exceptions. In certain instances, the authors or the printers certainly specified the presumed readers. Going further, the patrons themselves perhaps read the books as well. In this sense one may discern the identity not only of those who paid for publication, but that of the readers as well. I have left out the dedications referring to uncertain audiences, listing only those alluding to the social status of readers.

In 1539, Honter dedicated a text edition to Queen Isabella. In 1552, Caspar Heltai dedicated a dialogue on drunkenness to a distinguished Transylvanian lord, Antal Kendy. One year later, Heltai dedicated his small volume providing reading material for individual meditation to Anna Báthori, a member of the powerful Báthori family. In 1555, Valentin Wagner dedicated one of his text editions to the son of the town judge of Brassó, Johann Bengner. This same year, Mátyás Csabai dedicated a song glorifying the successful defense of the Castle of Eger against the Ottomans in 1552 to István Ruszkai Dobó, the commander of the Hungarian forces at the castle who had subsequently become the Voivode of Transylvania. Teacher Michael Siegler of Nagyszeben (Sibiu, Romania) dedicated a pedagogical work to the son of the city judge, Thomas Bomel. In 1558, an unknown author dedicated a song regarding John Sigismund and his mother Queen Isabella to the chancellor Mihály Csáky. Beginning in 1558, Ferenc Dávid dedicated several works to John Sigismund, and in the same year, Gál Huszár dedicated his printed sermons to Archduke Maximilian. In 1559, Huszár published one of Mihály Sztárai's dramas under the title *A semnici, kremenci és besztercei bölcs tanácsoknak és mind az egész Magyarország bányáin lakozó Krisztus híveinek* [To the Wise Councils of Semnic, Kremenc and Beszterce and the Believers in Christ Living at Mines in All of Hungary]. Beginning in 1560, Transylvanian Saxon writer and printer Caspar Heltai dedicated several books to John Sigismund. In 1561, theologian and Reformed Bishop of Debrecen Péter Melius Juhász dedicated the preface of a book of his sermons to "the Hungarian and trading peoples" and another book to the

"Debrecen council." Also in 1561, Caspar Heltai dedicated a Hungarian-language New Testament to Anna Nádasdy, the widow of the former Voivode of Transylvania, István Majláth. In 1562, Péter Melius Juhász dedicated his work written against Tamás Arany to János Enyingi Török, the Debrecen landlord, his brother and the "Christian kinsman of Debrecen." There is no reason to specify further dedications, which at most contain new names, though do not refer to new social categories.

The composition of readers whom the authors of these books presumed were not intellectuals was thus extremely diverse, including monarchs, distinguished lords and ladies as well as citizens. With the inclusion of Debrecen, the targeted audience also encompassed market town communities and dwellers. However, some of the individuals identified in the dedications manifestly belonged to the intellectual élite. Neither Queen Isabella nor Archduke Maximilian can be classified in the average category of Hungarian erudition, though is it impossible to make a satisfying selection of those among the entire group who could be qualified as meeting expressly domestic standards.

Based on the data regarding all printed matter published in Hungary, the only thing that becomes clearly apparent is that prior to the year 1571, intellectuals or others with a similar degree of education were the primary users of readily accessible intellectual culture in Hungary. The lay audience is of mixed social composition and, as the low number of printed matter designated for them demonstrates, was relatively small.

Data regarding the popular printed matter that comprised the lowest grade of literate culture (Tables 4/1, 5/1 and 6) present a similar picture. Such works constituted 16 percent of the printed matter published during the period, while in terms of structure they were almost completely identical to the entirety of published works. Theology, text editions and "other sciences" predominate here as well. Only the proportion of literary fiction is significantly higher, representing 23 percent of popular works compared to 6 percent of all printed matter.

The proportion of vernacular works among popular printed matter published during the period is also relatively small. Vernacular works are far from exceeding those in dead languages. Their proportion here compared to that among all works is barely higher: vernacular works constituted 36 percent of the entire output and 23 percent of popular printed matter. The proportion is significantly higher only in the literary fiction category: half of the works of this genre were in the vernacular.

Thus between 1529 and 1570, the lowest level of intellectual culture does not differ significantly from the average. Literary fiction composed a greater proportion of such works than they did at higher levels. However, the variety of printed matter in this category is very broad, extending from polemical works to guild regulations.

The contents of the category are composed of the following works: Sebastian Pauschner's German-language book of health advice from the year 1539; a nice little popular edition of Honter's *Rudimenta Cosmographica* in Latin from the year 1541; and Thomas Bomel's Hungarian historical outline "from the first incursion of the Huns into Pannonia until 1556," the year of publication. Literary fiction beyond occasional poetry includes Mihály Szátrai's comedy about the marriage of priests from the year 1550; Mátyás Csabai's report in song about the defense of the Castle of Eger from 1555; *Comoedia Balassi Menyhárt árultatásáról* (Comedy on the Treachery of Menyhárt Balassi) from 1569; and Péter Ilosvai Selymes's history in verse, *A nagy szent Pál apostolnak életéről* (On the Life of the Great Saint Paul) from the year 1570. All these works are in Hungarian, while the occasional poetry is in Latin.

Therefore, the audience for the lowest level of intellectual culture could have been very similar to the average, that is, most of them were intellectuals. Here one must likely think of *domi doctus* village preachers and schoolmasters. However, in comparison to the higher ones, at the lowest levels there was a larger number of people with secular interests, as demonstrated by the relatively greater number of popular literary fiction published in the vernacular.

In fact, here the situation might be the same as it was with regard to the intellectual élite. The data regarding publications in Hungary do not reflect their intellectual culture, though we are familiar with a few libraries that do reflect it.[93] The contents of the largest library catalogues suggest that the intellectual élite did not constitute a social category, but a group of people who wished to receive some of the fruits of culture in accordance with their material possibilities and level of education. The library of the wealthy burgher businessman Hans Dernschwamm was no less interesting or comprehensive than that of a powerful aristocrat such as Boldizsár Batthyány, while that of János Zsámboki—the most learned intellectual living on an imperial salary as court librarian—was just slightly larger, though no more diverse in composition. Popular prints display an identical aspect at the lowest level of culture: the intellectuals and other laypeople with the same degree of wealth and education constitute a single audience group. A portion of citizens and some market town inhabitants certainly belong to this group, though nobles might as well have belonged to it too. Anyway, it is a sure fact that between 1529 and 1570, some non-intellectuals from the lower social strata also became consumers of printed culture.

93 István Monok (ed.), *Magángyűjtemények Magyarországon 1551–1721. Könyvjegyzékek bibliográfiája* [Private Collections in Hungary, 1551–1721. Bibliography of Book Catalogues] (Szeged, 1981).

The Golden Age: 1571–1600

Two radical transformations are apparent in the data pertaining to the period from 1571 to 1600 (Tables 1/2 and 2/2): the thematic structure of published materials changed; and the amount of published printed matter rose sharply. The immense increase in the number of popular publications that appeared during this period can also be regarded as a structural change (Table 6). During the previous period, popular publications constituted just 17 percent of all published printed matter; between 1571 and 1600, such publications constituted 45 percent of all published printed matter. The internal, thematic arrangement of popular printed matter appearing during this period underwent an even more prominent transformation than it did in the case of printed material as a whole. All in all, the transformations suggest that the audience for printed matter had increased enormously and undergone a structural shift.

The quantity of all printed works more than doubled between 1571 and 1600, resulting in a general growth of publications in all thematic categories except for text editions. The whole character and structure of printed culture changed.

The sharp rise in the number of calendars was the most conspicuous, rising more than twentyfold from 3 to 70. Calendars constituted 12 percent of all published material during the period, compared to just 1 percent during the previous period. The increase in literary fiction is somewhat smaller, though still considerable, rising to 31 percent of all published material appearing during the period, compared to 6 percent during the previous period. All in all, printed material became more secular: although the number of theological works rose, their proportion of all printed works dropped from 60 percent to 42 percent. One might say that secular themes and theological themes switched places.

Secularization entailed a significant increase in the number of vernacular works. Again with the exception of text editions, the proportion of vernacular publications grew astonishingly in all categories of printed matter, rising tenfold among theological works, fifteenfold among literary fiction and almost twentyfold among calendars after the year 1571.

If, as with works published during the previous period, we regard printed matter appearing in the vernacular in non-scientific genres as evidence of a non-intellectual audience, then the increases specified above are staggering.

The number of vernacular works rose more than tenfold. Demand among the lay audience and the size of this audience both increased dramatically between 1571 and 1600. The number of those reading scientific works in their mother tongue rose by a significantly lower degree, though grew nonetheless: there were 105 vernacular works published before 1571 and 378 after that year, representing a roughly threefold increase. This suggests that the number of those who read scientific works in other than dead languages grew considerably.

Although both the works published during this period as well as their readers underwent secularization, an analysis of theological works appearing during these years (Table 3) reveals extremely significant phenomena. I did not classify printed matter according to religious denomination in the previous period, though it is certain that after the late 1540s only Protestant and Eastern Orthodox works were published in Hungary, while beginning in 1571 Catholic works appeared as well, constituting 12.9 percent of all theological works published after that year. However, Protestant works continued to predominate even after 1571, comprising 78 percent of all theological works published during this period.

Alongside the reemergence of Catholic publications, another important development that took place during the period after 1571 was the initial appearance of works in Slovak, Slovenian and Croatian in addition to the three vernacular languages in which books had been published until that year (Hungarian, German and Romanian). With the exception of one legal work published in Croatian, all the other printed matter that appeared in the three new vernacular languages were theological works, similarly to the seven theological works in Romanian in the previous period. The publication of such works may denote the existence of secular Hungarians, Germans, Romanians, Slovaks, Slovenes and Croats who took an interest in ecclesiastical matters. What is, however, certain is that even if theological publications consisted simply of handbooks written by priests who lacked a higher degree of education, they did reflect an important fact: after the year 1571, all the peoples living in Hungary began to produce a relatively broad variety of printed works representing vernacular intellectual culture.

Along with the explosive rise in the demands of the lay reading audience, the appearance of Slovak, Slovene and Croatian vernacular works represented the most characteristic change of the post-1571 period. The dedications of printed matter that appeared during this period suggest that the social composition of readers had not changed. The proportion of intellectuals obviously decreased as a result of secularization, while the rest presumably were residents of cities and market towns as before. One of the dedications—that contained in Mihály Sztárai's history in verse about Bishop Athanasius—cites the market towns of Debrecen and Tolna. It is questionable, however, whether it is worthwhile to use the category of market-town burgher in this relation. An analysis of popular publications inspires this reasoning.

There was a conspicuous increase in the number of popular works published between 1571 and 1600 and a transformation of the audience for such works, as was the case with regard to all printed matter during the period (Tables 4/2 and 5/2). The number of works published in popular form rose almost fivefold. Popular works constituted 44 percent of all works published during this period, up from 16 percent during the previous period (Table 6). At the same time, the number of theological works declined radically. On the other hand, the number of works of literary fiction published in vernacular languages rose to 186 during the period, up from 18 during the previous period—a nearly tenfold increase that was nearly unparalleled during these years.

Thus the demand for the products of popular printed culture accessible without the knowledge of dead languages grew by an unprecedented degree after 1571. Data pertaining to other categories of printed matter also shows increasing demand, though to a lesser degree: the number of theological works in the vernacular doubled as did the number of scientific works; 50 vernacular-language calendars appeared in popular form—the first time such calendars had ever been published; and all works in the "other" category appeared in the vernacular. Only text editions and political works showed some deviation: one Latin-language work appeared in each of these categories, thus they were essentially negligible.

The nearly tenfold increase in vernacular printed matter during this period pertained primarily to Hungarian-language works. There were 177 popular works published in the Hungarian language during this period, compared to 12 the previous period, and 19 such works published in the German language during the period, compared to just 4 the previous period. Thus there were nearly nine times more popular works published in Hungarian during the period than there were in German.

The data therefore shows that demand for the lowest grade of intellectual culture in Hungary grew primarily among Hungarians. However, it is important to note that this does not mean that demand for such intellectual culture among the German-speaking population living in Hungary stagnated or failed to grow commensurately at this time, since they also acquired works from the foreign German-language book market. Information is available with regard to only a single German book peddler, showing that he offered published works of all genres, from peasant calendars to popular novels and dramas.[94] Data regarding works published in Hungary simply fails to reflect demand for printed matter among the German-speaking population of the country.

Demand from the Hungarian-speaking population at the lowest level of reading culture thus grew in comparison to its own needs in the previous period and not in comparison to the needs of the German-speaking inhabitants of Hungary. Returning to the problem of social categories: Hungarian-language literature was certainly not intended for citizens, who during this period were predominantly German-speaking. Therefore, the large number of Hungarian-language popular works were designed to satisfy the enormous intellectual demands of lay readers belonging to the lower social strata.

94 Lajos Kemény, "Gálién János könyvkereskedő hagyatéka 158-ból" [The Legacy of Book Merchant János Gálién from the Year 1583], *Magyar Könyvszemle* 12 (1887): 136–38.

This might be identified with the burghers of market towns if the popular Hungarian-language publications, including the rapidly growing number of works of literary fiction, did not provide cause for further reflection. It is questionable whether the unprecedented abundance of such works did not exceed demand in market towns and consequently enter villages. Perhaps it would be more accurate to identify the Hungarian-speaking lay audience at the lowest level of intellectual culture simply as the higher strata of peasants rather than as market-town burghers. The demand for intellectual culture grew to the greatest degree among this group during the period from 1571 to 1600.

Finally, one may assert that during the final three decades of the sixteenth century, the intellectuals came to form the minority of the audience for printed matter in Hungary, both at the lowest level of intellectual culture as well as higher levels.

Decay: 1601–1635

The final period (Tables 1/3 and 2/3) is conspicuous for two reasons: the trends of secularization and a vastly increasing number of publications essentially came to an end. The total number of works published between 1601 and 1635 grew by only 14 percent.

Theological works constituted 42 percent of all printed matter published during the period, identical to the previous period. Paradoxically, the proportion of Protestant works among all theological works published between 1601 and 1635 rose to 87 percent, compared to 78 percent between 1571 and 1600, in spite of the fact that the former period is associated with the advance of the Counter-Reformation in Hungary (Table 3). This increase is so surprising that I decided to examine the Hungarian works published abroad as well. Taking the latter into account, 77 percent of publications that appeared between 1601 and 1635 were Protestant and 23 percent were Catholic, which means that they did not alter the Catholic-Protestant proportions.

Another very significant phenomenon during this period: although the number of Eastern Orthodox living in Hungary increased greatly with the movement of people into Hungary from the war-affflicted regions, works associated with this denomination disappeared entirely. A total of 11 Eastern Orthodox works were published in Hungary between 1529 and 1570, including 5 in Romanian and 2 bilingual publications, while 18 Eastern Orthodox works appeared in the country between 1571 and 1600 and none between 1601 and 1635. In fact, Hungarian and German were the only languages in which theological works were published in Hungary during the latter period.

The composition of secular publications underwent a significant transformation during the period: between 1601 and 1635, the number of works of literary fiction and works regarding secular sciences decreased by one-third as compared to the previous period. Literary fiction constituted 19 percent of all secular works published between 1601 and 1635, compared to 31 percent between 1571 and 1600. However, the number of secular calendars published during the period doubled in comparison to the previous period, while the number of publications classified in the "other" category rose threefold. Texts of Diet legislation represented the large majority of works placed in the latter category.

Vernacular works constituted 71 percent of all works published between 1601 and 1635, compared to 67 percent between 1571 and 1600. Vernacular calendars and Hungarian-language texts of legislation adopted in the Transylvanian Diet propelled this increase. Literary fiction published in the vernacular underwent a dramatic decrease between 1601 and 1635, dropping from 186 works recorded between 1571 and 1600 to just 132 works—or 19 percent of all works published. Hungarian-language literary fiction decreased by two-thirds.

The changes that took place during this period with regard to popular works (Tables 4/3 and 5/3) were simply startling. Although the number of popular works rose to 53 percent of all printed matter published between 1601 and 1635—up from 45 percent of all works that appeared between 1571 and 1600—their numerical increase was just 37 percent, compared to 472 percent in the latter period as compared to the years 1529 to 1570. This was primarily the result of a threefold increase in the number of legal publications and a rise in the number of political works and calendars. The proportion of literary fiction decreased to 32 percent of all works published between 1601 and 1635, down from 53 percent of all works published between 1571 and 1600. A total of 49 works of popular theology were published between 1601 and 1635, down from 53 such works between 1571 and 1600, representing a decrease of over 7 percent.

The change with regard to vernacular works during the period was also remarkable. The number of vernacular literary fiction published between 1601 and 1635 dropped to just 41, compared to 140 between 1571 and 1600, and the number of German-language works of literary fiction also decreased. Only the number of theological works in vernacular grew considerably, and the number of vernacular-language calendars even doubled, as compared to the previous period. There were no books falling under the "other sciences" category published in the vernacular between 1601 and 1635, compared to three popular Hungarian-language works in this category during the previous period. The number of vernacular theological works dropped to 30 between 1601 and 1635, down from 33 between 1571 and 1600. The number of vernacular-language calendars published during the period more than doubled compared to the previous period. There were five vernacular-language political works published in popular form between 1601 and 1635, compared to none during the previous period. Finally, there was a ninefold increase in the number of vernacular-language works classified in the "other" category during the period, again primarily the result of books containing the texts of legislation adopted at the Transylvanian Diet.

The number of popular works published in the Hungarian language rose somewhat between 1601 and 1635, yet their percentage among all works published dropped nonetheless. It is interesting to note that the number of Hungarian-language popular works published between 1571 and 1600 rose nearly fifteenfold compared to the numbers of the previous period.

This data suggests that the demand for printed matter by and large stopped growing during the years 1601–1635. Within these conditions of general stagnation, the content of printed matter transformed significantly, while the audience identified as the higher strata of peasants declined sharply and the entire grouping underwent realignment.

The fundamental transformation of content pertains to the culture of German-speaking citizens. Although it is undoubtedly true that they acquired a considerable amount of printed matter from abroad, domestic printing houses undoubtedly satisfied one of their needs. Occasional poetry meeting the needs of the German-speaking citizens of Hungary was not likely published extensively abroad, though even if it was, the relatively large amount of such poetry written for their festivities would merely receive even greater weight. Occasional poetry constituted 57 percent of all literary fiction published between 1601 and 1635, compared to 22 percent between 1571 and 1600. One must add: these works of just a few pages could easily be destroyed, thus the number of those printed presumably exceeds by a considerable number those known today. The large majority of such works were published in Latin.

In addition to the numerical increase of occasional poetry, a unique change also occurred with regard to the audience for them. Demand for such poetry was originally based in the highest social strata. Most occasional poetry consisted of laudatory verse. The first such verse appeared with the publication in 1564 of a poem glorifying King John Sigismund and continued with a long succession of such poetry honoring kings, princes and archdukes. At the beginning of the seventeenth century, two high-ranking lords and the Archbishop of Esztergom Péter Pázmány were also among the addressees of laudatory verses; the genre unambiguously continued to satisfíy demand from the highest social circles. The situation was the same with elegies, the first of which was written to mourn the death of King John Sigismund and the majority of which were written in honor of the members of the social élite.

Amid such circumstances it is surprising that among the many glorified monarchs and aristocrats, citizens also arise as patrons of literature in the year 1630 in the town of Lőcse (Levoča, Slovakia). And in addition to several preachers, municipal senators Niklas Kirschner and Andreas Payer also appear. There were 4 commoners among the 14 deceased mourned in elegies prior to 1601. After that year citizens—the wives of preachers, town judges, senators, mine owners, teachers, printers and physicians—became the primary subjects of mourning poetry. Wedding poems, however, represented a typically civilian genre from the very beginning. Between 1571 and 1600, 9 of 12 wedding poems were written for burghers' marriage ceremonies, while after 1601, 12 of 23 were.

The large amount of occasional poetry written for citizens entails two conclusions. First, the fact that almost all such poetry was published in Latin, although it was written for the family feasts of the urban population, obviously shows that the German-speaking citizenry continued to use this dead language. Thus data regarding German-language printed matter do not reflect its role in Hungarian intellectual culture. The German-speaking population of the country may have used Latin-language products of intellectual culture in many other spheres of their lives in addition to family holidays.

Second, and perhaps more importantly, by appropriating this originally aristocratic genre, the German-speaking citizens wished to resemble the nobility that stood above them in the social hierarchy. This effort was in large measure successful, resulting in the production of occasional poetry for both aristocrats and burghers. Half of wedding poems were written for commoners at a time when four collections of such poetry were published for the wedding of Prince of Transylvania Gábor Bethlen and Catherine of Brandenburg. The situation was the same with regard to elegies. After 1601, when commoners constituted the majority of those for whom elegies were written, such mourning poetry was also published in honor of the aristocrats Ferenc Nádasdy, Kristóf Thurzó, Judit Kornis and Gábor Bethlen.

The culture of urban citizens, at least in terms of ambition, started to resemble that of the nobility. Both the intimate use of Latin as well as the adoption of rituals of family feasts reflect this change.

Two seemingly contradictory facts reflect the internal transformation of the audience: the eightfold increase in political works after 1601 and the 29 percent decrease in literary fiction. The two changes are not inconsistent with one another, because they are not interdependent. They do not pertain to the same stratum of the audience.

Political works reflect the demand of the nobility as well as the social expectations toward it. The composition of this type of publication is very colorful, including works such as the pamphlet that Péter Alvinczi wrote for Prince Gábor Bethlen in 1619, an account of the 1622 coronation of Queen Eleonora Gonzaga and János Pataki Füsüs's *Királyoknak Türköre* (The Royal Mirror) from 1625, and András Prágai's 1628 *A fejedelmek serkentő órája* (The Dial of Princes, a translation of the *Golden Book* of Antonio de Guevara). These works refer to the gentry to which most people engaged in politics belonged. They either intended to gain the allegiance and support of the gentry or expressed their ideas. Political literature written for aristocratic political leaders was not produced in Hungary during this period.

Another category of printed matter, legislative texts and legal works, was also related to the demands of the noble audience. Classified as part of the "other" and "other sciences" categories in the tables, there were 38 such works published between 1601 and 1635, compared to just 12 between 1571 and 1600. Prominent among political works that appeared during these periods was István Werbőczy's collection of customary law, entitled *Tripartitum*, which was published three times during 1571 and 1600—once in Latin, once in Hungarian and once in Croatian—and twice more between 1601 and 1635, on both occasions as a bilingual Latin-Hungarian edition. By the early seventeenth century, the texts of Diet laws had eclipsed Werbőczy: between 1601 and 1635, 29 publications containing laws were published.

Thus the number of publications intended for a noble audience—political and legal works as well as legislative texts—quadrupled from 11 between 1571 and 1600 to 44 between 1601 and 1635. The number of vernacular-language publications intended for a noble audience also radically increased, rising from just 3 between 1571 and 1600 to 33 between 1601 and 1635. Publications from no other category underwent such a sharp increase between the former and latter periods.

Data regarding works related to noble culture thus illustrates the cultural advance of the gentry from 1601. As the growing influence of noble culture coincided with an increase of vernacular prints, the nobility seems to have lacked a higher degree of education and was consuming primarily vernacular texts. The large number of works published for a noble readership in the vernacular during this period also serves to refute the popular belief that Latin was generally used among members of the ruling classes in Hungary at this time.

The decline in literary fiction naturally reflects decreasing demand for such works. An analysis of specific data reveals more information regarding the precise audience groups that accounted for this fall in demand. The decline in demand for literary fiction essentially did not manifest itself among the urban population, the cultural demand of which did not decrease, but merely underwent transformation —as demand for Latin-language occasional verse demonstrates. However, this decline was conspicuous among the audience for Hungarian-language publications, including readers of Hungarian literary fiction published in popular form: the number of works of literary fiction published in Hungarian declined 72 percent between 1601 and 1635 in comparison to the period from 1571 to 1600.

The post-1601 transformation deprived the upper strata of the peasantry of the repositories of intellectual culture. Between 1601 and 1635, the calendar became the practical equivalent to the book at this lowest level of culture: among popular works published in the vernacular, only calendars were published in larger number between 1601 and 1635 than during the previous period. The number of calendars published in popular form in the Hungarian language tripled between 1601 and 1635. An examination of the calendars intended for the broadest strata of society will provide a clear insight into the content of this culture.

Finally, data regarding printed matter published in Hungary characterizes cultural conditions according to external criteria: only classifications of genre provided information regarding content. In theory, the numerical decline or stagnation may have concealed intellectual growth. However, this, in fact, did not occur. The numerical decrease recorded after 1601 was accompanied by narrowing content.

The shrinking of the intellectual horizon after the turn of the century is reflected most conspicuously, though in light of the numbers unsurprisingly, in the category of literary fiction. Works of this genre that were published between 1571 and 1600 represented a popular version of those held in contemporary humanist libraries. The works of classical authors such as Aesop, Homer, Plutarch and Virgil were published in rendered form as Hungarian-language verse. Péter Ilosvai Selymes's didactic poem *"Sokféle neveknek magyarázatja"* (Explanation of Many Kinds of Names) constitutes the dictionary category. History in verse form extended from the Longobards to the nearly contemporary events in England concerning Archbishop Cranmer.[95] Geographical themes were designed to satisfy interest in distant lands, Africa, Asia and Mediterranean pirates. Those who listened to singable verses of the time could be, with some divergence corresponding to their lower level of education, versed in matters of culture like members of the intellectual élite. Popular literary fiction included no themes regarding the natural sciences, though the many vernacular calendars published after 1571 transmitted the issues that occupied the greatest minds of the age to this lowest grade of culture.

After 1601, Africa and other distant lands disappear from popular literary fiction, while the majority of such works are those of sixteenth-century authors. Of the 40 works of Hungarian-language literary fiction published between 1601 and 1635, a total of 28 had already been published before. Therefore, the composition of literary fiction published during this period could have theoretically been nearly identical to that published between 1571 and 1600. But this is not the case. Among popular literary fiction published in the decades after the turn of the century, only medieval history, tales and ancient history remained. One might also say that works that could be determined as unrealistic published between 1571 and 1600 were not republished during the following period. It is revealing, for example, that Péter Ilosvai Selymes's three histories were published between 1601 and 1635, though his poem "Sokféle neveknek magyarázatja" explaining the meaning of words was not.

95 Sztárai Mihály, *Cranmerus Tamás érseknek az igaz hitben való álhatatosságáról* [About Archbishop Thomas Cranmer's persistence to true faith] (Debrecen, 1582).

Many of the works written and published after 1601 were intended to regulate morality, such as János Munkácsi's biblical history in verse on the life of Tobiah and Gáspár Decsi's history of the love of King David, both of which attempt to teach the morals of a good marriage. What is, however, surprising is that nobles emerge within and behind these new themes as well. In 1610, János Debreceni Szappanos wrote a history in verse regarding the conspiracy of Transylvanian aristocrats against Prince Gábor Báthori that was likely popular only among the noble readers who were familiar with the main characters of the work. In a work published this same year, János Petki, who had himself served as chancellor of Transylvania, published a work stating in its title that it was intended to serve as a "lesson to the noble Transylvanian youth."

Therefore, in addition to a sharp numerical decline and narrowing thematic range, this lowest level of written culture, as with the average, was characterized by an advance of the nobility lacking a higher level of education.

At the same time, the cultural opportunities of the higher strata of peasants declined in comparison to that of the nobility. The behavior of the citizenry imitating customs of the nobility reflects the rising influence of the latter.

Conclusion

The data regarding printed matter published in Hungary during the periods in question thus support the hypothesis formulated on the basis of economic history arguments. Cultural tendencies closely resemble the direction of economic changes in that the conditions of intellectual culture underwent a negative transformation after the year 1600.

The features of the run-up phase largely corresponded to those of European culture in general in the sixteenth century.[96] In spite of the wars, this phase arrived in Hungary no later than it did to lands that lay distant from the original scenes of the Reformation. The beginnings of religious reform in England are likewise placed in the 1520s. Here the humanist influence also made itself felt: the abundance of classical text editions in Hungary is very surprising in light of the fact that by this time, following the destruction of the Bibliotheca Corviniana no codices of ancient texts could be found in Hungary. Although I am unfamiliar with the proportions in other parts of Europe in this regard, I doubt that their 24 percent share of all printed matter published in Hungary during the initial period could be regarded as comparatively low. However, the decline in this category during the final third of

96 Tibor Klaniczay, "A magyar irodalom reneszánsz korszaka" [The Renaissance Era of Hungarian Literature], in Klaniczay, *Reneszánsz és Barokk* [Renaissance and Baroque] (Budapest, 1961), 7–38.

the sixteenth century certainly conforms to the general rule, since as in other places where this process took place, the category "other sciences" grew along with the decline in text editions. Printed matter classified in the latter category, along with works regarding linguistics, declined 44 percent after 1571, although works pertaining to other sciences increased by 91 percent. Therefore, the entire number of works dealing with secular science increased by 153 percent in the course of the sixteenth century.

The secularization of culture in general is, in this way, regular, and went hand in hand with the decline in theology taking place in the final decades of the century. The receding of dead languages into the background represented a general characteristic of the sixteenth century. The threefold rise in vernacular works in Hungary between 1571 and 1600 can be regarded as very significant and the nearly tenfold rise in vernacular literary fiction published in popular form as downright astonishing.

This data reveals an enormous expansion of the audience and an unprecedented growth in the lay consumers of the products of printed culture. This diffusion of the products of written culture among the non-intellectual social strata has been observed in Hungary, as in other countries of Europe such as England and France, beginning in the sixteenth century.[97]

Culture thus transformed in largely the same way throughout Europe in the sixteenth century. The changes that took place in Hungary during this period were of the same nature as those in countries that later achieved a much higher level of cultural niveau.

However, certain facts that were perceptible already in the sixteenth century show that although the transformation of culture moved along a similar path, there nevertheless existed some numerically perceptible divergences. A number reflecting such disparities is that the share of Latin-language literary fiction remained at 59 percent. Data showing that the number of works of vernacular literary fiction published in popular form grew to an immense degree, even though half of such works still appeared in Latin, also reflects these divergences. By this time there was practically no literary fiction being written in dead languages in England or France. Written culture likely permeated a broader segment of society in these countries during the sixteenth century than it did in Hungary.

The faster pace of cultural changes among the Hungarian and German-speaking populations of Hungary than among the other peoples inhabiting the country represents another significant difference. Between 1529 and 1570, theological works in Romanian represented only printed matter published in any language

97 For an intensive study of popular culture on the basis of printed material see Robert Mandrou, *De la culture populaire aux 17e et 18e siècles. La Bibliothèque bleu de Troyes.* (Paris, 1964).

besides Hungarian and German. Only the cultural explosion that took place after the year 1571 brought other vernacular languages spoken among the inhabitants of Hungary to the surface.

The data reveals that within the culture that developed in Hungary in accordance with general European trends during the sixteenth century, another tendency emerged in the country, one that gained momentum after 1571. This trend, although somewhat delayed, followed the general movement of culture, beginning with theology. This is how the last three decades of the sixteenth century became the golden age of intellectual culture for all the peoples living in Hungary. All languages spoken in the country reached the level of getting into print.

The change that occurred at the turn of the seventeenth century brought a ruthless end to this golden age.

The events of the scientific revolution took place in the parts of Europe that underwent more fortunate further development at a time when cultural growth came to a halt in Hungary.[98] The level of intellectual culture among the German-speaking people of the country essentially stagnated, while that of the Hungarian-speaking, particularly at the lower levels of culture and society, declined significantly and the nobility made advances vis-à-vis the commoners. Moreover, the promising sixteenth-century initiatives of the other peoples of Hungary either disappeared or did not continue to move forward.

Data relating to printed matter published between 1529 and 1635 ultimately shows that the "divergence" in the conditions of intellectual culture became apparent earlier than it did compared to economy. The divergence became obvious in cultural terms beginning in 1601, while in economic terms it manifested itself only in the middle of the seventeenth century. Going even farther, one arrives to another conclusion: cultural standards in Hungary not only lagged behind those in the countries of Europe that continued to develop in a more beneficial manner, but also failed to maintain its own strengthening trend that it had established in the sixteenth century. Not only did Hungary miss out on the benefits of the scientific revolution, but in cultural terms it fell into a period of stagnation and, from certain perspectives, decline after the year 1601.

98 I found the treatment of science-society interrelatedness most convincing in Alan Smith, *Science and Society in the Sixteenth and Seventeenth Centuries* (London, 1972).

Tables

Table 1: Thematic Structure of All Works Published in Hungary

1/1: 1529–1570

Theme	Number of Works	Percentage of All Works
Theological and Ecclesiastical	174	60.2
Text Editions and Linguistics	70	24.3
Other Sciences	22	7.6
Politics	0	0
Literary Fiction	18	6.2
Calendars	3	1
Other	2	0.7
Total	289	100

1/2: 1571–1600

Theme	Number of Works	Percentage of All Works	Change from 1/1
Theological and Ecclesiastical	255	42.1	+ 46.5 %
Text Editions and Linguistics	39	6.4	– 44.1 %
Other Sciences	42	7	+ 91 %
Politics	1	0.2	
Literary Fiction	186	30.7	+ 933 %
Calendars	70	11.6	+ 2233 %
Other	12	2	+ 500 %
Total	605	100	+ 109.3 %

1/3: 1601–1635

Theme	Number of Works	Percentage of All Works	Change from 1/2
Theological and Ecclesiastical	294	42.4	+ 15.3 %
Text Editions and Linguistics	32	4.6	– 21.9 %
Other Sciences	28	4.4	– 33.3 %
Politics	9	1.3	+ 800 %
Literary Fiction	132	19	– 29 %

(Continued)

Theme	Number of Works	Percentage of All Works	Change from 1/2
Calendars	159	22.9	+ 127 %
Other	38	5.4	+ 216.6 %
Total	692	100	+ 14.3 %

Table 2: Language Distribution of All Works

(Vernaculars have been indicated the following: H = Hungarian; G = German; C = Croatian; R = Romanian; S = Slovak; Sl = Slovene, according to the definition of languages in RMNY 1 and RMNY 2.)

2/1: 1529–1570

Theme	All	Vernacular		Vernacular's percentage
Theol. ecclesiastical	174	84:	H 66 G 11 R 7	48.3
Other sciences	22	7:	H 6 G 1	3.8
Politics	0			
Literary fict.	18	9:	H 9	50
Calendars	3	3:	H 3	100
Other	2	2:	H 1 G 1	100
Total	219	105		47.9

2/2: 1571–1600

Theme	All	Vernacular		Vernacular's percentage	Change from 2/1
Theol. ecclesiastical	255	160:	H 135 G 20 S 2 C 1 R 1 Sl 1	62.7	+ 90.5 %
Other sciences	42	15:	H 7 C 1 G 7	35.7	+ 115 %

(Continued)

Theme	All	Vernacular		Vernacular's percentage	Change from 2/1
Politics	1	0			
Literary fiction	186	140:	H 136 G 4	75	+ 1455 %
Calendars	70	58:	H 57 G 1	83	+ 1833 %
Other	13	5:	G 4 H 1	38	
Total	567	378		66.6	+ 260 %

2/3: 1601–1635

Theme	All	Vernacular		Vernacular's percentage	Change from 2/2
Theol. ecclesiastical	294	234:	H 203 G 25 Sl 4 C 2	79	+ 14 %
Other sciences	28	12:	H 11 G 1	43	+ 33 %
Politics	9	5:	H 5	55	+
Literary fiction	132	41:	H 40 G1	31	− 29 %
Calendars	158	149:	H 125 G 24	94	+ 156
Other	38	32:	H 31 G 1	92	+ 59 %
Total	659	473		71	+ 25 %

Table 3: Distribution of Theological Works according to Religious Denomination

	1571–1600			1601–1635		
	Catholic	Protestant	Eastern Orthodox	Catholic	Protestant	Eastern Orthodox
Dead Languages	11	67	18	12	48	0
Vernacular	22	133	4	27	207	0
Total	33	200	22	39	255	0
Percentage	13	78,4	8,6	13,3	86,7	0

Table 4: Thematic Structure of Popular Works

4/1: 1529–1570

Theme	Number of Works	Percentage of All Popular Works
Theological and Ecclesiastical	25	53.2
Text Editions and Linguistics	6	12.8
Other Sciences	3	6.4
Politics	0	0.0
Literary Fiction	11	23.4
Calendars	0	0.0
Other	2	4.2
Total	47	100.0

4/2: 1571–1600

Theme	Number of Works	Percentage of All Popular Works	Change from 4/1
Theological and Ecclesiastical	53	19.7	+ 112.0
Text Editions and Linguistics	1	0.4	– 16.6
Other Sciences	17	6.3	+ 466,6
Politics	1	0.4	
Literary Fiction	143	53.1	+ 1200
Calendars	50	18.6	
Other	4	1.5	+ 100
Total	269	100.0	+ 472.3

4/3: 1601–1635

Theme	Number of Works	Percentage of All Popular Works	Change from 4/2
Theological and Ecclesiastical	49	13.0	– 6
Text Editions and Linguistics	0	0	
Other Sciences	12	3.2	– 29
Politics	8	2.1	+ 700
Literary Fiction	119	31.7	– 17
Calendars	152	40.4	+ 204
Other	36	9.6	+ 800
Total	376	100.0	+ 37

Table 5: Language Distribution of Popular Works

5/1: 1529–1570

Theme	All	Vernacular		Vernacular's percentage
Theol. ecclesiastical	25	10:	H 7 G 3	40
Other sciences	3	1:	G 1	33
Politics	0			
Literary fiction	11	7:	H 4 G 3	64
Calendars	0			
Other	2	2:	H 1 G 1	100
Total	41	20		48

5/2: 1571–1600

Theme	All	Vernacular		Vernacular's percentage	Change from 5/1
Theol. ecclesiastical	53	33:	H 18 G 14 Sl 1	62	+ 230 %
Other sciences	17	4:	H 3 G 1	23	+ 200 %
Politics	1	0			
Literary fiction	143	108:	H 107 G 1	75	+ 1443 %
Calendars	50	50:	H 49 G 1	100	
Other	4	3:	G 3	75	+ 50 %
Total	268	198		74	+ 890 %

5/3: 1601–1635

Theme	All	Vernacular		Vernacular's percentage	Change from 5/2
Theol. ecclesiastical	49	30:	H 22 G 8	53	– 39 %
Other sciences	12	3:	H 2 G 1	25	– 25 %
Politics	8	5:	H 5	62	
Literary fiction	119	33:	H 30 G 3	28	– 69 %

(Continued)

Theme	All	Vernacular		Vernacular's percentage	Change from 5/2
Calendars	152	148:	H 121 G 27	97	+ 216
Other	36	36:	H 32 G 4	100	+ 800 %
Total	376	255		68	+ 29 %

Table 6: Percentage of Popular Works among All Works

Period	Total Works	Popular Works	Percentage	Change
1529–1570	289	47	16.3	0.0
1571–1600	605	269	44.4	+ 109.3 %
1601–1635	692	376	54.3	+ 14.4 %

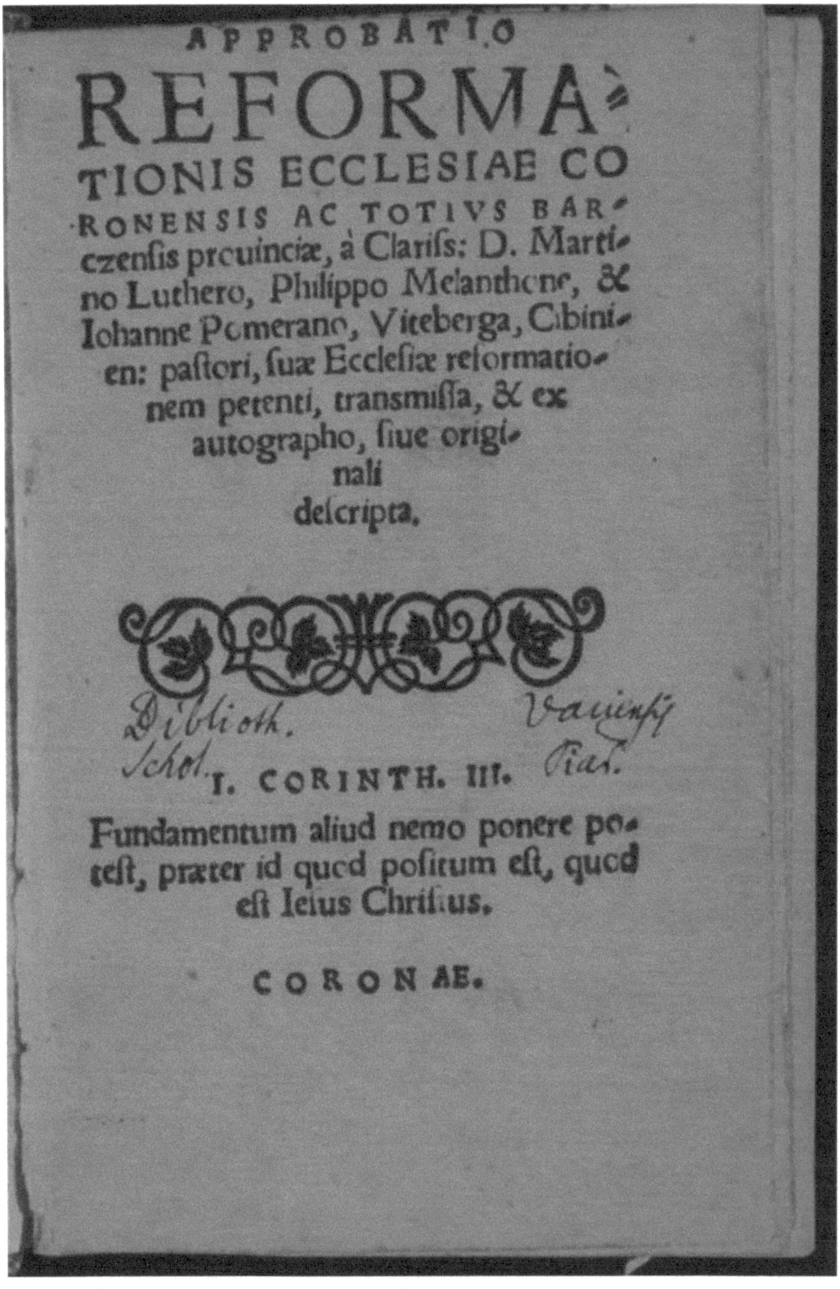

APPROBATIO
REFORMA-
TIONIS ECCLESIAE CO-
RONENSIS AC TOTIVS BAR-
czenſis prouinciæ, à Clariſs: D. Marti-
no Luthero, Philippo Melanthone, &
Iohanne Pomerano, Viteberga, Cibini-
en: paſtori, ſuæ Eccleſiæ reformatio-
nem petenti, transmiſſa, & ex
autographo, ſiue origi-
nali
deſcripta.

I. CORINTH. III.
Fundamentum aliud nemo ponere po-
teſt, præter id quod poſitum eſt, quod
eſt Ieſus Chriſtus.

CORONAE.

Fig. 9. *Reformatio ecclesiae Coronensis ac totius Barcensis provinciae.* Corona, 1543. Front Page

4 Hungarian Schooling in Transylvania in the Sixteenth and Seventeenth Centuries

The Opportunities for Learning

The Hungarian Reformed teacher and scholar János Apáczai Csere best described the conditions surrounding education in Transylvania during the middle of the seventeenth century. According to Apáczai Csere, the sons of tenants so "abundantly filled" schools in the principality that the "sons of free and noble parents" had nearly been squeezed out.[99]

This is an astonishing statement. It is difficult to believe, because during the time in which Apáczai Csere was active, the preponderance of students from the lowest social strata hardly signified one of the attributes that could be used to characterize schooling in other countries of Europe. Any doubts in this regard could easily be dispelled in regions more fortunate than Hungary where it is possible to simply consult extant matriculation registers containing full lists of student names. In Hungary, to which Transylvania also belonged in the mental map of contemporary people, such records have rarely survived from this early period and the scarce extant ones are insufficient to define the social origin of students.[100] The opinion of contemporaries must, therefore, be regarded as conclusive. Contemporary observers, including Apáczai Csere, referred with conspicuous frequency to the peasants who could not be pushed out of the schools.

99 János Apáczai Csere's frequently quoted statements regarding education in Transylvania appear in: János Apáczai Csere, *Az iskolák fölöttébb szükséges voltáról* [The Exceedingly Necessary Nature of Schools], ed. Lajos Orosz (Budapest, 1956), 170. This chapter first appeared in Hungarian: "Az erdélyi magyar iskolázás a 16. és a 17. században," in *A Ráday Gyűjtemény Évkönyve* 7 (1994): 3–13.

100 Due to inadequate sources, it was not even possible to analyze the social origin of students who attended the prestigious college in Nagyenyed (Aiud, Romania) before the year 1818, although documentation regarding this school is otherwise abundant after the year 1662. See Zsigmond Jakó and István Juhász, *Nagyenyedi diákok 1662–1848* [Nagyenyed Students, 1662–1848] (Bucharest, 1979), 7–80.

At the beginning of the seventeenth century, preacher János Kecskeméti Alexis declared that "The knowledge of Latin has become the domain of bag-toting mendicant apprentices."[101] József Hermányi Dienes complained much later that the sons of tenants were attempting to climb the social ladder through learning.[102] These authors did not write about the sons of tenants who attended school as a sign of recognition, but in order to contrast them with the intellectually lazy nobility, partially out of concern for the standard of education and partially because they feared the consciousness of the learned peasant. Apáczai Csere wrote the most clearly regarding this issue as well:

> since they would otherwise have to serve in a perpetual state of serfdom or continual great poverty, in order to get this heavy misfortune off their backs, they flee to the altars of the schools and demonstrate clearly that they have given their souls to study not out of love for the sciences, but merely out of fear of physical miseries.[103]

Kecskeméti Alexis refers to the social consequences: "It is no wonder then that there is such a lot of ruckus."[104]

In a certain sense, some of the smartest people shared this opinion regarding the rise in the number of students of meager social origin at the expense of their noble counterparts, frequently castigating sons of the nobility who failed to attend school. However, regardless of what lay on the flip side of this phenomenon, it would be difficult to state anything more commendable about the relationship between society and education than that the sons of tenants could climb the social ladder through the schools. Naturally not everybody performed well in school: complaints about idlers probably appeared along with the institution of the school and would only cease with them as well. The grumbling of recognized intellectuals does not, however, qualify a society. The opinions of Apáczai Csere and his associates are important also because they said good things despite their contrary intentions. They intended their statements to be criticisms, while in retrospect we cannot imagine anything more positive about the educational conditions in a given country than schooling being accessible to a broad segment of society. With regard to seventeenth-century Transylvania, the described concerns regarding the large number of tenants attending schools in the principality demonstrate that the opportunity to learn and those who took advantage of this opportunity both reached down to the humblest layers of society.

---

101 József Barcza, (ed.), *A debreceni református kollégium története* [History of the Debrecen Reformed College] (Budapest, 1988), 34.

102 Jakó and Juhász, *Nagyenyedi diákok*, 19.

103 Apáczai Csere, *Az iskolák fölöttébb szükséges voltáról.*

104 Barcza, (ed.), *A debreceni református kollégium története.*

The opportunity to learn for tenants in Transylvania is usually attributed to Prince Gábor Bethlen, who indeed initiated the adoption of a law in 1624 that provided the sons of serfs with the freedom to attend school. However, the Transylvanian Diet did not proclaim this freedom per se, but merely stipulated that fines be imposed on landowners who, in contravention of customary law, either prevented the sons of tenants from attending school or forced them to leave school.[105] The fine for breaking this law was heavy: 1,000 forints—the cost of a small landholding. The Transylvanian Diet presumably prescribed a fine of such magnitude because landowners frequently violated the longstanding customary law.

The 1624 law regarding the freedom of the sons of tenants to attend school does not therefore represent a turning point, though it is nevertheless very important in terms of understanding educational affairs in Transylvania for two reasons. First, the law confirms that the sons of tenants attended school according to established custom. Although the explanation of the law does not expand upon than the appraisal of Apáczai Csere and his fellow intellectuals, it still must be highlighted because it corroborates the stunning statement regarding the many sons of serfs who studied at school. Second, the law draws attention to the pre-Gábor Bethlen period during which the custom of the sons of peasants attending school emerged.

This approach does not imply an attempt to diminish the merits of Gábor Bethlen, who—in addition to his other accomplishments—was unquestionably one of the greatest figures in the cultural history of Transylvania. Therefore, there is no reason to credit him with achievements in which he did not play the main role. It was the estates that put pressure on rulers of Transylvania to support schools in the form of new foundations, scholarships, and all other forms of protection. The estates of course did not have to initiate such pressure against the will of Bethlen, but much earlier, long before he came to power. At this time, the estates elevated their ruler, Queen Isabella Jagiellon, to the role of supreme secular head of all churches. The princes of Transylvania later followed Isabella's example, though were probably unaware that she served as their model.

105 EOE 8, 236.

Catholic Rulers Forced into the Role of Supreme Patron of the Protestants

Queen Isabella, who very consciously remained Catholic, first took action as a supreme secular authority in the Protestant sense of the term in 1543. In this year, Isabella—contrary to the intentions of the official leaders of the Roman Catholic Church—sanctioned and confirmed the Lutheran Confession of certain Saxon congregations in Transylvania.[106] During the famous Council of Torda in 1557, she assented in both her name and that of her son, John Sigismund, to the notion that "everybody should follow the faith of their choice" and as a matter of principle that "we are obliged to defend every church according to our royal office and dignity."[107]

By this time, the majority of the inhabitants of Transylvania belonged to Protestant denominations. Most of them were Lutherans, though many gravitated toward the Helvetic Confession as well. The Transylvanian Calvinists held their first synod together with followers of this faith in the Kingdom of Hungary in the year 1559.[108] Thus in practical terms, "to defend" in this case meant that the queen did not turn against the majority of her subjects. Isabella, who generally had great difficulty resigning herself to unchangeable situations, chose to concede with regard to religious affairs and build a relationship with the Protestant denominations that was unparalleled throughout all of Europe. The nature of this uniqueness is obvious: the sovereigns of Europe customarily stood with or above those of their own religious denomination. However, the Catholic rulers of Transylvania maintained the role that Isabella had assumed. Prince Stephen Báthory reached the farthest as the supreme patron of the Protestants, receiving even the right of excommunication from the Transylvanian Diet in 1572.[109] John Sigismund's changes of religious affiliation at times of internal political crisis provide an explanation for this peculiar royal behavior.[110] All evidence indicates that in Transylvania, the power of the Protestant estates determined the nature of relations between the principality's rulers and Protestantism. The Transylvanian estates seem to have been much more decisive in their stance toward religion than they were in other regards. The severity of the estates vis-à-vis religion is reflected in the fact that freedom

106 For the relevant document and a bibliography of literature regarding it, see RMNY 1, 52.
107 EOE 2, 78.
108 This early period of the Reformation is still best described by Jenő Zoványi, *A reformáció Magyarországon 1565-ig* [The Reformation in Hungary until 1565] (Budapest, 1922).
109 EOE 2, 528.
110 See Katalin Péter, "A reformáció és a műveltség a 16. században" [The Reformation and Culture in the Sixteenth Century], in *Magyarország Története* [History of Hungary], ed. by Ágnes R. Várkonyi, vol. 3. (Budapest, 1985), 524 et seq.

of religion was suspended for Catholics in Transylvania during the period from 1566 to 1581, the final decade of which occurred during the dominion of the Catholic Stephen Báthory. Still, no Catholic ruler of Transylvania ever attempted to implement forced Counter-Reformation. It is true that the conduct of the Roman Catholic Church in Hungary helped the Protestant estates of Transylvania to a great degree. The Roman Catholic Church in Hungary identified with the kingdom and the rulers of Transylvania maintained no official relations with Catholicism. This circumstance had complex ramifications with regard to relations between the rulers and estates of Transylvania but they are not associated with the train of thought concerning education in the principality.

The decision of the estates in 1557 to force the state to run higher level Protestant schools is relevant to the issue of schooling. They did not easily attain this objective. The Transylvanian Diet first addressed the matter in 1556, on Queen Isabella's return from exile in Poland. At this time, she promised to establish new schools after the consolidation of the position of the Catholic Church in Transylvania. Yet the queen did not debate the status of the school in Gyulafehérvár that had originally belonged to the cathedral chapter, instead simply assuming the obligation to finance the operation of this school along with control over the episcopate's property.[111] In the spring of 1557, the estates again advocated the foundation of new educational institutions "because barbarism is intensifying and growing as a result of the failure to educate the youth."[112] Finally, in the autumn of 1557, they managed to pass a law at the Transylvanian Diet stipulating that the queen would establish more schools "in accordance with the public will" at monasteries that had been left empty following the expulsion of the monks from Transylvania. Queen Isabella consequently opened educational institutions at the Franciscan cloisters in Marosvásárhely and Nagyvárad (Oradea) and at the Dominican cloister in Kolozsvár.[113] The text of the relevant laws reveals that the estates wanted to establish a very high standard of education. The Transylvanian Diet that convened in the spring of 1557 provided the most complete expression of this ambition, proclaiming that there should be secondary schools in the principality at which "gently and graciously knowledgeable men who are familiar with languages teach every branch of the sciences."[114]

These laws refer explicitly to newly founded schools. Certain school histories suggest that new buildings were added to previously existing schools in ac-

111 EOE 2, 60.
112 Ibid., 74.
113 Ibid., 79.
114 Ibid., 74–75.

cordance with the Transylvanian Diet's legislation. However, the ostensibly donated schools have been defined in an extremely contradictory manner. This situation was particularly conspicuous in the city of Kolozsvár, where there were undoubtedly several schools operating already before the year 1557. The initial religious affiliation of the educational institutions in question has also been the subject of scholarly debate. More precisely: conflicting viewpoints have emerged regarding the specific branch of Protestantism to which these schools adhered in the middle of the sixteenth century.[115] The disagreements may or may not be resolved; in either case they do not exercise an impact on the overall issue of education in Transylvania.

Consolidated School System in the Middle of the Sixteenth Century

The important circumstance with regard to the general advance of education in Transylvania was that the demands of society compelled the Transylvanian Diet to establish the relevant schools. Works on the history of education would define the required level of education differently according to their use of either traditional or more modern criteria.[116] However, it is clear that the lords believed that it was necessary to establish a level of instruction at these schools that went beyond elementary education.

Their desire to introduce higher-level schooling performed by "knowledgeable men who are familiar with languages" obviously meant that there were young people in Transylvania who were capable of learning at this level. The endeavor to establish higher-level educational institutions suggests that there existed an extensive network of urban and rural primary schools in the principality.

This conclusion is important because the Reformation and the disappearance of the Catholic Church as a factor in Transylvanian society may have disrupted education in the principality. One of the greatest Hungarian cultural historians, Vilmos Fraknói, long ago recognized this fact with regard to Hungary and, particularly, Transylvania. In 1873, Fraknói wrote that, along

115 See István Török, *A kolozsvári református kollégium története* [History of the Kolozsvár Reformed College], vol. 1 (Kolozsvár, 1905); Kelemen Gál, *A kolozsvári unitárius kollégium története 1568–1900* [History of the Kolozsvár Unitarian College, 1568–1900], vol. 1 (n.p., 1935); József Koncz, *A marosvásárhelyi református kollégium története* [History of the Marosvásárhely Reformed College] (Marosvásárhely, 1899); and Péter Cséplő, *A nagyváradi római katolikus főgimnázium története* [History of the Nagyvárad Roman Catholic Main Secondary School] (Nagyvárad, 1896).

116 Jenő Szűcs, "A középkori iskolázás Sárospatakon" [Medieval Schooling in Sárospatak], in *A sárospataki református kollégium története* [History of the Sárospatak Reformed College] (Budapest, 1981), 8 et seq.

with Catholicism, "they destroyed the old schools, while new ones arose only slowly."[117] However, scholarship in Hungary did not subscribe to this idea. The cultural history of other peoples long lacked similar ideas as well. Viewpoints describing the "catastrophic" impact of religious renewal on the state of culture first emerged with regard to Germany, presumably in response to the unambiguously positive appraisal that the Reformation and its emphasis on vernacular education have usually received in terms of their cultural influence.[118]

However, this thesis is not universally valid: on the one hand because the events associated with the spread of the Reformation varied greatly from country to country as did the consequences of the disappearance of Catholic institutions; and on the other hand, regardless of the magnitude of momentary decline resulting from the collapse of Catholicism in places where such collapse actually took place, the advance of the Reformation in the vernacular everywhere entailed a cultural boom. In England, where the Reformation is most frequently described as having caused a cultural "catastrophe," a true scientific revolution eventually took place under the auspices of Protestantism.[119]

In Transylvania there likewise emerged during the final third of the sixteenth century a cultural golden age, albeit one of less brilliance than that which took place in England.[120] The effort to establish schools offering a high level of education indicates that, regardless of what had taken place previously, the renewal of culture in Transylvania had undoubtedly happened by the end of the 1550s. The lords who were involved in negotiations with Queen Isabella based their demand for schools on the need to combat the barbarity that they claimed was devastating Transylvania. This demand appears to support the catastrophe theory. However, certain facts demonstrate that, all in all, it was not necessary to save education and culture from total destruction at this time.

The number of students from Transylvania who attended foreign universities provides the most revealing evidence. The number of students fluctuated; the presence of students from the principality at the great universities of

117 Vilmos Frankl, *A hazai és külföldi iskolázás a XVI. században* [Domestic and Foreign Education in the Sixteenth Century] (Budapest, 1873), 9.

118 For a summary of this issue, see Richard Gawthrop and Gerald Strauss, "Protestantism and Literacy in Early Modern Germany," *Past and Present* 104 (1984): 31–56.

119 See John Lawson, *Medieval Education and the Reformation* (London and New York, 1967); Christopher Hill, *Intellectual Origins of the English Revolution* (Oxford, 1965); and Tibor Klaniczay, "A reneszánsz korszakolása és értelmezése" [Periodization and Interpretation of the Renaissance], in Klaniczay, *Hagyományok ébresztése* [The Awakening of Traditions] (Budapest, 1976), 245 et seq.

120 This golden age occurred prior to the period of cultural decline in the seventeenth century. See in the present volume Chapter 3 (Part II) entitled "Golden Age and Decay in Intellectual Culture at the Turn of the Seventeenth Century."

Europe was continuous during the sixteenth century.[121] Although the number indeed underwent a conspicuous decline following the acceptance of the Reformation in Transylvania in the decade after 1531, this should not be interpreted as proof that the educational system in the principality had completely collapsed. The continual enrollment of students from Transylvania at foreign universities suggests that the operation of secondary schooling, which prepared students for university studies, was likewise continuous. Events connected to the spread of the Reformation in Transylvania prompt similar conclusions. The new faith arrived peacefully to the principality and became predominant without violence.

It would not be logical to presume in Transylvania, where Protestantism supplanted Catholicism essentially without struggle, anything other than that the transition was peaceful in the domain of education as well.

Great Intellectual Demand, Narrow Opportunity

The events that transpired after the consolidation of the school system in Transylvania are among the most frequently mentioned episodes in the cultural history of Hungary. Two of them deserve to be highlighted because they provide an accurate reflection of the connection between society and culture.

One of these was the establishment of schools for girls via a resolution adopted at the Reformed synod held in Szatmárnémeti (Satu Mare, Romania) in 1646.[122] This synod is noted for its contradictory decisions. On the one hand, it prohibited János Tolnai Dali and other preachers who espoused Puritan beliefs from exercising their offices. On the other hand, it defined one of the main objectives of Puritanism—the education of women—as one of the nearly official missions of the Reformed Church. The synod decreed that schools teaching girls to read and write in the vernacular be established in all Reformed congregations. The importance of this decision was immense. In terms of form, it was important because it proposed the introduction of a new type of school to Transylvania's educational system. In terms of content, it was important be-

121 The following book is the source of all data in this volume on the number of Transylvanian students enrolled at foreign universities: Miklós Szabó, "Erdélyi diákok külföldi egyetemjárása a XVI–XVII században" [Attendance of Transylvanian Students at Foreign Universities in the Sixteenth and Seventeenth Centuries], in *Művelődéstörténeti Tanulmányok* [Cultural History Essays], ed. Elek Csetri and Zsigmond Jakó (Bucharest, 1980), 152 et seq.

122 See Jenő Zoványi, *Magyarországi protestáns egyháztörténeti lexikon* [Hungarian Protestant Church History Encyclopedia], ed. Sándor Ladányi (Budapest, [3]1977), 580. Imre Révész, *A szatmármegyei nemzeti zsinat* [The Szatmárnémeti national synod], (Budapest, 1947. reprint 1993. 9–26.

cause it aimed to extend the opportunity to learn to a large segment of society that had, until that time, been largely excluded from participation in cultural affairs. This represents a significant change from the sixteenth century, when even aristocratic women regarded learning to write to be a true success.

We do not know if the decision of the Szatmárnémeti synod served to increase the number of literate women because we have no information on the actual establishment of schools for girls. One may presume that not many schools for girls were founded within the foreseeable future after the synod. The council's decree regarding the foundation of schools for girls is nevertheless significant, demonstrating that the cultural consequences arising from an appreciation of the role of women in the family had gained acceptance within the intellectual life of Transylvania.

The other outstanding event related to seventeenth-century education in Transylvania was the foundation of an educational institution that is usually described as the college of Gyulafehérvár in 1622.[123] This is also indicative of the relationship between society and culture, only in a much more complex fashion than the foundation of schools for girls. The complexity is due, partly, to the exceptionally poor quality of sources—notably their lack of distinction between information referring to the intentions of Prince Gábor Bethlen and those on the actual college in Gyulafehérvár—and, partly, to the fact that the prince's intentions were not realized.

No light has been shed upon the contradiction between intention and reality, perhaps as a result of the inadequacy of the relevant sources, although the text of the 1622 law speaks clearly about it. The law refers to the institution to be erected as "academia," "Common Academia" (*Közönséges academia*) and "chief professors" (*főprofesszorok*), words that the people of seventeenth-century Transylvania used in relation to universities.[124] Miklós Bethlen, chancellor of Transylvania, for example, described in his memoirs his education at Heidelberg University as "my academic studies" and used the terms "schola" and "collegium" to describe the institutions in Transylvania where he had also been a student.[125] In this same sense, János Apáczai Csere wrote "We have ... not a single academy ..."[126] Moreover, the register of students at the college in Nagyenyed, as all records of this kind, showed if they had gone on to a foreign university using phrases such as "in academias Belgicas" or simply "in aca-

123 See István Mészáros, *Középszintű iskoláink kronológiája és topográfiája* [The Chronology and Topography of our Secondary Schools] (Budapest, 1988), 191.

124 EOE 8, 96–97.

125 Miklós Bethlen, "Élete leírása magától" [His Own Description of His Life], in *Kemény János és Bethlen Miklós művei* [Works of János Kemény and Miklós Bethlen], ed. Éva Windisch V. (Budapest, 1980), 566, 540 et seq.

126 Apáczai Csere, *Az iskolák fölöttébb szükséges voltáról.*

demias" or "in academiam." They applied the phrases like "in scholam" or "in collegium" in reference to colleges in the principality.[127]

Therefore, the "Common Academia" referred to in the 1622 law obviously did not correspond to the educational institution known as the "college" (*főiskola*) in Hungarian school history. In 1622, the Diet must have conducted debates not simply about colleges that operated under the auspices of teachers specializing in various branches of science. The establishment of such colleges was inveigled from Queen Isabella much earlier.[128] In any case, it is certain that by 1622 the schools in Marosvásárhely and Nagyvárad, those belonging to the Reformed and Unitarian churches in Kolozsvár, as well as that in Debrecen, functioned as colleges.[129] There would have been no reason to make a big deal about this matter, one that was debated at the Diet.[130] It would have been particularly pointless to open another college in Kolozsvár, where two such institutions already operated.[131] The law is nevertheless clear, stating with regard to the "Common Academia" that it should "be in the city of Kolozsvár at the abandoned cloister that had been in the possession of the papists, which these days is vacant and stands derelict."[132]

Yet it was precisely Kolozsvár that would have been the most suitable location for a university. The presence of two functioning colleges in the city made it the natural place to establish the educational center of Transylvania. The foundation of a university in Kolozsvár would have certainly entailed such status if, in fact, the city had not already attained it prior to the decision of the

---

127 Jakó and Juhász, *Nagyenyedi diákok*, 95 et seq.

128 László Makkai defined colleges in Hungary as such. See Pál Zsigmond Pach (ed.), *Magyarország története* [History of Hungary], vol. 3 (Budapest, 1985), 1494, 1497.

129 See Török, *A kolozsvári református kollégium története*; Gál, *A kolozsvári unitárius kollégium története 1568–1900*; Koncz, *A marosvásárhelyi református kollégium története*; Cséplő, *A nagyváradi római katolikus főgimnázium története*; and Barcza, *A debreceni református kollégium története.*

130 For information regarding the antecedents in the Kingdom of Hungary during the years 1619–1620 to Gábor Bethlen's attempt to establish a university in Transylvania, see Kálmán Benda, "Bethlen Gábor és a magyar művelődés" [Gábor Bethlen and Hungarian Education], *Tiszatáj* 10 (1980): 65–75.

131 See János Herepei, *Adatok Bethlen Gábor academicum collégiumának előtörténetéhez* [Data regarding Gábor Bethlen's Academicum College] (Budapest and Szeged, 1965), *Adattár XVII. századi szellemi mozgalmaink történetéhez* vol. 1, 240. As the result of a translation error, Herepei published misleading information regarding the Reformed college, stating that Bethlen's 1617 donation pertained to intellectuals of mid-level education. The actual donation charter is as follows: "Cum itaque animadvertamus hanc patriam nostrum … non solum sapientum virorum, sed vel mediocriter etiam eruditorum inopia vehementer laborare, nostrae censimus partis esse, emolumento . . . alumnorum celeberrimi civitatis nostrae Colosvariensis gymnasy … prospicere." See Elek Jakab (ed.), *Oklevéltár Kolozsvár története második és harmadik kötetéhez* [Sourcebook for the Second and Third Volume of the History of Kolozsvár] vol. 2 (Budapest, 1988), 235.

132 EOE 8, 96.

Transylvanian Diet. It was perhaps for this reason that Kolozsvár was selected rather than the princely residence of Gyulafehérvár.

However, Prince Gábor Bethlen's planned university did not materialize. A regular university was established in Transylvania only much later amid different historical circumstances. The ceremonial inscription of the rights of the university did not take place either. According to the text of the 1622 law, the estates were aware only of a "*dispositio*" from the prince. They would formulate the operational conditions for the university "unanimously and via collective decision." If the prince actually built the university and invited professors to teach there, nobody could take the designated position and income.[133]

Construction of the university never began at the location that the estates had designated. Researchers generally attribute this to the opposition of the residents of Kolozsvár, the majority of whom were Unitarians. This explanation seems logical, though no direct data has been found to support it. Neither has any indirect data been uncovered to show why a university was not established elsewhere, if not in Kolozsvár. It is true that scholars have not dealt with this issue, since they argue that only the location of the educational institution, the foundation of which was discussed at the Diet of 1622, had moved from Kolozsvár to Gyulafehérvár.

However, no university was founded at the princely residence, thus the Gyulafehérvár college is not identical to the planned institution. Contemporaries never described the educational institution in Gyulafehérvár as an "*academia*"—referring to it as either a "school" (*skóla*) or a "college" (*kollégium*). One of its professors who had come from Germany called it a "seminarium."[134]

Thus it seems probable that the prince's development of the Gyulafehérvár college was unrelated to the planned university in Kolozsvár. With regard to this fact, the emphasis must be placed on the notion of "development," since the school that had evolved from the chapter school in Gyulafehérvár was operating at the college level before the year 1622. Using the regulations of the Hungarian *coetus* of the University of Wittenberg, the college in Gyulafehérvár established around the year 1580 the ordinance, which served as a model for other colleges subsequently located in Hungary. Despite the fact that the college had already existed for a long time, Prince Gábor Bethlen treated the institution as one of his own foundations and provided it with abundant donations. Contemporaries also considered the college to be the prince's school. They had

133 Ibid., 97.

134 János Herepei, "Adatok Bethlen Gábor academicum collégiumának előtörténetéhez," Idem, *Polgári irodalmi és kulturális törekvések a század első felében. Adattár XVII. századi szellemi mozgalmaink történetéhez* I. (Budapest, Szeged 1965.) 271–279.

every reason to do so. Gábor Bethlen's material and intellectual support for the college indeed served as the basis for the institution's fundamental renewal. Moreover, the earlier princely donations provided the college with the means to maintain its operations for years after it was forced to move in 1662.

Therefore, the judged fact of the foundation of the college of Gyulafehérvár in 1622 was, in the end, not important to emphasize because doing so would serve to uncover some previously unknown circumstance regarding this school. The contradiction between the original intention of the prince and the reality of the situation is important primarily for the reason that it sheds some light upon Gábor Bethlen's endeavor to establish a university. One may also phrase it this way: the number of known attempts to found a university in Transylvania increased by one.

The attempts to establish a university in the principality before the time of Bethlen are well-known. John Sigismund Szapolyai was the first to entertain the notion of founding a university in the principality, specifically around one of the great scholars of the age, Petrus Ramus. King of Poland and Prince of Transylvania Stephen Báthory was the next to try, going so far as to compose a deed of foundation for a university. According to this document, the university —to be located in Kolozsvár—would confer academic degrees that corresponded to those granted at academies in France, Germany, Spain and Italy.[135] However, the planned university was never established, though Báthory's efforts did result in the foundation of a very good educational institution that was the equivalent to a secondary school, which operated until its Jesuit teachers were expelled from Transylvania in 1588 and, again, in 1603. The Transylvanian Diet subsequently designated the same location on Farkas Street in Kolozsvár as Báthory had specified in his deed of foundation as the location for Gábor Bethlen's university.

The collective reason for the failure of these attempts to establish a university in Transylvania were certainly not the result of belatedness. That is, one cannot say that the idea of founding a university was no longer timely. In fact, there were a large number of universities established in Europe during the roughly 100-year period beginning with the first decades of the sixteenth century. Between 1537 and 1636, 10 universities of various sizes were founded in countries from Switzerland to Poland and including Bohemia.[136] Apparently the demand

135 For the most recent publication of the deed of foundation see: *István Mészáros, XVI. századi városi iskoláink és a "studius humanitatis"* [Our Sixteenth-Century Urban Schools and the studius humanitatis] (Budapest, 1981), 173 et seq.

136 See *The World of Learning*, 2 vol. (London, 1977). I once subscribed to the opinion that Bethlen's attempt to found a college in Transylvania in 1622 was no longer timely. However, this can today be regarded as an error on multiple accounts.

for people who had received education of the highest level grew suddenly, by historical standards, throughout Europe at this time.

Thus, the attempt of princes of Transylvania John Sigismund Szapolyai, Stephen Báthory and Gábor Bethlen to found a university placed them in the company of many other European sovereigns at this time: only their failure to transform intention into reality separated them from their peers. However, it would be worthwhile to consider the possibility that achievements realized in the domain of education in Transylvania established the foundations upon which efforts to found a university in the principality were based. The repeated failure to establish such a university raises the question, because this failure can be traced to a common cause and was thus not merely a question of happenstance.

It is not difficult to identify the concrete cause. Why, for example, would Petrus Ramus have abandoned his prestigious position in Paris in order to take up John Sigismund's offer? Stephen Báthory's immediate problem may have been that he brought in Jesuits to teach. The Unitarian citizens of Kolozsvár were, in fact, able to protest against Gábor Bethlen's intention to establish a university in the city.[137] However, we do not yet know what transformed these incidental occurrences into regular events: That is: there have only been a few, easily refutable, platitudes advanced to explain it.

Whether we use platitudes or the results of subsequent research to explain the repeated failure of attempts to found a university in Transylvania, the essential fact remains that a significant counterforce was working against them. If one takes these forces into account, the attempts themselves can be considered successes reflecting the intellectual demands that arose in Transylvania despite many difficulties and obstacles. On the one hand, the princes of Transylvania required educated people to fill ecclesiastical and secular offices, while on the other hand, there were numerous people in the principality, apt and determined to learn, who yearned for university studies. The latter conclusion is not groundless. Data showing that an average of around 100 Transylvanian students attended foreign universities every year serves to corroborate it. Even a portion of these students would have been enough to sustain a Transylvanian university. The princes of Transylvania sent their people to study at foreign universities and engaged the services of students who returned from such universities. Those Transylvanians who were the most determined to

137 According to Gyula Szekfű, Transylvanians generally regarded Bethlen's ideas regarding the foundation of a university as "alien" because they were based on a foreign, Catholic model. This reasoning is incomprehensible, since in spite of the fact there was no university in Hungary, those who dealt with the issue were obviously aware of the many Protestant universities that operated in Europe. See Gyula Szekfű, *Bethlen Gábor* (Budapest, 1929), 197–98.

gain social and intellectual advancement undertook the hardships of studying at distant universities. Transylvania ultimately derived some benefit from this situation. The principality's intellectual effervescence was due in no small measure to the fact that Transylvanian students who had studied abroad returned home bearing the most important scientific knowledge and cultural ideals of the age. However, lacking their own university and in the absence of scientific life that had sprung organically from domestic soil, Transylvanian intellectuals, regardless of their significant social prestige, often languished in an uncomprehending environment.

The Democratization of Education and Culture

It would be possible to cite many scattered accounts regarding the relationship between those who had studied at the highest level and their intellectual environment. They would most likely reveal that the social prestige of the intellectuals grew following the Reformation in the sixteenth and seventeenth centuries. This phenomenon did not necessarily correspond to intellectual understanding. Teacher, preacher and, eventually, bishop István Geleji Katona, for example, was undoubtedly part of the social élite of Transylvania during the sovereignty of both Gábor Bethlen and György Rákóczi I. At the same time, one has the feeling that virtually nobody either read or was able to understand his lengthy theological works.

The rise in the social standing of intellectuals in Transylvania may have been a complex function of the increasing number of educated people in the principality and the consequent heightening exposure of society to culture. It is again worthwhile to cite the most valuable data regarding the cultural history of Transylvania—namely that showing the number of students from the principality who attended foreign universities. According to this data, the proportion of students of village origin among all Transylvanians who studied at foreign universities rose from 15 percent before the year 1521 to 36.7 between 1521 and 1700. Data showing that 30.7 percent of Transylvanians who had received the highest level of education at foreign universities pursued non-intellectual occupations after their return to the principality is perhaps even more significant.[138]

These numbers ultimately serve to confirm the statements of Apáczai Csere and other intellectuals of his time quoted at the beginning of this chapter. In fact, numbers may be even more revealing than contemporary statements from

138 Miklós Szabó compared his data with those of Sándor Tonk. See Szabó, "Erdélyi diákok külföldi egyetemjárása."

the past because they pertain to students who attended universities rather than colleges. The proportion of students from lower societal strata increased at the highest level as well. Although one could question the precise numbers indicated in the data, the overall trend is indisputable: more and more people gained access to culture and education. In other words, culture and education underwent democratization in Transylvania during the sixteenth and seventeenth centuries.

Many other facts regarding the cultural history of Transylvania support this conclusion. All of these facts indicate that Transylvanians satisfied one of the greatest demands of the Reformation—the expansion of knowledge through schools. The religious reform did not formulate abstract concepts, but articulated proposals regarding the solution to social problems. The great desire for schooling among the inhabitants of Transylvania indicates that this demand was satisfied in the principality.

Fig. 10. The Castle of Fraknó (Forchtenstein, Austria), engraving, 1644.

5 Actions and Ideas: Religious Resistance in the Four Congregations of the Fraknó Manor in 1638

This chapter portrays the behavior of members of four seventeenth-century congregations that was triggered by the Counter-Reformation measures of their landlord.[139] In addition to a simple description of behavior, it seeks to identify possible connections between the disobedience and the religious knowledge of those who defied the landlord's disposition. The problem is not a retrospective construction: the secular authority already speculated at the time that there was a connection between the ideas and actions of the people involved in the matter.

This secular authority was the landlord, Miklós Esterházy, while the four congregations lived in Fraknóalja (Forchtenau) and Nagymarton (Mattersdorf) as well as in their two filial churches in Neustift and Wisen. These communities were located on one of Esterházy's landholdings in western Hungary (today Burgenland, Austria), the Fraknó manor. Exceptionally rich source materials, which had been already published, make the present analysis possible.[140] Relevant documents reveal that Esterházy issued a decree in 1638 ordering the parishioners in question to convert to Catholicism by Easter of that year. Many of the parishioners complied with his decree. Precise data exists with regard to the heads of household. A total of 43 percent of heads of household in Fraknóalja and Neustift—locations for which data was not compiled separately—converted to Catholicism in observance of the decree, compared to 54 percent in Nagymarton and 90 percent in Wisen. Therefore, 57 percent of heads of households in Fraknóalja and Neustift, 46 percent in Nagymarton and 10 percent in Wisen did not convert to Catholicism.

139 This chapter was first published in Hungarian: "Cselekedetek és eszmék. Vallási ellenállás a fraknói uradalom négy gyülekezetében (1638)" in *Művelődési törekvések a kora újkorban. Tanulmányok Keserű Bálint tiszteletére* [Cultural Pursuits in the Early Modern Period. Studies in Honor of Bálint Keserű], ed. Zsuzsanna Font, Gizella Keserű, and Péter Ötvös (Szeged, 1997), 479–86.

140 István Monok and Katalin Péter, "Felmérés a hithűségről 163-ban" [A Survey of Religious Loyalty], in *Lymbus. Művelődéstörténeti Tár* [Lymbus. Cultural History Collection] vol. 2, ed. István Monok and Áron Petneki (Szeged, 1990), 111–42.

This event took place at a time when Miklós Esterházy also served as Palatine of Hungary, thus exercising dual authority over the people who lived on his estates. He had manifested no interest in the religious affairs of his subjects for a long time. He had received Fraknó manor along with the Kismarton (Eisenstadt, Austria) manor after the 1621 Peace of Nikolsburg and the Protestants who thus came under his authority were able to live undisturbed in their religious affiliation until 1637, when he invited missionaries from the Austrian province of the Society of Jesus to work in and around Kismarton.[141]

According to the account of the Jesuits, their activity in and around Kismarton ended in the use of violence. The Jesuits first attempted to convert people both at their homes and in public, though the inhabitants' resolute opposition to this effort resulted in the deployment of mercenary soldiers. This compelled some to convert, while others escaped or were banished and very few people converted "voluntarily." The account is full of emotional elements that reflect the disposition of the Jesuits.

Esterházy did not attempt to conduct such proselytization on the Fraknó estate. Here, immediately after the violent events that had taken place at the Kismarton manor, residents were informed at the time of the annual village assembly of the landlord's decree obliging them to convert from Protestantism to Catholicism.[142] No information exists regarding the motives of those who complied with this decree. The notion that they did so merely out of fear or under the impact of violence that had occurred at the Kismarton manor appears to be a simplification. There is no evidence of any trepidation among those who had adhered to their religion and no common cause can be found for their resistance. Perhaps no single motive impelled the converts to relinquish their religion either. The lack of relevant sources makes meditation upon this problem futile. However, there is a document resembling a manorial survey that displays information regarding the heads of household who refused to comply with the lord's decree.[143] It seems that the matter was regarded as a manorial affair and thus, as was the case with regard to all landowner-imposed obligations, pertained only to heads of household.

Thus we hardly know anything about the behavior of women, since the large majority of heads of household were men. It is important to take this fact into account, because women likely behaved differently than men in this regard. The significant number of households that were mixed in terms of religious affiliation reflects this probable disparity. The highly detailed data regarding the village of Wisen, for example, shows that 21 of 119 households at this location were of

141 For the account of the Jesuits, see ibid., 139–42.
142 Ibid., 112.
143 Ibid., 112–36.

mixed religious affiliation.[144] The Jesuit account of the events at the Kismarton manor specifically describes the unique behavior of women. This account ended with the assertion: "Of the people, only the members of the female gender were more stubborn as they regard themselves less dependent on authority."[145] This same account does not mention the events that took place at the Fraknó estate, though there is no reason for us to presume that the stubbornness of women caused fewer problems here than it had during the attempt to convert the inhabitants of the neighboring manor.

Some men, such as the following, took the opinions of their wives into account: Thomas Koler of Fraknóalja stated that he must talk to his wife about what to do in the future;[146] Casparus Moser of Wisen claimed that he had to keep the promise he had made to his wife that he would not convert;[147] and Sebastianus Scheichenstuhl declared that he would move away from this village because his wife wished to do so.[148] And data showing that the proportion of female heads of household was very small, though the fact that three of those who had resisted Esterházy's decree—Christiana Gieffing of Fraknólja, widow Sebastian Frahler of Nagymarton and widow Johannes Kratzer of Neustift—were women appears to be characteristic of the situation in general.[149]

However, there is no information available indicating the number of female heads of household who complied with the landowner's decree to convert to Catholicism. Data in the sources regarding the latter group is purely numerical, thus we know the names of only a few converted Catholics. The document regarding those who failed to obey Esterházy's decree is, to the contrary, detailed.[150] The first column of this carefully prepared document shows the name of the person in question. The next two columns display the answers to questions that were intended to obtain the following information from respondents: first, the reason for their failure to comply with the landlord's decree;[151] second, their degree of religious knowledge; and third, their future intentions with regard to the issue of conversion.[152]

144 Ibid., 120, 135.

145 "Solae proceruum genus foemina negotium facessebant eo contumacius, quo ad imperia solutiores se arbitrabantur," ibid., 139.

146 "Vult tamen prius antequam id (conversionem) fecerit, uxorem suam consulere interea vult et Deo et superiorı́bus Se commendare," ibid., 114.

147 "promisit uxori olim," ibid., 121.

148 "uxor eius vult abire, ergo et ipse debet sequere uxorem," ibid., 136.

149 Ibid., 116, 117, 130.

150 Ibid., 112, 136.

151 The text of the first heading: "Rationes cur non conversi et satisfecerint mandato illustrissimi principis," ibid., 112, 122, 129, 133, 135.

152 The text of the second heading: "Enunciata et quid facturi," ibid.

Judges summoned those who failed to meet the deadline stipulated in the decree to appear before a committee for questioning, which the document refers to as *examen.* The document reveals that some people ignored these citations and that such instances of delinquency were entered into official records using descriptions such as "cited several times by the judge, they nevertheless did not appear."[153] The members of the committee that conducted these hearings were Catholics, almost certainly both laypeople and clergymen.

The fact that the members of the hearing committee were Catholic is not surprising. Protestants were unlikely to have been chosen to deal with such a delicate matter. There is also clear reference to this in the document: the judge in Nagymarton indicated in one of his filings that he had already donated 500 forints, according to the Jesuit account, "templo nostro" (for our church), and he would give even more money if he were permitted to remain in his faith.[154] This church was obviously a Catholic one.

The form of the document as well as the application of manorial practices in the specification of heads of household imply the presence of secular, presumably manorial, representatives. And these records were apparently compiled with the objectivity applied to manorial affairs, reporting the words of respondents in an unbiased manner. The statements of those questioned were abbreviated as such: "he will not change even at the command of the Lord but remains steadfast" or "he hopes to die in his own faith."[155] Inquiries regarding the religious knowledge of those questioned suggests that Catholic clergymen were also present. The task of conducting such inquiries would hardly have been entrusted to laypeople.

Thus those who had ignored Esterházy's order to convert to Catholicism were forced to provide recorded testimony regarding the causes of their disobedience and their religious convictions before the committee composed of several members whom they considered to be people of authority. Appearing before this committee likely required more courage than defying the landowner's decree. Evidence suggests that those who had failed to meet the deadline for conversion had to report to the committee without receiving individual citation, though somebody obviously kept track of this or else they would not have known precisely whom they were summoning.

Under these circumstances, some of the statements made before the committee are surprising. Some people, for example, simply asked for permission to remain in their faith. According to the records of these hearings, Georgius Fri-

153 "citati aliquoties per iudicem, noluerunt parere." For example, ibid., 133.

154 Ibid., 22.

155 "etiam ad mandatum illustrissimi principis non desistet, sed constans permanebit" and "sperat se in hac fide permansuram." Ibid., 113, 116.

dericus Stötner requested that he "be permitted to believe as before."[156] The hearing records state that Andreas Gschichel "requests to be allowed to keep his faith."[157] In the village of Wisen, where almost everybody had submitted to the order to convert, Laurentius Klamppfer "asks to be permitted to die in this faith."[158] Klamppfer and several others cited their old age or general vulnerability, while some did not attempt to justify their requests to remain in their faith. Statements such as that which the widow of Johannes Kratzer made before the committee are likewise surprising. According to the hearing records, she had declined to convert because "she did not yet receive the command" but "if she is forced, she will do it."[159] Stephanus Rubacher made a similar statement with regard to his future intentions: "if his grace gives the command, he will do it."[160] And some others who were summoned to appear before the committee said that they would convert if the landlord seriously—*serio*—ordered them to do so. The hearing records indicate that 22 people responded to the committee's questions with answers which, given their situation, seem astonishing. Their responses suggest that the given communities regarded religious conversion to be a manorial affair—just as the authority did—and that some members of these communities chose not to obey the official order because they hoped to receive an exemption from this duty as they had with regard to other obligations. These people apparently regarded the notion of an order that applied to everybody to be unusual and therefore required an individual command. The behavior of the six people who simply did not show up for their hearing, or the two who traveled to another location to avoid citation, reflects a similar attitude.

Without knowing that the majority of those affected apparently converted to Catholicism before the deadline without being subjected to external compulsion, we might conclude that, as a result of their previously positive experiences, the inhabitants of the Esterházy estates did not believe even after the events that had taken place at the Kismarton manor that seigniorial pressure would be applied in a consequential manner. However, taking into account those who converted without protest, perhaps it would be more accurate to state that there were significant individual disparities in the assessment of the situation.

Those answers that, from an external and retrospective viewpoint, may be regarded as suitable for the situation were not uniform either. The answers to the first inquiry seeking to determine the motive for disobedience can be divided into three categories: the first has nothing to do with religion, citing ignorance of the decree as the reason for delinquency; the second claimed that the person in

156 "permittatur sic credere uti hactenus," ibid., 115.
157 "petit et obsecrat, ut in sua fide permittatur," ibid., 129.
158 "petit ut in hac fide permittetur mori," ibid., 36.
159 "hactenus illi non iniunctum fuit" and "si autem cogeretur, tunc faciet," ibid., 117.
160 "si illustrissimus princeps mandaverit, tunc illico faciet," ibid., 116.

question had always been "of this faith" or had been baptized "in this faith" or had been raised "in it"; and the third referred to the religious affiliation of parents or other ancestors, who had always been "of this faith." There are, additionally, some strange responses. Michael Sparrabitz of Fraknóalja, for example, declared that he had not noticed that he was attending a non-Catholic church.[161] Johannes Wilffing of Nagymarton asserted that he had not obeyed the lord's order, because he was a "catholicus natus" (born Catholic), though promised that he would convert by the time of the Feast of the Ascension.[162] Gallus Dorner of Nagymarton provided no reason or excuse for his failure to convert by the stipulated deadline.[163]

As to the inquiry about religious knowledge, either not all those summoned before the committee faced those questions or their answers were not always recorded. In fact, the relevant column of the hearing records in the majority of cases contains no reference to responses about religious knowledge. And the recorded answers to such questions are so extremely diverse that they cannot be divided into categories. For example, saddler Christian Wolff of Nagymarton engaged in a debate with committee members regarding the sacraments in general—and the visible features of the two Lutheran sacraments in particular—that was based on carefully considered knowledge that had not merely been learned by rote.[164] At the same time, fellow Nagymarton resident Matthias Binder told the committee that he was also familiar with the "six" sacraments, which he identified as the Lord's Prayer, the Ten Commandments, faith, baptism, the keys and the Lord's Supper.[165]

The responses to the third question cannot be placed into categories either. Of the 164 heads of household who responded to this question, 73 declared that they did not want to convert to Catholicism in the future, while 37 stated that they would convert if others, such as neighbors, converted, 33 indicated that they would convert only under compulsion or in response to another command from the lord, 9 asserted that they would convert if they could continue to take communion under both kinds, 6 promised to convert before the prescribed deadline, and another 6 said they were still uncertain as to their future decision. One could logically conclude that there existed some correlation between the responses. It would be logical to surmise, for example, that those who provided indifferent responses to the first question would be among those who agreed to convert in some form, or that those who displayed a high degree of religious

161 Ibid., 116.
162 Ibid., 125.
163 Ibid., 129.
164 Ibid., 134.
165 Ibid., 126.

knowledge would adhere stubbornly to their religion. Reality did not necessarily turn out that way.

Christian Wolff, who entered into a debate about the sacraments and whom the hearing records indicate to have behaved in a condescending manner toward committee members, indeed rejected the notion of converting at some time in the future. Others maintained that they had failed to comply with the lord's command because they had not heard about it. Among those who made this claim was Georgius Prunhuber of either Fraknóalja or Neustift, who revealed his lack of religious knowledge when he stated that he believed in five sacraments—*coena, sanguis, baptismum, matrimonium* and *ordo* (supper, blood, baptism, marriage and the holy orders). Nevertheless, he also declared that he wanted to keep his faith "usque ad mortem" (until his death).[166]

We have the least information regarding the most significant of the three questions that the committee members posed to those who had failed to convert in compliance with the landlord's decree—that concerning religious knowledge. The responses reveal that this question pertained to the number of sacraments, though the fact that only answers reflecting either conspicuous religious ignorance or extraordinary religious knowledge were recorded suggests that most of those summoned to appear before the committee simply cited the two evangelical sacraments—baptism and the Lord's Supper.

The incorrect answers to questions regarding religious knowledge show that respondents regarded the Lord's Supper to be more important than anything else. The 31 incorrect responses that appear in the records refer to the Holy Communion in 20 instances, sometimes along with other sacraments or within very odd contexts. Examples of such strange contexts reported in the hearing records are "he confessed ... two sacraments, which are the two kinds"[167] and Andreas Machel's assertion that "it is written that each time you gather and each time you drink, those are the sacraments from the Lord's chalice."[168] Some of those who did not mention communion in their responses evidently misunderstood the question. The hearing record stated with regard to Joannes Mandel, for example, "believes in the three sacraments of his evangelical faith, 1. God the Father, 2. God the Son, 3. God the Holy Ghost,"[169] while with regard to another respondent, it indicated "he said ... that he believes in three evangelists, Matthew, Mark and Saint Paul."[170] Three others understood the question, but

166 Ibid., 129.

167 "fatetur ... 2 sacramenta, quae sunt 2 species," ibid., 113.

168 "scriptum est, quotiescunque societis et quotiescunque bibetis, tot sunt sacramenta ex calice Domini," ibid., 119.

169 "credit tamen in sua evangelica professione esse 3 sacramenta, 1 Deus Pater, 2 Deus Filius, 3 Deus Spiritus Sanctus," ibid.,124.

170 "dicit se ... credere 3 Evangelistae, Mattheum, Marcum et Sanctum Paulum," ibid., 125.

were still unable to answer it correctly—a fact that they themselves recognized. The hearing records show that Balthasar Klampffer provided the following incorrect response: "He confesses three sacraments but does not know their names. He believes, however, in God Almighty, as a good Christian."[171]

However, even such incorrect and unclear answers reflect some degree of knowledge regarding the teachings of religion. Moreover, the general level of religious knowledge manifested in the responses far exceeds that which one might expect among the residents of two rather insignificant market towns and two small villages. The circumstances under which the hearings were held support this assertion. People usually acquire their religious knowledge in church. The hearings were held at some official location. Those who appeared before the committee were forced to retrieve knowledge that they had acquired during catechism lessons as children in response to questions posed to them as if they were the accused at a manorial court. Presumably even many of those who in the course of a personal conversation could have comfortably discussed religion became flustered during such questioning.

The extremely concisely composed records indicate that those called before the committee responded in a much more relaxed manner if they did not feel as if they were being interrogated. And their answers to the question concerning their future intentions perhaps revealed more about their religious knowledge than the direct inquiry on this subject. For example, Matthias Reisner, although he could not correctly identify the number of sacraments, was able to apply Luther's teaching regarding the "two empires" to his own situation. According to the records, Reisner "regards himself to be in sufficiently good faith as he fulfills his superior obligation to perform manual labor diligently."[172] This subtle expression of the obligation to obey secular authorities was, from the mouth of a laboring peasant, simply astounding. Many responses were much less refined formulations of the same teaching: Laurentius Reisner, for example, said "He does not want to resist because from his teacher he learned God's words to obey God and the superiors."[173] Others made similar statements. However, it is striking that although most of those who made such declarations intended to convert to Catholicism upon the landlord's issue of a new decree to do so, some planned to ignore the repeated seigniorial command even though they were familiar with the teaching regarding obedience toward secular authorities. The hearing records indicate that Michael Ossing, for example, declared that "he does not leave his

171 "Fatetur 3 sacramenta, sed quae sint et quomodo appellantur, ignorat. Credit autem (inquit) in Deum Patrem omnipotentem, uti bonus christianus." Ibid., 132.

172 "putat se esse in satis bona fide, et sufficere, quia superioribus suum debitum roboth cum diligentia perficit," ibid., 114.

173 "Non vult resistere, quia a suo pastore didicit ex Verbo Dei obediere Deo et superioribus." Ibid., 116.

faith even on the demand of his Grace,"[174] while with regard to Adamus Weiner, the relevant rubric noted "he does not consider conversion even if his Grace obligates him."[175]

The committee members saw the facial expressions of the people who entered the room for questioning and were likely already familiar with these individuals, thus enabling them perhaps to determine the reasons for which they, as a group, had ignored the powerful landowner's decree to convert. As an outsider studying these hearings in retrospect, one cannot discern any characteristic features that would serve to identify even the most resolute group of recalcitrants.

That group was composed of the previously mentioned 73 heads of household who asserted during the hearings that they were not prepared to convert to Catholicism under any circumstances. Eight of these people declared that they would rather die than convert. One of them, a tailor named Johannes Koch who lived in the household of another person, likely talked about his intention in detail, because the report indicates that he stated it twice:

> he is ready to die in his evangelical faith, rather than to convert to the Catholic faith. Even if his Grace obliges him to convert, he refuses to do so and prefers to die.[176]

The eight heads of family who claimed they would choose death over conversion included, in addition to the tailor, citizens from both Fraknóalja and Nagymarton and cotters from the villages of Neustift and Wisen. The other heads of family who refused to convert to Catholicism were similarly of diverse social status and the answers they provided during the hearings differed from one another as well. Among those who belonged to this group was the religiously well-informed saddler from Nagymarton, but otherwise they seem to have been people of average religious knowledge. Eight of them articulated the religiously neutral claim that they had failed to convert because they had not been home when the decree was issued or for some other reason had not heard about the landowner's command.

The situation at the Fraknó manor did not turn violent as it had at the neighboring Kismarton manor. Here Miklós Esterházy did not resort to the use of armed force against the members of the four congregations who showed resistance, but the Catholic mission continued. In 1659, more than 20 years after the issue of the original decree, there were still Lutherans living on the Fraknó manor, at least in Fraknóalja and the villages of Neustift and Wisen. During this year, a total of 28 new converts to Catholicism were recorded at these three

174 "non desistet a sua fide etiam demandante illustrissimo princepe," ibid., 129.
175 "etiamsi illustrissimus princeps injungeret illi, nullo modo cogitat converti," ibid., 131.
176 "paratus est cum sua evangelica doctrina potius in mortem ire, quam ad fidem catholicam converti, etiamsi illustrissimus princeps illi iniungeret, non faciet, sed mavult mori." Ibid., 134.

locations. Some of the converts were the sons, daughters and, perhaps, spouses of the heads of household who had most resolutely refused to obey the 1638 decree. The fact that their descendants converted indicates that the fathers were resilient in their intentions: they had remained steadfast in their old religion. One might attribute the refusal to convert to personality factors if the 73 people in question did not constitute nearly half of those who had initially failed to comply with the relevant decree and around one-third of all members of the congregation living in the two market towns and two villages located on the Fraknó manor. This many unique personalities certainly did not live together at four locations. In fact, these people lived not together, but scattered throughout the manor.

However, there is no room in history for sheer guesswork. We must simply resign ourselves to the fact that the tools of historical scholarship can be used to describe many past events, but cannot find explanations for all of them.

Subject Index

Index of Places

Index of Persons